Psychological Passives and the Agentive Prepositions in English

A Historical Study

Susumu TAKETAZU

KAIBUNSHA LTD
TOKYO

Contents

Preface iii
Acknowledgments v
Abbreviations vi

Chapter 1　The 'passive of *surprise* + *by*' construction in the Computer Corpus and the *OED* 1

Chapter 2　The passive of *surprise* + *at* or *by*?: The choice of preposition in Present-day English 20

Chapter 3　Psych-passives with agentive prepositions: the historical shift from Early Modern English to Present-day English 37

Chapter 4　How Dickens used psych-passives with *at* or *by* 70

Chapter 5　The semantic shift of psych-passives + *by* 97

Chapter 6　The decline of gerunds with psych-passives 114

Chapter 7　The rise and growth of *how*-clauses with psych-passives 130

Chapter 8　How Onions treated the 'passive of *surprise* + *by*' construction in the *OED* 151

Chapter 9　How Bradley treated the 'psych-passive + *by*' construction in the *OED* 167

Chapter 10　Psych-verbs in the past-participle form: Adjectives or passives? 192

Chapter 11　Concluding Remarks 200

Bibliography 205
Dictionaries 212
Computer Corpora 212
Index 215

Preface

Surprised by Joy is C. S. Lewis's autobiographical work of his early life. The title has been said to be inspired by Wordsworth's poem, which begins with the line 'Surprised by joy—impatient as Wind.' The book's title struck me as odd since we learnt at school that the passive form of *surprise* generally occurs with the agentive preposition *at*, not *by*. Together with this, the occasional encounters with the sentences of the 'passive of *surprise* + *by*' construction in novels, newspapers and magazines became an inspiration to begin the research into this construction.

Emotions are inherent in humans. We have joy, grief, surprise, fear, sadness and so on. These emotions can be expressed in numerous ways in human language. In English, they take various syntactic representations: adjectives (*I am happy*), nominal phrases (*She had a great joy*) and a variety of verbal constructions, which include intransitives (*He marveled*), transitives (*She fears spiders*), passives (*They were amazed*), reflexives (*He delighted himself*) and historically impersonals (*Me pleases*).

What is striking is that passive sentences with psychological verbs (psychological passives or psych-passives) are much utilized in English. Why does English resort to passives to convey emotional conditions when there are structurally simpler intransitive sentences available? Although the structure is that of the passive, prepositions other than *by* have been generally employed to show the agent. This is why the title *Surprised by Joy* sounded unusual to me. The truth is that the *by*-agent has been observed to occur with the passive form of *surprise* quite frequently in Present-day English, which made me very curious and inquisitive.

My curiosity got the better of me and set myself to launch an investigation into the passives of *surprise* and synonymous verbs occurring with the agentive *by* from a historical perspective. I will deal with such issues as are related to the psych-passives: to what extent the agentive *by* has been increasing historically; what are the determining factors for the choice of *at* or *by* with the passive of *surprise* in Present-day English; Charles Dickens' preference for the agentive *by*; the semantic shift of the 'psych-passive + *by*' construction; the decline of gerunds and the growth of *how*-clauses with psych-passives; the *OED* editors' treatment of the psych-passives with the agentive *by*; and the identity of the past participles of psych-verbs whether they are adjectives or passives.

In discussing these issues, I will show some historical shifts of linguistic phenomena, or language changes, which are likely to be an increase or decrease of a certain phenomenon. The most effective way to show the changes in an objective way would be to use statistics in tables or graphs. Graphs are especially useful to see the change visually and many of them are presented throughout the book. With the emergence of computer corpora in recent decades, a large amount of data are easily available and consequently, the statistics are useful, or may even become indispensable when presenting data.

The verbal constructions mentioned above are more or less related to each other. I once presented a hypothesis that the psych-passives may have been replacing reflexives or impersonals to express emotions in the history of Modern English. Leaving this theme behind, I was, so to speak, sidetracked and engaged myself in the present research. The research instigated by a simple curiosity turned into a long-term endeavor, which almost occupied the latter half of my scholarly life. This book will be a witness to how a simple and naïve curiosity could make a tiny bud of academic interest bloom into a flower, albeit a humble flower it may be.

Hopefully, this book will be read by many readers. I expect them to be not only researchers but also English instructors and university students majoring in English. For the sake of non-researchers, for whom the theme itself should not be so difficult to handle, the book is written in fairly plain English. May the readers share with me the pleasure and enjoyment in reading this book and find something beneficial and enlightening.

Susumu TAKETAZU

Acknowledgments

I owe many thanks to many people in publishing this book. First of all, I would like to extend my gratitude to Emeritus Professor of Kyushu University, Dr. Matsuji Tajima. Dr. Tajima has constantly given me assistance and encouragement in academic matters for the past quarter century. He kindly read the whole manuscript and gave me many beneficial comments. I have received a lot of benefits from the members of the Japanese Association for Studies in the History of the English Language (*Eigo-shi Kenkyu-kai*), which Professor Tajima established twenty years ago.

I would like to thank Mr. Nicholas Caine, one of my colleagues, who kindly read the whole draft of this book and assisted me in emending my English. Mr. Caine's generous assistance is such that I can hardly find words to express my gratitude to him. My thanks also go to the former professor of Kitakyushu City University, Ryuichi Uemura and Mr. Stephen Rife, another colleague of mine, who also proofread the manuscripts and gave me many useful comments. Needless to say, the responsibility for any remaining errors or irregularities is mine.

I am thankful to the corpus creators who have provided many computer corpora, indispensable for this type of research. I thank Professor Mark Davies of Brigham Young University for allowing researchers to use a dozen corpora freely. I am also thankful to Professor Mitsuharu Matsuoka of Nagoya University, who created the Victorian Literary Studies Archives. Without these corpora, this book may not have seen the light of day.

I have felt obliged to my mentors at my alma mater: the late professors Eiichi Hayashi, Atsumu Kanayama and Fumio Morizuka. I owe a special debt to Professor Hayashi, who was so generous as to assist me in graduating from the alma mater while I was in the US. May they rest in peace.

I thank my family for their patience with my scholarly, therefore more or less self-centered life. I thank my daughter Sakura, who assisted me in the statistics and the charts. I am indebted to my parents who supported my early life as a scholar and made me what I am today.

Last but not least, I am deeply thankful to Mr. Yohichi Yasui, the president of Kaibunsha Publishing Co., for kindly publishing this book.

Abbreviations

psych-verb	psychological verb
psych-passive	psychological passive (passive of a psych-verb)
N	noun

OE	Old English
ME	Middle English
EModE	Early Modern English (= Early ModE)
LModE	Late Modern English (= Late ModE)
PE	Present-day English

BNC	British National Corpus
CASO	Corpus of American Soap Opera
COBUILD	Cobuild Direct Corpus
COCA	Corpus of Contemporary American English
COHA	Corpus of Historical American English
EEBO	Early English Book Online
MEC	Modern English Collection
TIME	*Time* Magazine Corpus
VLSA	Victorian Literary Studies Archives

MEG	*A Modern English Grammar on Historical Principles*
OED	*The Oxford English Dictionary*

Chapter 1
The 'passive of *surprise* + *by*' construction in the Computer Corpus and the *OED*

"Surprise!" is an interjection that the participants at a surprise party shout at a timely moment to the unsuspecteing person for whom the party is held. It is an interesting fact that a 'surprise party' is recorded to have appeared as early as 1835–45 in *Random House Dictionary*. The *OED* also records it as an American term with an illustrative quotation of 1872 but with a slightly different meaning from the current meaning.

I. Introduction

You may be pleasantly surprised to hear the interjection "Surprise!" at a surprise party thrown for you. When you hear it, would you be surprised at how discreetly and secretly the party had been planned? Would you not be surprised by the sweetness and kindness of your friends who had been good enough to hold the party for you?

The preceding two sentences in the passage above contain examples of the two constructions that are the focus of this book. It may be a trivial matter whether to use *at* or *by* with the passive of *surprise*,[1] but it has been a matter of great concern to me. This had been intriguing me for quite a while before my naïve curiosity overcame me and induced me to launch an investigation to find out the mystery of agentive prepositions occurring with the construction.

---

1) 'The passive of *surprise*' can be a misleading term as the construction also functions as an adjective. '*Be surprised*' may be an alternative choice, but it is also misleading because other linking verbs such as *seem*, *look*, *appear* are neglected. 'The past participle form of *surprise*' may be another alternative but it is too cumbersome to use. An incomplete-looking '*surprised*' without a copula or a linking verb can be used where necessary for convenience' sake. No terminology is a perfect formula to describe the construction. A suitable one will be used depending on the context.

Paperback novels are not only fun to read but are also a good resource filled with samples of any linguistic issue. Ken Follett, a popular and successful novelist, writes many novels set in medieval England. In one of his best-selling novels titled *A Place Called Freedom* (1995), Follett uses the sentences containing the construction in question, as in (1).

(1) a. He was **surprised by** the withering scorn in his own voice. (p.21)
b. Jay was **surprised at** how riled his father was. (p. 31) [2]

Follett uses a noun phrase with *by* on one page and a dozen pages later uses a *how*-clause with *at*. It seems that the novelist makes a distinction in the use of preposition, depending on the type of a prepositional complement.

Traditional school grammars have taught that the passive of *surprise*, when used psychologically, generally takes *at*, not *by*. The construction, however, occurs with *by* quite frequently in Present-day English (PE), as in (2) below.

(2) For as I say, as I motored on in the sunshine towards the Berkshire border, I continued to be **surprised by** the familiarity of the country around me. (Kazuo Ishiguro, *The Remains of the Day*, 1989); As a long-time Japan watcher I am continually **surprised by** the Japanese capacity for tolerance and forgiveness of both private and public infractions. (*The Lancet*, June 19, 1993); During an interview with Fox News, Ivanka Trump said she is **surprised by** the viciousness of the media covering President Trump. (CNN, June 12, 2017); etc.

In fact, it occurs with such an unexpectedly high frequency in novels, magazines, newspapers and TV or radio news that the real linguistic conditions seem to run counter to conventional grammatical ideas of the construction.

Historically, sentences of this construction are observed in the works of eminent writers of Late Modern English (Late ModE, LModE) such as Jane Austen, Charles Dickens, Anthony Trollope, Joseph Conrad and so forth, as in (3).

---

[2] Bold letters to highlight the word or phrase in question in sample sentences are mine. This practice will be adopted throughout this book.

(3) I should not have been at all **surprised by** her Ladyship's asking us on Sunday to drink tea and spend the evening at Rosings. (Austen, *Pride and Prejudice*, 1813); "Oh, you're here, are you, sir?" said John, rather **surprised by** the quickness with which he appeared. (Dickens, *Barnaby Rudge*, 1845); Its failure never surprised me; but I have been **surprised by** the success of Doctor Thorne. (Trollope, *Autobiography*, 1883); Mr. Powell was **surprised** not only **by** being engaged in conversation, but also **by** its character. (Conrad, *Victory*, 1915); etc.

Then we might come up with such questions as: When did the *by*-agent begin to occur when *at* had been the norm? To what extent has the agentive *by* been used? Has *by* been competing against *at* for supremacy and possibly replacing *at*?

To answer these questions would have been very difficult or even impossible a few decades ago. However, with the advent and development of computer corpora, a situation has emerged where an enormous amount of data, which ordinarily might take a lifetime to collect, can be obtained in an instant and with almost flawless accuracy. This favorable situation has enabled me to undertake this research from a historical perspective. This chapter attempts to clarify the historical shift of the agentive prepositions occurring with the passive of *surprise* used in a psychological sense, as seen in (2) and (3).

II. Data collection

2.1 Computer corpora

To collect data, the following computer corpora are used in this chapter:

(i) the *OED* on CD-ROM for Modern English and the Early English Book Online (EEBO) for Early Modern English
(ii) the Modern English Collection (MEC) and the Victorian Literary Studies Archives (VLSA) for Late Modern English
(iii) the British National Corpus (BNC), the Cobuild Direct Corpus (COBUILD) and the Wordbanks for present-day British English

(iv) the Corpus of Contemporary American English (COCA) and the Corpus of American Soap Opera (CASO) for present-day American English
(v) the Corpus of Historical American English (COHA) for Late Modern English and Present-day English

2.2 The procedure of data collection

With these corpora, such collocations as *surprised* + *at* (*by*, *with*, etc.) and its variant forms (*surprized, surpris'd, surpriz'd*, etc.) are searched. Retrieved samples are sieved and inappropriate ones are excluded. Non-psychological sentences (*The troop was surprised by a guerrilla force, We were surprised by a snowstorm*) are naturally discarded and so are the ill-collocated ones (*I was much surprised at first*) and the title of a book (*Surprised by Joy* by C. S. Lewis).

Syntactically, not only complete sentences (*I was surprised at the welcome I got*) but non-finite clauses such as participle constructions (*Much surprised by her change of heart*) are also taken into account. The sentences in which such linking verbs as *seem, look, sound* or *feel* function as a main verb (*I felt surprised at myself*), elliptical sentences (*She looks as if surprised at his modesty*) and object complements (*He found himself surprised by her friendly greeting*) are also considered.

There are ambiguous examples that border on mental or physical interpretation (*No potential thief likes to be surprised by a 500 watt halogen floodlight*) and therefore are hard to determine whether psychological or not. There may be examples overlooked in dealing with a large amount of data. Utmost attention has been paid to collecting and counting the data but an allowance must be made for possible miscounting or oversight, especially for three- or four-digit figures of data. These shortcomings, however, do not seem to affect the occurrence rate of *at* and *by* as they are very marginal.

It would be essential to read texts carefully and collect data but to read hundreds or thousands of texts would be very difficult or even impossible within a limited amount of time. Computer corpora are, therefore, extremely useful and may be indispensable, especially in searching for words or phrases which appear only a few times in one volume.

The data from computer corpora, however, are after all secondary information and an automatic search of a certain word or phrase may retrieve inappropriate samples such as those mentioned above. In some corpora, the same sentence is retrieved as two or sometime three samples. We have to make sure that the retrieved sample sentences are authentic, not inadequate ones and should be careful not to let inappropriate samples mislead us into an erroneous observation.

III. The *OED* on CD-ROM

The *OED* on CD-ROM is considered to be a very useful historical corpus as Fisher (1997) aptly explains. The size of this corpus is estimated to be about 35 million words in text quotations.[3] It is a huge corpus in its own right and its size is such that the results obtained may be said to have some significance in this research.

3.1 The definition of *surprise* in the *OED*

Before conducting an investigation with this corpus, let us first examine one of the definitions of *surprise*, sense 5a of the verb used psychologically.

> SURPRISE 5.a. To affect with the characteristic emotion caused by something unexpected; to excite to wonder by being unlooked-for. † Formerly also in stronger sense (cf. SURPRISE *n.* 4 a), to astonish or alarm; also, to excite to admiration. Often *pass.*, const. *at* († *with*) or inf.; colloq. *to be surprised at* = to be scandalized or shocked at; also as a retort: *you'd be surprised*, the facts are not as you would think.

---

[3] Personal communication with the academic division of Oxford University Press. It has been suggested that the figures for the number of words contained within the text of the quotations cited in the *OED* will be approximately 60 per cent of the figures for the number of words in the *OED* database, which is estimated to be 59 million. It follows that approximately 35 million words will be the figure for the number of text quotations.

Fischer (1997: 162), on the other hand, provides a figure of 25 million words. Her estimation is: "the *OED* on CD-ROM contains nearly 2.5 million illustrative quotations. If an average quotation is assumed to be ten words long, the quotation corpus of the *OED* totals about 25 million words . . ."

It tells us that the verb *surprise*, often used in the passive, formerly accompanied *with*, which is now obsolete, and then *at*, as an agentive preposition. No mention of *by* is made in the definition.

There are five illustrative quotations in which *surprise* is used in the passive and occur with agentive prepositions. Three of them accompany *with* and two take *at*. No quotation containing *by* is adopted. Let us show some of the illustrative quotations.

(4) People were not so much Frighted, as they were **Surpriz'd at** the Bigness, and Uncouth Deformity of the Camel. (L'Estrange *Fables*, 1692); I was exceedingly **surpriz'd with** the Print of a Man's naked Foot on the Shore. (Defoe *Crusoe*, 1719); You'll be **surpriz'd**, Sir, **with** this visit. (Goldsmith *Good-n. Man*, 1768); Macbriar was . . . **surprised at** the degree of agitation which Balfour displayed. (Scot, *Old Mort*, 1816)

This does not seem to reflect the real linguistic situations of the 19th century since the search into the corpora retrieves numerous samples of *surprised* occurring with *by*.

3.2 A text-search

A text-search of the phrases *surprised + at* (*by*, *with*, etc.) and their variant forms was conducted to retrieve the illustrative quotations containing the construction in question. *Surprised* itself was also searched to find quotations in which the verb and the preposition are separated by intervening words.

Retrieved samples are screened, with inappropriate quotations discarded. *Of* and *among* are also found but they are not included here because of very few occurrences (*of* 4, *among* 1). Let us provide some of the instances obtained.

(5) [*with*] 1576 Fleming, I am not **surprised with** the incantations and sorceries of vaine glorie; 1639 Wotton, I was then **surprized with** an advertisement from Court, of the death of . . . my dear nephew . . . ; 1740 Johnson *Life Drake* Wks., Were **surprized with** the sight of seven

Spanish shallops; etc.

[*at*] 1670 Cotton, **Surprizíd at** so slight, and so crude an answer; 1753 T. Gray, I am **surprised at** the print, which far surpasses my idea of London graving; 1824 L. Murray *Eng. Gram.*, In the history of Henry the fourth, by Father Daniel, we are **surprised at** not finding him *the* great man; 1852 Mrs. Stowe *Uncle Tom's C.*, Andy looked up innocently at Sam, **surprised at** hearing this new geographical fact.; etc.

[*by*] 1786 F. Burney *Diary*, At the desert I was very agreeably **surprised by** the entrance of Sir Richard Jeb . . . ; 1794 C. Pigott *Female Jockey Club*, She faints at the approach of a mouse; if **surprised by** the sight of a black lobster, she screams unmercifully; 1838 Lytton *Alice* Miss Merton was . . . **surprised by** the beauty . . . of the young fairy before; 1855 Macaulay *Hist. Eng.*, In the spring of 1691, the Waldensian Shepherds . . . were **surprised by** glad tidings; etc.

Figure 1 shows the statistical results of the occurrence of the agentive prepositions with *surprised*:

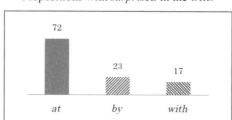

Figure 1
Prepositions with *surprised* in the *OED*

It shows that *at* is the preposition used most often, then comes *by* in a distant second and *with* in third place. *By* is used more than *with* but the definition of *surprise* in the *OED* does not reflect this. Why is this? The century-by-century distribution of the prepositions shown in Figure 2 below will clarify this question.

Figure 2
The century-by-century distribution of *at*, *by* and *with* in the *OED*

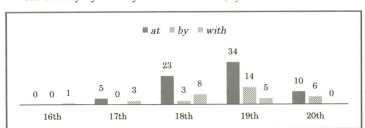

The passive of *surprise* in a psychological sense is observed to have occurred with the agentive preposition *with* in the 16th century. *At* occurred in the 17th century and has been the most predominant preposition throughout the Modern English period, especially in the 18th and the 19th centuries. It seems to show a sign of a relative decrease, however, in the 20th century. *With* was used with less frequency than *at* from the 16th to the 19th century and seems to have been declining in the 20th century. A search into the EEBO is able to partially confirm the observations made here.[4]

By appeared in the 18th century for the first time and has been on the increase ever since: 24 percent occurrence in the 19th century and 38 percent in the 20th. The late appearance of *by* seems to be the reason for its absence in the definition in the *OED*.

It seems that the frequency gap between the two rival prepositions, *at* and *by*, seems to have been narrowing century by century. If we give the value of one to *at*, the ratio of *at* and *by* for each century would be 1 : 0.1 for the 18th century, 1 : 0.4 for the 19th and 1 : 0.6 for the 20th century, which is a clear indication of the increase of *by* and the relative decrease of *at*. If this trend should continue, it could be expected that *by* will catch up with, or overtake, *at* as an agentive preposition of the passive of *surprise* in the near future.

---

[4] The EEBO is a corpus of the Early Modern English period, covering the 1470s through to the 1690s. The following are among the earlier instances: 1588 the good king primaleon olde and decrepite, was so **surprised with** these newes, as he imagined he heard some fantastical illuding voice; 1652 i was **surprised at** this encounter, and guess'd, though with some repugnance the truth of his commission; etc.

This assumption will be confirmed through the investigation into computer corpora in the following sections.

IV. Late Modern English

To further substantiate the results obtained from the *OED*, let us utilize the two computer corpora, the MEC and the VLSA, of Late Modern English (1700–1900) and examine how agentive prepositions occurred with the passive of *surprise*.

4.1 The MEC

The MEC is a corpus created at the Electronic Text Center of the University of Virginia and it is assumed to contain 50 million words of British and American English, with texts from the 16th to the early 20th century. The corpus became unavailable a couple of years ago and the data used here is what was obtained for writing my 2002 and 2015(c) articles.

The search of *surprised* + *at* (*by*, *with*, etc.) and the screening of inappropriate samples yields the statistics in Figure 3 below, together with the data from the VLSA. *With* is also retrieved but is not taken into consideration because of the relatively small number of its occurrence. The occurrence ratio of *at* and *by*, with the value of one given to *at*, is approximately 1 : 0.3.

4.2 The VLSA

The VLSA is a corpus created by Professor Mitsuharu Matsuoka of Nagoya University. It contains more than a hundred British writers of the Victorian period and fifty American writers of the same period, together with some twenty writers of the Early Modern English period. I chose twenty-plus writers each from Britain and America and collected data. After the same procedure, we obtained the result in Figure 3. The ratio of *at* and *by* is roughly 1 : 0.34 and it is quite similar to that obtained from the MEC. (How each writer of this period used *at* or *by* with the passive of *surprise* is shown in Appendix.)

4.3 The results

The data obtained from the two corpora yields the statistics in the following chart.

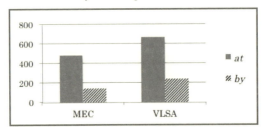

Figure 3
At and *by* with *surprised* in LModE

The ratios of *at* and *by* have turned out to be very similar and they are also very similar to the ratio obtained from the *OED*.[5]

The search also discloses that not a small number of famous and popular writers of the Late Modern English period used *by* with *surprised*, as well as the standard *at*. These writers include Samuel Johnson, Jane Austen, Charles Dickens, Anthony Trollope, Joseph Conrad, Nathaniel Hawthorne, to name a few. It was Dr. Johnson, one of the most renowned men in the literary history of the Modern English period, who used the *surprised + by* construction apparently for the first time. Dickens, another great writer of the period, particularly favored *by*. It is somewhat surprising that a host of writers used *by*, contrary to our belief that *at* was considered to be the standard usage. It does not mean, however, that every writer of the period used *by* with *surprised*. A number of other writers adhered to the conventional preposition *at* and hardly used the newcomer.[6]

---

5) The *OED*'s ratio of *at* and *by* during the period of LModE (i.e. the 18th and the 19th centuries) is 1 : 0.3.

6) They are Lewis Carroll, Sir Arthur Conan Doyle, Charles Darwin, Andrew Lang and so forth.

Chapter 1

V. Present-day English

Present-day English may be referred to as the English of recent decades. Since the texts of the BNC covers the period from 1975, we consider the PE period to be the period which begins from the 1970s in this study. To collect data to cover the period, we used three British corpora, the BNC, the COBUILD and the Wordbanks and two American corpora, the COCA and the CASO.

The COBUILD and the Wordbanks, both created in Britain, contain British and non-British texts. However, as the non-British texts constitute less than a quarter of all the texts, I include them as the British corpora for convenience' sake.

5.1 British corpora
5.1.1 The BNC

The BNC is a 100 million-word corpus with a collection of more than 4,000 texts of modern British English basically from 1975 to 1993, containing both spoken texts (10 percent) and written texts (90 percent). The written texts include such a wide range of genres as fiction, magazine, newspaper and academic. I used the data obtained from the original BNC when I wrote my 1999(a) article.

The statistics obtained after the same process of searching and screening are shown in Figure 4 below, together with the results of the other corpora. Only *at* and *by* will be taken into consideration, disregarding other prepositions with a small number of occurrences.

The outcome of this search is very different from those of the corpora of Late Modern English. The occurrence of *by* has increased a great deal and the ratio of *at* and *by* has become roughly 1 : 1.[7]

---

7) The search into the BNC provided by Brigham Young University yields the different statistics: *at* occurs 366 times and *by* 392 times. This may have to do with the period that the texts of the corpus cover: from the 1980s to 1993, later and shorter than that of the original BNC.

5.1.2 COBUILD

This is a 50 million-word corpus and the texts with a variety of genres range from 1983 to 2000.[8] A search of the same phrases and screening yields the statistics in Figure 4.[9] This corpus is quantitatively half as large as the 100-million word BNC, and the amount of data is approximately half of that of the BNC. The results show a slight increase of *by* and a decrease of *at*, with the approximate ratio of *at* and *by* to be 1 : 1.2.

5.1.3 Wordbanks

This is a 100 million-word corpus and the COBUILD is a subset of this corpus. It contains a variety of texts of multiple countries: Britain, America, Australia, Canada and South Africa. The texts cover the period from 1974 to 2010. The search yields the ratio of *at* and *by* to be approximately 1 : 1.4.

5.1.4 The results

The data obtained from the three corpora yields the statistics in Figure 4.

Figure 4
At and *by* in PE (Britain)

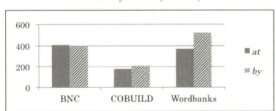

What is to be observed is the shift of the ratios of *at* and *by*. The chart shows the relative increase of *by* from the earlier corpus (BNC) to the later corpus (Wordbanks). A rather large difference of the ratios between the Wordbanks and the BNC or the COBUILD may be explained by the fact that the texts of

---

8) Australian news (OZ news), UK books, UK ephemera, UK magazines, UK spoken, US books, US ephemera, BBC World Services (BBC), National Public Radio (NPR), *The Times* newspaper and *Today* newspaper.

9) The data was obtained when I was writing my articles of 1999.

the Wordbanks cover the first decade of the 21st century, when the occurrence rate of *by* seems to be on the rapid increase.

5.2 American corpora
5.2.1 The COCA

The COCA is a corpus created at Brigham Young University. The corpus is described to contain "more than 560 million words of text (20 million words each year 1990–2017) and it is equally divided among spoken, fiction, popular magazines, newspapers, and academic texts. It is probably the most widely-used corpus of English."[10]

For writing this chapter this corpus was partly utilized; namely, the data for the 1991–95 period and for the 2011–15 period are collected. This time difference has unexpectedly produced significant results, which are shown in Figure 5 below, together with the outcome of the CASO.

5.2.2 CASO

This is also a corpus created at Brigham Young University and it is described to contain "100 million words in more than 22,000 transcripts of ten American soap operas from 2001 to 2012. It provides very useful insight into informal, colloquial American speech."[11] The search of the corpus yields the statistics in Figure 5 below. The ratio of *at* and *by* is roughly 1 : 1.2.

5.2.3 The results

The results in Figure 5 below are obtained from the search into the American PE corpora.

---

10) This is a description provided in the introductory remarks of the corpus. The COCA was not available when I was writing my 1999(a) article, on which this chapter is based.
11) This description is also provided in the introductory remarks of this corpus.

Figure 5
At and *by* in PE (America)

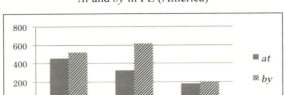

The difference of the two timespans of the COCA has turned out to show some variation between the ratios of *at* and *by*. The ratio for the 1990–94 period is 1 : 1.2, while the ratio for the 2011–15 period unexpectedly shows an astonishing 1 : 1.9. This is a surprising change in that a considerable increase of *by* and the decline of *at* have taken place. The occurrence rate of *by* has surpassed a great deal that of *at* and *by* is used nearly twice as frequently as *at* in the English of the most recent decade.

The ratio of the CASO is approximately 1 : 1.2, similar to the result of the COCA (1). Considering the period the texts of this corpus cover, the outcome should be closer to that of the COCA (2). Why is this? This may be attributed to the fact that as many as forty samples of *I'm surprised at you* (and its variations[12]) are retrieved probably because this corpus consists of the texts of spoken English. Forty occurrences of *at* in this expression seem to push up the figure of the total occurrences, resulting in this ratio.

5.3 The shift of the ratios from Late ModE to PE

The results of the search into the eight corpora from Late Modern English to Present-day English are presented in Figure 6 below, in which the occurrence rate of *at* and *by* in each corpus or sub-corpus are shown. The corpora are arranged according to the period that the texts of each corpus cover.

---

12) Variations include *I am really surprised at you*, *I'm a kind of surprised at you*, *I ain't surprised at you* and so forth.

Figure 6
The occurrence rates of *at* and *by* from LModE to PE

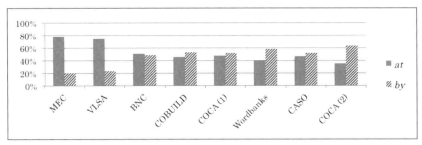

The occurrence rate of *by* was a little over 20 percent in Late Modern English, while in Present-day English the rate has risen to as high as 50 percent and more than 60 percent in the most recent decade.

The data from the eight corpora can be combined to exhibit the shift of the ratios of *at* and *by*, with the value of one given to *at*, in the following figure.

Figure 7
The shift of ratios from LModE to PE

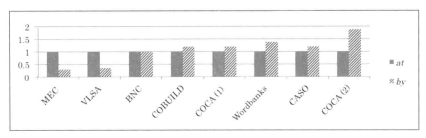

It is evident that the rate of occurrence of *at* has gradually declined, especially in the last two decades, while that of *by* has seen a considerable increase from Late Modern English to Present-day English and an abrupt increase has taken place for these twenty years. The rise and fall of the two prepositions result in the reverse of the occurrence rate in the late 20th century and the ascendancy of *by* over *at* during the recent couple of decades.

5.4 COHA

It is fortunate to be able to have access to another corpus, the Corpus of Historical American English (COHA), also provided by Brigham Young University. The COHA is a corpus of 400 million words of American English, containing texts from 1810 to 2009. The period this corpus covers is such that it will be able to confirm the results we have obtained so far. A search of *surprised* + *at* (*by*) yields the results in Figure 8.

Figure 8
At and *by* with *surprised* from LModE to PE (COHA)

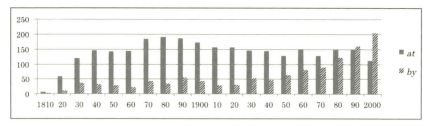

What is particularly noticeable is that *by* began to increase during a couple of decades after the war and it has continued to rise up until the present-day. Let us show the ratios of *at* and *by* on the following chart. The first one hundred fifty years are divided into three parts and after that, the results are illustrated according to each decade. The ratio, with the value of one given to *at*, will be shown for each timespan.

Figure 9
The shift of ratios from LModE to PE (COHA)

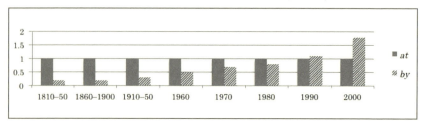

This confirms the results we have shown so far. The occurrence rate of *by* was roughly a quarter or one third in the 19th century and it has kept increasing in the 20th century. The rate of *at* gradually decreased in the first half of the 20th century and kept declining through the latter half of the 20th century. The occurrence rate of *at* and *by* is reversed during the last decade of the 20th century and *by* has become so dominant that it occurs nearly twice as frequently as *at* in the most current English.

VI. The historical shift of agentive prepositions

In Present-day English, passives occur mainly with the agentive preposition *by*. Historically, however, this is not the case and a variety of prepositions have been used. *Of*, for instance, was used as an agentive preposition in Middle English and its heritage can be seen in Present-day English.

The *I am afraid of* construction often used in Present-day English is a vestige of the passive of the verb *affray*, now obsolete or archaic. The verb, when used in the passive, occurred with *of* as an agentive preposition in older English.[13] The active use of *affray* gradually fell into disuse and the surviving past-participle form is felt like an adjective, with *of* no longer considered to be an agentive preposition after *by* has become dominant as a passive preposition (see Jespersen, *MEG* III, 1927: 318).

Not only *of* but other prepositions were used as the agentive preposition in earlier English. Mustanoja (1960: 442) says, "The ME prepositions expressing agency are *by*, *from*, *mid*, *of*, *through*, and *with*." Visser (1973: §§1987–2000) gives the following prepositions: *among*, *at*, *between/betwixt*, *be/by*, *for*, *fram/from*, *mid*, *of*, *to*, *þruh/through*, *with*. *By*, however, ousted other prepositions and has now become the principal agentive preposition in English passives today.

Let us illustrate this shift using the sentences from Chaucer (c1343–1400) and Shakespeare (1564–1616). The following examples from *The Canterbury*

---

13) The definition of *affray* in the *OED* is as follows: "To frighten, to affect with fear; especially in the passive voice to be affrayed or Afraid. *arch.*" and the illustrative quotation is: 1637 Gillespie, If Papists . . . were so affrayed of Conformists.

Tales by Chaucer in (6) and from the plays of Shakespeare in (7) would be a good illustration.

(6) And bathed every veyne in swich licour **Of** which vertu engendred is the flour; (And bathed every sap-vessel in moisture, **by** virtue of which the flower is produced, *General Prologue*, 3–4); The grete Theseus, that of his sleep waked **With** mynstralcie and noyse that was maked, (Great Theseus was awoken out of his sleep **By** minstrelsy and noise . . . , *Knight's Tale*, 2523–24)

(7) There lies the man, slaine **by** young *Romeo*, (*Romeo and Juliet*, III.i.144); I shall be saved **by** my husband. (*Merchant of Venice*, III.v.19); Be govern'd **by** your knowledge, (*King Lear*, IV.vii.18)

It shows that in Chaucer's time, *of* or *with* was commonly used as an agentive preposition, whereas in Shakespeare's plays two centuries later, *by* became the chief preposition of agent.

Considering the usurpation of the agentive prepositions of passives with *by* in the history of the English language, it looks as if the same encroachment of *by* has been taking place for the passive of *surprise*, and possibly for other psychological passives, especially for the passives of psych-verbs synonymous to *surprise*.

VII. Summary

The historical shift of agentive prepositions occurring with the passive of *surprise* in a psychological sense has been examined, utilizing the eight computer corpora of Late Modern English and Present-day English as well as the *OED* on CD-ROM.

A search into the *OED* shows that the agentive *with* began to appear with the passive of *surprise* in the 16th century and *at* in the 17th century. It also shows that *at* has been a predominant preposition throughout the centuries, while *with* has gradually fallen into decline after coexisting with *at* for a couple of centuries. *By* appeared in the 18th century and seems to be on the rise ever since, showing a sign of catching up with the occurrence rate of *at*.

The search into the eight corpora from Late Modern English to Present-day English shows that the ratio of *at* and *by* was approximately 1 : 0.3 in Late ModE and that *by* has been on the increase at such a rate that it has overtaken *at* and now has surpassed it in PE with the result that the ratio has become 1 : 1.9 for the most recent decade.

The increase of *by* with the passive of *surprise* reminds us of the historical shift in which the agentive *by* has replaced a variety of agentive prepositions (*of*, *from*, *through*, etc.) with the English passives in general. The *by*-agent, which ousted rival prepositions, may be replacing *at* with the passive of *surprise* as well. This will be further examined in Chapter 3 for the passives of synonymous verbs to *surprise*.

Appendix

At and *by* with *surprised* used by LModE writers

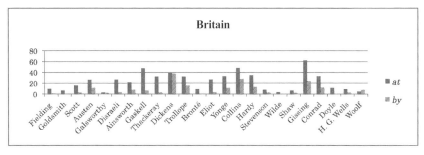

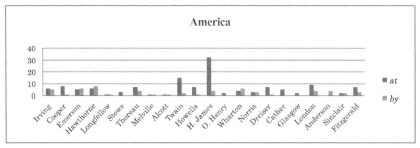

Chapter 2

The passive of *surprise* + *at* or *by*?: The choice of preposition in Present-day English

"To be or not to be, that is the question" is a well-known soliloquy uttered by Hamlet. To choose one from the two alternatives could have been a tough decision to make for an indecisive person like Hamlet. This may be true of a linguistic choice as well. There are many cases in which a person has to choose one linguistic form over the other. The title of this chapter is a case in point. If I am tempted to say "To use *at* or to use *by*, that is the question," would it sound a bit presumptuous for comparing oneself to a great dramatic figure or slightly frivolous for mimicking a famous utterance? The choice of preposition, *at* or *by* with the passive of *surprise*, is the topic we will deal with in this chapter.

I. Introduction

The investigation in Chapter 1 reveals that the rate of occurrence of *by* with the passive of *surprise* was a little over twenty percent in Late Modern English, whereas in Present-day English, the rate has risen to fifty percent and even more than sixty percent in the most recent decade. The use of *by* with *surprised* has shown such a rapid increase that it has caught up with the occurrence rate of *at* and shows a clear dominance over the rival during the most recent decades.

How, then, has the choice of *at* or *by* been made in Present-day English, especially when *at* and *by* are used almost in equal numbers during the last few decades of the 20th century? Are there any crucial factors, linguistic or stylistic, involved in the choice of preposition?

Grammar and usage books have not been particularly eloquent about the choice of preposition. Traditionally, whether the construction is to be treated as an adjective or a passive seems to determine the choice of preposition. A more recent and detailed explanation about the choice is given in Kenkyusha's *Luminous English-Japanese Dictionary* (2005, 2nd ed.) by dictionary advisors Bolinger (an American linguist) and Ilson (a British lexicographer). It goes as follows: "*by* is a colorless preposition used to mention a fact, whereas when *at* is used, a strong shock or an emotional response or reaction can be felt"[1] (s.v. *surprise* v.). Although this is a useful description as the first of this kind and explains very well the difference in the limited space of a dictionary, it does not seem to do full justice to the examples found in the corpora.

This chapter will attempt to discuss the determining factors that govern the choice of *at* or *by* occurring with the passive of *surprise* in Present-day English, by using the data obtained from the PE corpora.

II. *At* with adjectives and *by* with passives?

2.1 *Surprise* in the past-participle form: an adjective or a passive?

Some grammarians have presented claims to the effect that the past-participle form of *surprise* is adjectival if it is static in meaning and is followed by *at*, whereas it is a passive if it occurs with *by* and has a dynamic meaning (Close, 1975; Leech and Svartvik, 1975; Konishi, 1980; etc.). The following sentences from Close exemplify this.

(1) a. I am very surprised at you.
    b. I was surprised by a knock at the door. (Close, 1975: §11.3)

The sentence (1a) is adjectival use, while (1b) is used as a passive. Sentences like (1b) and (2) below (presented by Swan, 1995), however, do not seem to be appropriate examples.

(2) The burglar was surprised by the family coming home unexpectedly.
(Swan, 1995, §405)

---
1) This is a translation from the Japanese description.

21

First, they have a slight physical connotation,[2] and naturally require *by* as an agentive preposition. Second, these sentences are observed to have occurred in the Late ModE corpora but rarely appear in the data of the PE corpora.[3] They would sound rather outdated and look like the type of sentences, reused as a 'second-hand' example in grammar or usage books.

Quirk *et al.* (1985: §3.76) call the adjectival construction like (1a) "semi-passives", which have both verbal and adjectival properties and occur with prepositions other than *by*. In another section (§ 9.63), however, they present two sentences that are exactly the same except for the preposition, as in (3).

(3) a. I was surprised by their rejection of the offer.
b. I was surprised at their rejection of the offer.
(Quirk *et al.*, 1985: § 9.63)

They call the first sentence a passive and the second a participial adjective, obscuring the reasons for the prepositional choice.

Palmer (1988: §5.2.2) also calls the construction of adjectival type "semi-passives", which "appear to have corresponding actives, yet exhibit adjectival features." Palmer further says that these "can occur not only with *by* but also with other prepositions." Palmer rather seems to treat the construction as a passive, but does not provide reasons for the choice of preposition.

Declerck (1991: §6.1) calls the construction occurring with *by* a "true passive" and one taking other than *by* a "pseudo-passive".

(4) a. I was surprised by what she said.
b. She seemed surprised at your behaviour. (Declerck, 1991, §6.1)

---

2) I will discuss this issue in Chapter 5, arguing that these sentences are at the 'intermediate' stage between physical and psychological. They are more likely to have occurred in Late Modern English. In this sense, they are somewhat outdated.
3) My investigation into the prepositional complements of *surprised* shows that there are abundant cases in which abstract nouns are used after a preposition, especially after *by* (e.g. *He is perhaps surprised by her composure*). It also shows that gerunds after the prepositions (e.g. *She was surprised at seeing the curtain drawn aside*) have been declining.

Declerck's pseudo-passives are what other grammarians treat as adjectival sentences. Although Declerck uses a different term, his treatment of the constructions seems to be similar to that of the grammarians who argue for the adjectival theory.

Psychological passives and adjectival constructions are sometimes difficult to distinguish as Denison (1998: 229) says that "the borderline between a passive and BE + predicate can be a murky one," as the following sentences illustrate:

(5) a. Jim was amused by her tirade. [passive]
 b. Jim was amused.
 c. Jim was amused at her tirade. [predicative] (Denison, 1998: 229)

Denison claims that the sentence (5b) could be analyzed as either verbal or adjectival.

Huddleston and Pullum's (2002: 1,436) terminology "adjectival passives" (vs. "verbal passives") to refer to a sentence like *They were very worried* may be more appropriate. At any rate, psych-passives including the passive form of *surprise* show a great deal of ambivalence whether they should be treated as passives or adjectives.

2.2 Two problematic issues

Before discussing the choice of preposition, let us note the two problems involved in this issue. First, discussions so far seem to have been based on more or less outdated data, especially those presented by adjectival theorists.[4] Fortunately, thanks to computer corpora, today's researchers have been able to obtain an enormous amount of data quickly and accurately without the risk of human oversight. It has enabled us, therefore, to examine English usages from a far more advantageous position than our predecessors, who were obliged to analyze a language with a comparatively meager amount of data

---

4) We have seen the drastic increase of *by* and the decrease of *at* with *surprised* from Late Modern English to Present-day English. Furthermore, there has been a shift of types of complements characterized by the increase of *how*-clauses and the decline of gerunds from earlier English to current English. Some grammarians' judgments seem to have been made on the data of earlier English.

and may have inevitably been led to misleading conclusions.

Secondly, the choice of preposition itself has not been much of an issue when the preposition *at* has been considered to be the norm and no clear-cut criterion for the factors governing the choice has been discussed except for such an explanation as was provided by Bolinger and Ilson mentioned above.

Let us now show how the adjectival theory seems to become more or less inappropriate in Present-day English, where *by* has been showing a great deal of increase and there are a number of counter-examples to the claim. The adjectival theory can be contradicted by the examples (6) and (7) below.

In (6), *very* modifies *surprised*, which means that the predicate is used as an adjective according to the adjectival theory. However, because its occurrence with *by* means that the predicate is also used as a passive,[5] it runs counter to the adjectival argument.

(6) At first I was very **surprised by** the average standard of play. (BNC, Magazine, 1991); I'm very **surprised by** what Tony said. (Wordbanks, News, 2005); I am very **surprised by** the book's title. (COCA, Spoken, 1996); etc.

By the same token, the examples in (7) will become counter-examples to the adjectival theory.

(7) a. Louisa was **surprised by** the arrival and glad of it.
(BNC, Fiction, 1989)
b. The doctor never seemed **surprised by** Ted's strange speech patterns.
(Wordbanks, USbooks, 1990)
c. No one was more **surprised by** it than I was. (COCA, News, 1996)

In (7a), the coordination of *surprised* and the adjective *glad* means that

---

5) Konishi (1980: 1551) says that sometimes *surprised* modified by *very* occurs with *by* as in the following: *I was very surprised by the great amount of work done by many students in America.* Swan (1995, §405) also says, "With some words referring to emotional states and reactions, usage is divided" and gives the following examples: *I was very amused / much amused / very much amused by Miranda's performance.* These examples, however, seem to contradict the adjectival claim.

surprised is used adjectivally. In (7b), *surprised* is used as an adjective as it follows a linking verb (*seem*, *look*, *appear*, etc.), and in (7c), the occurrence of *surprised* with the comparative *more* means that the predicate functions as an adjective. However, the use of *by* with *surprised* in each sentence means that it is used as a passive, contradicting the adjectival theory. The claim that the past-participle form of *surprise* is adjectival and occurs with *at* can be refuted.

2.3 'Agentivity' and the choice of *by*

The claim that *by* is chosen if the construction is treated as a passive can be narrowed down to a discussion that there is a correlation between an agent noun signifying 'agentivity'[6] and the choice of *by*. Declerck (1991) and Swan (1995), for instance, suggest that there is a high degree of agentivity in the agent nouns of the following sentences:

(8) a. They were surprised by the guard suddenly entering the room.
(Declerck, 1991: §6.1)
b. The burglar was surprised by the family coming home unexpectedly.
(Swan, 1995: §405) (= (2))

Their claim, however, can be challenged on two counts. First, these sentences are ambiguous, in that they can be interpreted to entail a physical meaning, which naturally requires *by* as an agentive preposition.

Secondly, an investigation into the corpora has revealed that sentences of this type, which are occasionally met with in the Late ModE corpora, rarely occur in the PE corpora. It seems that the claim for the correlation between agentivity and the choice of *by* has become somewhat irrelevant.

Furthermore, the investigation into the PE corpora also shows that the

---

6) I refer to Quirk *et al.* for the terms of semantic roles. They use the term 'agentive' and define it as "animate being instigating or causing the happening denoted by the verb" (Quirk *et al*. §10.19). An agent is a grammatical concept, while agentive is a semantic one (ibid: §3.15). By 'agentivity' I mean such a set of semantic properties in agentive noun phrases as <animacy>, <action> and <volition>. Agentivity will be considered high if an agent is an animate being, especially a human, rather than an inanimate object, and the agent does something to affect another entity with an intention.

majority of agent nouns are abstract nouns, which are supposedly low in agentivity. The following examples, in which abstract nouns are used as agents, illustrate the co-occurrence of nouns with a static meaning (i.e. low in agentivity) with *by*.

(9) He was **surprised by** his impatience for the party to end. (BNC, Fiction, 1993); She was **surprised by** her own endurance . . . (COCA, Fiction, 1992); etc.

In addition to these, samples with abstract nouns as agents are abundant in the data. As the agents of these examples do not show a high degree of agentivity, the claim that the characteristic co-occurrence of *by* with an agentive phrase conveying a sense of activity (or a dynamic meaning) does not seem very convincing. What, then, are the determining factors in choosing *at* or *by*, especially when they exist side by side as equal rivals? In the next section we will discuss how the choice was made between *at* or *by* with *surprised*.

III. The choice of preposition

In discussing the choice of preposition, we will use the following corpora: the BNC, the Wordbanks, the COCA, the COHA and the CASO. The COCA (1990–1994), and the COHA (1970–2000) are used as sub-corpora and these are the periods when *at* and *by* are used in almost equal numbers. In additon, the size of each corpus becomes approximately 100 million words, almost equivalent to that of the other corpora. The CASO covers the period from 2000 to 2012, but since it shows a similarity in the ratio of *at* and *by* to the BNC or the COCA (1990–1994), this corpus is also taken into consideration.

3.1 *How*-clauses with *at* and nominal phrases with *by*

The 'passive of *surprise* + *at* (*by*)' constructions are not only followed by noun phrases but also clauses. Both *at* and *by* are followed by various types

---

7) There are several examples which contain two heterogeneous complements with *surprised at*. They are counted as two samples. The following is an example in which

of complement:[7] abstract nouns and other nouns,[8] pronouns, gerunds, *how*-clauses[9] and *what*-clauses. The frequency of occurrence of each complement is shown in Figure 1.

Figure 1
Types of complements and the frequency of occurrence in PE

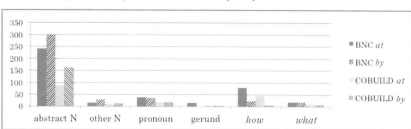

It is apparent that *at* occurs not only with nominal and pronominal phrases, but also with gerunds and clauses, especially *how*-clauses, while *by* occurs chiefly with nominal and pronominal phrases, and with fewer clauses and very few gerunds. Although both *at* and *by* can occur with the same types of complements, what is particularly characteristic of the two prepositions is the stronger tendency for the co-occurrence of *how*-clauses with *at*, and the closer relationship of the nominal phrases, especially abstract noun phrases with *by*. This characterization may be exemplified by the following sentences:

(10) a. But you'll be **surprised at** *how* soon you will become accustomed to

---

an abstract noun and a *how*-clause constitute two different types of complement: *I'm surprised at my abilities and how easily it has come to me.* (BNC, Magazine, 1992)

8) The classification of nouns into abstract nouns and other nouns is due to the fact that the former is static in meaning, while the latter may involve a dynamic meaning, which may affect the choice of preposition. For the classification, I refer to Otsuka and Nakajima (1982: 6–7) and Leech (1989: 9–12). Several nouns are difficult to determine as to whether they are abstract or concrete. The given statistics should be regarded as approximate for the reason that some are ambiguous whether abstract or concrete. Ambiguous cases, however, are so marginal that they are unlikely to influence the general ratio between abstract and other nouns.

9) This includes synonymous *the way*-clause construction as in *He would have been surprised at the way people speak about him.*

the taste of food without salt. (BNC, Non-fiction, 1989); You'd be **surprised at** *how* many people give money to the cause. (BNC, Fiction, 1993); etc.

b. Inwardly he was **surprised by** *the vehemence* in Frank's voice. (BNC, Fiction, 1991); He was **surprised by** *the finesse* with which Nona played. (COCA, Fiction, 1992); etc.

Let us now go back to examine Bolinger and Ilson's view by considering the characteristic occurrence of *by* with abstract nouns, and *at* with *how*-clauses. Abstract nouns are meant to convey cognitive meanings or concepts with little emotional nuances, while most *how*-clauses in the corpora are exclamatory sentences, which naturally express highly emotional conditions. If we interpret Bolinger and Ilson's view in terms of 'emotion', it may be possible to say that *by* occurs with complements carrying little emotional meaning, while *at* occurs with complements highly charged with emotions. If our interpretation were correct, then Bolinger and Ilson's view would be very apt and to the point.

3.2 *I'm surprised at you!*

In a sentence like *I'm surprised at you!*, *at* is the choice and *by* never occurs (except one instance found in the corpus of spoken English) simply because the sentence may be said to be idiomatic.

(11) **I'm surprised at you**, Sarah. (BNC, Fiction, 1993); Why, Virgil, **I'm surprised at you!** (COCA, Fiction, 1994); **I'm surprised at you**, Luke. (CASO, *General Hospital*, 2009); etc.

Table 1 below shows the frequency of occurrence of *I'm surprised at you* and its variations such as *I'm quite surprised at you, I am kind of surprised at you, I ain't surprised at you* and so forth.

This near-idiomatic sentence occurs typically in dialogue and its very frequent occurrence in the CASO explains it. It conveys a strong emotional, exclamatory or even accusatory nuance and together with *how*-clauses, may have led to Bolinger and Ilson's observation.

Table 1
Frequency of *at* in *I'm surprised at you*

	at	*by*
BNC	11	0
Wordbanks	2	0
COCA	8	0
COHA	6	0
CASO	40	1

It is surprising, however, that an instance of *I'm surprised by you* has been found in the CASO (*General Hospital*, 2005) and this may be an exceptional case instigated by the increasing use of *by* with *surprised* in the recent decades.

3.3 Reflexive pronouns with *at*

When an agent is a reflexive pronoun, *at* is almost invariably chosen.

(12) Gaily was **surprised at** *himself*, at his own reactions. (BNC, Fiction, 1969); **Surprised at** *himself*, Jeff grabbed her hand. (Wordbanks, Fiction, 1993); She breaks off suddenly, breathless and **surprised at** *herself*. (COCA, News, 1994); etc.

The frequencies of occurrence of reflexive pronouns and *at* in the PE corpora are shown in Table 2.

Table 2
Frequency of *at* and *by* with reflexive pronouns

	at	*by*
BNC	11	0
Wordbanks	6	0
COCA	11	0
COHA	18	1
CASO	2	1

This is presumably because the complement is not felt to be a genuine agent, which tends to require *by*, but a "semi-agent" that denotes "stimulus". *At*, one of whose functions is to signal "stimulus" (Quirk *et al.*, 1985: §9.51, §9.63), may therefore be chosen.

However, there are two instances of a reflexive pronoun used with *by*, as in (13).

> (13) She was endlessly **surprised by** *herself*. (COHA, Fiction, 2009); Yes, Honey, I'm as **surprised by** *myself* as you are. (CASO, *Young and Restless*, 2008)

Just like there is an instance of *I'm surprised by you* found in the CASO, the rapid increase of *by* may be causing an exceptional case to be occurring and it is likely that there will be more exceptions to appear in the future.

3.4 Double psychological passives and *by*

When *surprised* is coordinated with another psychological verb in the passive, *by* is more likely to be chosen. This is probably because the other predicate requires *by* as in (14a), or because the mutual preposition is not *at*, *by* may have been chosen as a concession, as in (14b).

> (14) a. I realized that I had been more **saddened** than **surprised by** the fact that someone would shoot the Pope. (*TIME*, 1981); Children and adults will in turn be **spellbound** and **surprised by** the wickedly clever use of puppets. (BNC, Ephemera, 1992)
> b. "Well, we have a lot of things to do," he says, apparently **disappointed** but not **surprised by** the MPAA decision. (COCA, News, 1994); He was **pleased** and **surprised by** the flowers and cards that he had received from United supporters. (Wordbanks, *Time*, 1996)

When *surprised* and another psychological passive occur in succession, if not in exact coordination, the other predicate, if it requires *by* as its agentive preposition, may trigger *surprised* to take *by* as well, as in the following:

> (15) I'd been **impressed by** the Spirit R/T, **surprised by** the agility of its

handling. (BNC, Magazine, 1990); Was the U.S. as **taken aback**, as **surprised by** that as apparently some others in the European Community were? (COCA, News, 1992); etc.

In these examples, the predicates *impressed* and *taken aback* both occur with *by*, so it may be possible that these verbs cause *surprised* also to occur with *by*.

3.5 'Suddenness' complement and *by*

I have already noted that the passive of *surprise* used in the original physical sense (i.e. 'to attack suddenly or unawares') takes *by* as its agentive preposition. The passive of *surprise* used in a psychological sense, if accompanied by an agent with a modifier conveying 'suddenness', 'unexpectedness' or 'abruptness', seems to be more likely to take *by* as its preposition, presumably because it is affected by its original physical meaning.

(16) She was **surprised by** *the sudden change* of subject. (BNC, Fiction, 1987); We will be all the more **surprised by** *her sudden illumination* in our midst. (COCA, Academic, 1993); You know, I was a bit **surprised by** *the suddenness* of your invitation. (CASO, *General Hospital*, 2010); etc.

This is a general tendency, not a rule. Although there is the occasional occurrence of sentences in which *at* is employed with a 'suddenness' modifier, *by* occurs with the modifier far more frequently. The occurrences of a 'suddenness' modifier with the preposition in the five corpora were counted and ratios of occurrence between *at* and *by* are shown in Table 3.[10]

Evidently, the 'passive of *surprise*' construction with a 'suddenness' agent phrase is more likely to occur with *by*, far more frequently than *at*.

---

10) In the data of the BNC, *by* with a 'suddenness' modifier occurs eight times and *at* occurs four times; in the Wordbanks, *by* occurs nine times and there is one example of at; in the COCA *by* occurs seven times and *at* four times; in the COHA *by* occurs eleven times and *at* eight times, in the CASO *by* occurs four times and *at* none. These figures lead to the ratios in Table 4 after adjustments are made to even out the differences of the total occurrences of *at* and *by*.

Table 3
The ratio of *at* and *by* with 'suddenness' modifier

	at	by
BNC	1	2
Wordbanks	1	7
COCA	1	1.7
COHA	1	1.6
CASO	0	4

3.6 Demonstrative and indefinite pronouns and *by* in spoken English

In CASO, whose texts are spoken English, *by* occurs quite often with such demonstrative or indefinite pronouns as *that*, *this*, *it* or *any*, as in (17).

(17) Hey, nobody's more **surprised by** *this* than me. (*Bold and Beautiful*, 2001); You can't be that **surprised by** *it*. (*Port Charles*, 2002); But I don't know why you should be **surprised by** *that*. (*Guiding Light*, 2004); 'Cause I'm not **surprised by** *that*. (*General Hospital*, 2008); You know, you don't seem too **surprised by** *any* of this. (*General Hospital*, 2008); etc.

Their frequencies of occurrence out of a total of 204 occurrences of *surprised by* are: *that* 46 times, *this* 23 times and *it* 7 times. Other than these examples, *any* occurs 7 times, *anything* 7 times, *all* 7 times and *anyone* 3 times. In fact, a majority of the prepositional complements occurring with *surprised by* in CASO are these pronouns. As far as spoken English is concerned, there seems to be a strong tendency of co-occurrence of *surprised by* with demonstrative and indefinite pronouns.

3.7 Journalism English and *by*

The choice of the agentive preposition may be made for a stylistic reason. The COBUILD is most convenient to use for research into the correlation between style and genre. The search of *surprised* + *at* (*by*) in the corpus yielded data from the following genres: Australian news (OZ news), UK ephemera, UK magazines, UK spoken, US ephemera, BBC world services

Chapter 2

(BBC), National Public Radio (NPR), UK books, US books, *The Times* newspaper and *Today* newspaper. Figure 2 below shows the frequency of occurrence of *at* and *by* in different genres.

Figure 2
At and *by* in the COBUILD

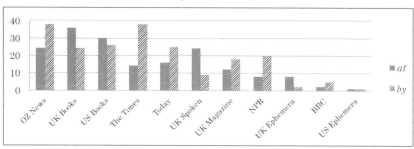

It is evident from the chart that *by* occurs with higher frequency than *at* in every field of journalism English: newspapers (OZ news, *The Times*, *Today*), magazines (UK magazine) and broadcast news (BBC, NPR). It may be said that *by* has become more common than *at* in journalism English, especially in newspaper English.

This preference for *by* in journalism English is confirmed by a search into *TIME* Magazine Corpus.[11] The search retrieves the results in Figure 3.

Figure 3
At and *by* in *TIME* Magazine Corpus

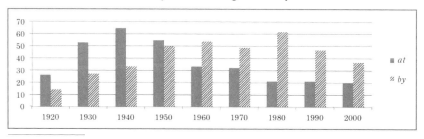

11) This is a 100-million-word American corpus created at Brigham Young University, covering the period from 1923 to 2006. An example from this corpus is already presented in (14a).

The occurrence of *by* surpassed that of *at* as early as in the 1960s in this corpus. It is surprising if we consider the fact that it is in the 1990s that *by* is observed to have begun to pass the occurrence rate of *at* in the findings obtained from the other corpora. This suggests that in journalism English such as *TIME* magazine, *by* seems to have been much more preferred to *at*, thus the correlation between journalism English and the agentive *by*.

It may be hasty to draw a conclusion from the research into only a couple of corpora. Furthermore, it is difficult to define what journalism English is in the first place, as Crystal and Davy (1969:173) point out, "everything that happens to be printed in a newspaper or magazine or written by a journalist is not going to be linguistically homogeneous." Nevertheless, the results obtained seem to be in agreement with our intuitions or empirical observations that *by* seems to be favored and occur more frequently than *at* in newspapers, magazines and TV or radio news. This inclination may be associated with the nature of what we call journalism English.

Newspaper reporters and editors may favor using new and novel expressions. At least they may not be inhibited from accepting them, as "the aim is to make a sudden impression on the reader . . ." (Foster 1968: 199). In addition, because newspaper reporters always face realities of society and are likely to meet people of all classes who speak varieties of English, they must be perceptive of the actual, if not acceptable, usages of English. They may even be susceptible to the changes in English that have been taking place in society and their writing may reflect this. The new usages or linguistic constructions may find their way into journalism English as "grammatical flexibility" or "grammatical daring" (Hughes 1989: 152), and the 'passive of *surprise* + *by*' construction may be an example of this.

3.8 Legal English and *by*

A search of the Corpus of US Supreme Court Opinions[12] yields the result of an unexpectedly frequent occurrence of *by* with the passive of *surprise*, as in Figure 4.

---

12) This is another corpus of Brigham Young University and it is described to "contain approximately 130 million words in 32,000 Supreme Court decisions from the 1790s to the current time."

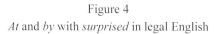

Figure 4
At and *by* with *surprised* in legal English

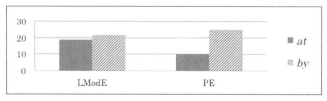

From the chart we find that the ratio of *at* and *by* is 1 : 1.2 in Late Modern English (1800–1900) and 1 : 2.5 in Present-day English (1970–2010). It shows an unusually high occurrence rate of *by* in legal English, considering the ratio of the day (1 : 0.3 in LModE and 1 : 1~1.9 in PE). Although this is the result obtained from the American corpus, it may be true of Britain since there should not be much difference in English in a technical field as law. British lawyers must have been reading the US Supreme Court decisions and may have known and favored this usage themselves.

This characteristic of legal English may have contributed to Dickens' preference for *by* with the predicate that we have touched on. Dickens had been a court reporter before he became a novelist. The future novelist may have heard this unusual usage during the trials and later may have been induced to use it in his writing.

IV. Summary

Determining factors have been examined for the choice of the preposition *at* or *by* introduced by the passive of *surprise*. There have been claims that the construction is adjectival if it has a static meaning and takes *at* as its agentive preposition, and that it is treated as a passive if it has a dynamic meaning and occurs with *by*. A number of counter-examples, however, have been found to refute the claim. Also the choice of the preposition seems to have little to do with the 'agentivity' of an agent noun phrase, contrary to the claims of some grammarians. What determines the choice of preposition seems to have to do with what type of prepositional complement the predicate occurs with.

Although both *at* and *by* take the same types of complements, *by* is most likely to be followed by noun phrases, especially abstract noun phrases, whereas *at* is characterized by being accompanied with a considerable number of *how*-clauses. This characterization seems to be reflected in Bolinger and Ilson's view of the choice of preposition.

In an idiomatic expression *I'm surprised at you*, *at* is chosen and *by* never occurs (except for one example in the CASO). When the preposition is followed by a reflexive pronoun, *at* is the choice (also two exceptions in the most recent data after 2000). When two psychological predicates occur in coordination or in succession, *by* is more likely to be chosen. When an agent noun is modified by a word meaning 'suddenness' or 'unexpectedness', *by* seems to be favored, presumably because of its association with the original physical meaning of the verb.

In spoken English, *by* occurs very frequently with such demonstrative or indefinite pronouns as *that*, *this*, *it*, *anything*, *anyone* and so forth. These pronouns make up of nearly half of the prepositional complements.

In journalism English, there seems to be a tendency to prefer *by* to *at*. This may have to do with the nature of journalism English, in which new and novel expressions are favored to make sudden impressions on readers. Furthermore, newspaper reporters may be susceptible to the changes of English and new constructions may find their way into their writings, thus the newspaper reporters' preference for *by*. This may be confirmed by the statistics obtained from the COBUILD and the *TIME*.

We have discovered that in legal English, the agentive *by* has been used with the passive of *surprise* at a much higher rate than the rate of the day. Dickens may have been aware of the construction uttered during the court trials, which in turn may have led him to use it so profusely in his novels.

Chapter 3

Psych-passives with agentive prepositions: the historical shift from Early Modern English to Present-day English

"History repeats itself" is said to be the statement made by an ancient Roman historian, Curtius Rufus. If Rufus were right, we might see the history repeated in a linguistic phenomenon of psych-passives in English, where the *by*-agent will be likely to become dominant as the agentive preposition, ousting other rival prepositions. This may have been the same path that the English passives had trodden in the past several centuries, thus the repetition of history.

I. Introduction

A language is abundant with emotional expressions and they are expressed in a variety of grammatical devices. In English, the passives of *surprise*, *please*, *frighten*, for instance, are used, along with such intransitive verbs as *marvel*, *rejoice*, *fear*, for expressing similar emotional conditions, respectively. Psychological verbs in the passive form (psych-passives), however, seem to be much more utilized in English than other constructions. What we are concerned with in this chapter is a history of psych-passives and the agentive prepositions they occur with from Early Modern English to Present-day English.

1.1 Agentive prepositions with psych-passives

The passives of psych-verbs have been observed to occur with a preposition other than *by* as an agentive preposition, as in (1).

(1) a. Sophia was much **pleased with** the beauty of the girl. (Fielding, *Tom Jones*, 1749)
   b. I was not a little **surprised at** his intimacy with people of the best fashion. (Goldsmith, *The Vicar of Wakefield*, 1766)

This is the normal and standard usage of the day and the *OED* gives the following descriptions about the agentive prepositions occurring with the passives of *please* and *surprise*.

Please 4.a. Passive. To be pleased. Const. *with*.
Surprise 5. Often *pass.*, const. *at* (†*with*) or inf.

The standard usage of the late 19th century dictates that when the verb *please* occurs in the passive, it takes *with* as an agentive preposition and the passive of *surprise* accompanies *at* or *with*.

1.2 Psych-passives + *by*

For a couple of centuries, however, the passives of these psych-verbs have been observed to be occurring with *by*, as in (2).

(2) a. Emma was particularly **pleased by** Harriet's begging to be allowed to decline it. (Austen, *Emma*, 1815); Was it folly in Tom to be so **pleased by** their remembrance of him at such a time? (Dickens, *Martin Chuzzlewit*, 1843–44)
   b. Rosamond was **surprised by** the appearance of the maid-servant. (Collins, *The Dead Secret*, 1857); They were **surprised by** the sudden opening of the door; a servant appeared to clear the table. (Gissing, *In the Year of Jubilee*, 1894)

Not only such eminent and renowned writers as Austen and Dickens but Collins, Gissing and many others are also observed to have used the passives of these psych-verbs with the agentive *by* in the 19th century, contrary to our conventional grammatical notions.

The examination of the developmental history of the passive of *surprise* occurring with *at* or *by* from Late ModE to PE in Chapter 1 shows that *at*

Chapter 3

was so prevalent that it occurred about three times more frequently than *by* in Late ModE but that in PE, *by* has been on the increase at such a rate that it has considerably surpassed the occurrence rate of *at*.

This chapter attempts to clarify how the passives of psych-verbs synonymous to *surprise* have occurred with the agentive prepositions from Early ModE through Late ModE to PE. My main concern is the shift of the prepositions from Late ModE to PE, but the examination of their occurrence in Early ModE would also be essential for a better comprehension of the shift of the agentive prepositions of later periods.

The comparison of the results of the three periods will reveal the developmental history of the agentive prepositions with psych-passives and the apparent dominance of *by* over *with* or *at*, which had been prevalent in earlier periods.

Finally, I will argue that this prepositional shift may have been the same shift that happened to the regular passives of English, where the agentive *by* replaced such other prepositions as *of*, *from*, *through*, etc. I will make a hypothesis that the dominance of *by* may be occurring with psych-passives as well with a few centuries' delay.

1.3 Synonymous psych-verbs

The verbs synonymous to *surprise* to be treated are: *alarm*, *amaze*, *appall*, *astonish*, *astound*, *baffle*, *bewilder*, *dismay*, *perplex*, *shock*, *startle* and *stun*. Let us show how synonymous these verbs are by consulting *Oxford Dictionary of English* (2003, 2nd), which offers the following definitions:

> *Amaze* is described as "surprise (someone) greatly; fill with astonishment", *appall* "greatly dismay or horrify", *astonish* as "surprise or impress (someone) greatly", *astound* as "shock or greatly surprise", *baffle* as "totally bewilder or perplex", *bewilder* as "cause (someone) to become perplexed and confused", *perplex* as "make (someone) feel completely baffled", *shock* as "cause (someone) to feel surprised and upset", *startle* as "cause to feel sudden shock or alarm", *stun* as "astonish or shock (someone) so that they are temporarily unable to react", *surprise* as "cause (someone) to feel mild astonishment or shock". *Alarm* is described as "to make (someone) feel

frightened, disturbed, or in danger" but a synonym dictionary lists "startle" and "dismay" for its synonym.[1] As for *dismay*, the dictionary gives "alarm" and "appall".

It is interesting to note that the definitions cited here are made by borrowing other synonymous words and in that sense these definitions may be more or less circuitous. These circular and roundabout definitions may be tantamount to saying that the verbs are used synonymously.

The fact that these verbs are synonymous may also be illustrated by the coordinated use of the two predicates, as shown in (3).

(3) **Astonished** and **shocked** at so unlover-like a speech . . . (Austen, *Sense and Sensibility*,1811); They were not however the less **astonished** and **dismayed** . . . (Shelley, *The Last Man*, 1826); Sam's fingers were trembling at the gaiters, as if he were rather **surprised** or **startled**. (Dickens, *Pickwick Papers*, 1836–37); Both the sisters seemed struck: not **shocked** or **appalled** . . . (Ch. Brontë, *Jane Eyre*, 1847); "Thy acts are like mercy," said Hester, **bewildered** and **appalled**. (Hawthorne, *The Scarlet Letter*, 1850); Poor Mrs. Edmonstone was **alarmed** and **perplexed** beyond measure. (Yonge, *The Heir of Redcliffe*, 1853); etc.

Synonymous as they may be, these verbs seem to have some slightly different shades of meaning from each other, as in (4).

(4) The fat butler seemed **astonished**, not to say **shocked**, at this violation of etiquette . . . (Disraeli, *The Young Duke*, 1831); Judith Malmayns, who appeared much **surprised**, and not a little **alarmed**, at the sight of so many persons . . . (Ainsworth, *Old Saint Paul's*, 1841); Those who . . . were **astonished**, and even **startled**, to perceive how her beauty shone out, (Hawthorne, *The Scarlet Letter*, 1850); He was **amazed**, and a little **startled**, (Collins, *The Queen of Hearts*, 1859); etc.

The writers, with the differences in mind, may have used them in an appropriate way in a suitable context. Basically, however, they seem to have

---

1) *The Penguin Dictionary of English Synonyms and Antonyms* (1992).

such identical or similar meanings as to be included as a group of synonyms.

1.4 Corpora and concordances

Four computer corpora were used to collect data: the VLSA and the MEC for Late Modern English and the BNC and the COCA for Present-day English. The COHA is also utilized for the comparative analysis of Late ModE and PE. We also made use of concordances for the collection and confirmation of the data for Spenser, Marlowe and Shakespeare.

The VLSA has a larger number of British writers,[2] compared to the MEC, generally with more works for each writer, which are not contained in the MEC. On the other hand, the MEC has more American writers and works, some of which are not contained in the VLSA.[3] The data from these corpora is, so to speak, a hybrid data but this would not be a detriment to our purpose of obtaining the overall ratio of *at* and *by* occurring with psych-passives during the periods we are concerned with. Using these corpora with the help of concordances, the data are collected in the same way as we did in the previous chapters.

II. Early Modern English

2.1 Writers examined

Now let us examine the behaviors of the construction in question during the period of Early Modern English (1500–1700). The writers and works to be treated are:

Edmund Spenser (1552?–99), William Shakespeare (1564–1616), The King James Bible (1611), Daniel Defoe (1660?–1731) and Jonathan Swift (1667–1745).

---

2) The exceptions are the following writers: Johnson, Prest, Lang, Stevenson, Doyle and H. G. Wells. Their data was obtained from the MEC.
3) Sedgwick, Child, Bird, Willis, Simms, Poe, Stowe, Curtis, Taylor and Cummins are such writers. Their data was also obtained from the MEC. The data of some writers (e.g. Cooper, Emerson, Hawthorne) are mixed data of the two corpora.

They are the major writers representing the period and their English may be considered to be typical of the literary English of the day.

Other writers we examined are:

Philip Sidney (1554–86), Francis Bacon (1561–1626), Ben Johnson (1572–1637), Christopher Marlowe (1564–93), Thomas Nashe (1567–1601), John Milton (1608–74), John Bunyan (1628–88) and John Dryden (1631–1700).

Their works, however, yield very few examples of these psych-passives in question. Only Marlowe, Milton and Bunyan produce meaningful results and, as each set of statistics obtained from these writers is not large enough to be treated individually, they are grouped together for examination in §2.7.

2.2 Spenser (1552?–1599)

The psych-verbs that Spenser mainly used in *The Faerie Queene* (*FQ*, 1590) and other works are *amaze, astonish* and *dismay*. *Appall*, *perplex* and *stun* are used but not in the passive. *Bewilder*, *shock* and *startle* do not seem to be in Spenser's vocabulary. Let us show some examples of psych-passives used with agentive prepositions in (5).

(5) She greatly grew **amazed at** the sight, (*FQ*, I.v.21); I stand **amazed At** wondrous sight . . . (*Amoretti*, iii.7); She was **astonisht at** her heavenly hew. (*FQ*, II.vii); Greatly there**at** was Britomart **dismayd**. (*FQ*, III. xi.22); **By** her I entering half **dismayed** was. (*FQ*, IV.x.36); etc.

The frequencies of occurrence of agentive prepositions are shown in parentheses, as follows: *amaze* (*at* 6, *with* 1); *astonish* (*at* 4, *with* 3); *dismay* (*at* 6, *with* 21, *by* 1). The agentive prepositions that Spenser mainly used are *at* and *with*. *At* has remained to be used till Present-day English, while *with* has gradually declined to fall into near disuse.[4] *By* appears only once in

---

4) This reminds us of the history of the passive of *surprise*. It first started with the occurrence of *with*, then followed by *at*, and the final entrance of *by*. Psych-passives with a meaning of 'surprise' or 'amazement' occurring with *at* may have already started before

Spencer, but this is a very significant instance because it seems to be one of the earliest examples in which *by* is used with a psych-passive.[5] Spenser's usage may be said to show a presage of the predominant occurrence of *at* and a forerunner of *by* to be used in Late Modern English.

2.3 Shakespeare (1564–1616)

The psych-verbs that Shakespeare used with an agentive preposition are *amaze* and *perplex*. *Amaze* occurs with *at* five times and *perplex* takes *with* once, as in (6).

(6) I am more **amazed at** his dishonour, Than **at** the strangeness of it. (*Measure for Measure*, V.i.384–5); I am **amazed at** your passionate words. (*M. N. Dream*, III.ii.220); What, **amaz'd At** my misfortunes? (*Henry VIII*, III.ii.374–5); for till you do return, I rest **perplexed with** thousand cares. (*1 Henry VI*, V.v.95); etc.

Appall and *dismay* are used in the passive but with no preposition. *Astonish* and *startle* only occur in the active voice. *Astound, bewilder, shock* and *stun* do not seem to be in Shakespeare's dictionary as Onions' *Glossary* (1911) contains none of them.

It may be Shakespeare's rhetoric but not showing agency in his many uses of psych-passives seems to be a little enigmatic, compared to Spenser's usage, in which agentive noun phrases are expressed more than forty times altogether. Shakespeare's use of psych-passives may be a reflection of the playwright being conscious that these predicates are felt to be adjectives, not passives.

Spenser's time. Interestingly enough, *surprise* had yet to be used in a psychological sense in Spenser and it was used in a physical sense (*He was surprised, and buried under beare*, *FQ*, III.iii.11.2). The psychological use was a later development and the first citation is 1692.

5) *Dismay* in the passive is used with *by* four times: three of them are used in a physical sense and one is psychological. This is the only instance of the psych-passive used with *by* in Spenser. This sort of overlapping use of *by* to cover physical and psychological uses may have triggered the extended use of *by* to other psych-verbs in general.

2.4 The King James Bible (1611)

The verbs used in the passive with a preposition in the Bible are *amaze*, *astonish*, *dismay* and *perplex*. Let us show some examples in (7).

(7) They were all **amazed at** the mighty power of God. (*Luke*, 9:43); And the disciples were **astonished at** his words. (*Mark*, 10:24); I was **dismayed at** the seeing of it. (*Isiah*, 21:3); Be not afraid nor **dismayed by** reason of this great multitude; (*1 Chronicle* 20:2); as they were much **perplexed** there**about**, (*Luke*, 24:4); etc.

The numbers of their occurrence with an agentive preposition are as follows: *amaze* (*at* 2), *astonish* (*at* 14), *dismay* (*at* 5, (*by* 1)), *perplex* (*about* 1). *At* is virtually the only preposition occurring with all the psych-passives in the Bible. *By* in "dismayed by reason of this great multitude" is a marginal and ambiguous example as to whether this is an agentive preposition or a part of an idiomatic expression of "by reason of" since in other versions the same line is translated as "dismayed at this multitude."

The overall absence of *by* with psych-passives except for this example may suggest that this *by* is not likely to be an agentive preposition. Nevertheless, there is a possibility that it was extended to the use of the agentive preposition in later usages.

The dominant occurrence of *at* in Spencer, Shakespeare and the King James Bible suggests that it was most widely used during the earlier part of the Early ModE period. Considering the continuous use of *at* till Present-day English, it is natural to think that *at* kept being used prevalently throughout the Late ModE period as well, as force of habit may have been working in the use of language.

2.5 Defoe (1660–1731)

The psych-verbs occur quite frequently in Defoe's works as they may be more likely to be used in adventurous novels like *Robinson Crusoe*, compared to the religious works of Milton or Bunyan. The verbs used in the passive are *alarm*, *amaze*, *astonish*, *perplex*, *shock*, *startle* and *stun*. Let us show some examples.

> (8) I was not **alarmed at** the news, (*Moll Flanders*); the country being **alarmed with** the appearance of ships of strangers upon the coast; (*Captain Singleton*); and all the Country was **alarmed about** them. (*A Journal of the Plague Year*); he seemed **amazed at** the sight of our bark, (*Singleton*); I was indeed **astonished at** the impudence of the men, (*Plague Year*); I was so **astonished with** the sight of these things, (*Robinson Crusoe*); Our men were **perplexed at** this, (*Singleton*); And now I was greatly **perplexed about** my little boy. (*Moll*); I was indeed **shocked with** this sight; (*Plague Year*); I was a little **startled at** that, (*Moll*); William was quite **stunned at** my discourse, (*Singleton*); etc.

The numbers of their occurrence are as follows; *alarm* (*at* 3, *with* 2, *about* 1), *amaze* (*at* 2, *with* 1), *astonish* (*at* 4, *with* 1), *perplex* (*at* 1, *about* 1), *shock* (*with* 1), *startle* (*at* 1), *stun* (*at* 1). *At* is the most frequently used preposition (12 times) and *with* comes second (four times), followed by *about* (twice).

Unlike Spenser, Shakespeare or other writers, Defoe used *surprise* in a psychological sense very frequently. The author uses the passive of the verb with *at* 18 times and with *with* 17 times and one of the sentences is used as an illustrative quotation in definition 5 of *surprise*, as we have seen in Chapter 1. The frequent use of *surprise* may have caused the writer to refrain from the use of other psych-verbs.

2.6 Swift (1667–1745)

The verbs that Swift used in the passive are *alarm*, *amaze*, *astonish*, *perplex* and *stun*. Some of the examples, all from *Gulliver's Travels*, are given below.

> (9) I was **alarmed with** the cries; He was **amazed at** the continual noise it made; they . . . were really **amazed at** the sight of a man . . . ; He was more **astonished at** my capacity for speech and reason . . . ; He was perfectly **astonished with** the historical account . . . ; I was quite **stunned with** the noise; etc.

The numbers of their occurrence are: *alarm* (*with* 3), *amaze* (*at* 4), *astonish* (*at* 1, *with* 1), *perplex* (*about* 1), *stun* (*with* 1). Compared to Defoe, Swift makes less use of these verbs and seems to prefer such older prepositions as *with* or *about*.

The usages of Defoe and Swift do not seem to be very different from those of their predecessors. The main verbs used are *amaze* and *astonish* and their passives occur mainly with *at* or *with*.

2.7 Other writers

Three writers are treated in this section: Marlowe (1564–93), Milton (1608–74) and Bunyan (1626–88). The verbs that Marlowe used in the passive with a preposition are *amaze* and *dismay*. Milton used *amaze*, *dismay* and *perplex*. Bunyan used *amaze* and *dismay*. The examples in (10) are the psych-passives that these three writers used with *at* or *with* as the agentive preposition.

(10) Marlowe: And hosts of soldiers stand **amazed at** us; (*1 Tamberlaine*, I. ii. 220); the Soldan is No more **dismayed with** tidings of his fall, Than in the heaven . . . (*1 Tamberlaine*, IV.iii.30).
Milton: and flocking birds, with those also that love twilight . . . **amazed at** what she means, (*Areopagitica*); All **amazed At** that so sudden blaze, (*Paradise Lost*, Book X); be not **dismayed**, Nor troubled **at** these tidings from the earth, (*Paradise Lost*, Book X); **Perplexed** and troubled **at** his bad success The Tempter stood. (*Paradise Regained*, Book IV).
Bunyan: I say, my Neighbours were **amazed at** this my great conversion; (*Grace Abounding*); for he, being **dismayed with** their coming upon him, (*Pilgrim's Progress*, Part I).

The variety of verbs and prepositions used by these writers are not much different from the earlier writers, showing the continuous use from the earlier period to this late Early ModE period. *Amaze*, *dismay* and *perplex* are the main verbs and their passives occur with such prepositions as *at* or *with*. The agentive *by* had yet to be used by these writers at this stage of Early Modern English.

2.8 Some characteristics of Early Modern English

We have seen the psych-passives used with the agentive prepositions in the works of the Early ModE period. The following table shows how each verb is used in the passive with a preposition *at* or *with* in each writer or work. The occurrence of *about* is so few that it is omitted from the table.[6]

Table 1
At or *with* occurring with psych-passives in EModE

		alarm	amaze	astonish	dismay	perplex	Total
Spenser	at	–	6	4	6	0	16
	with	–	1	3	21	0	25
	by	0	0	0	1	0	1
Shakespeare	at	0	5	0	0	0	5
	with	0	0	0	0	1	1
the Bible	at	0	2	14	5	0	21
	with	0	0	0	0	0	0
Defoe	at	3	2	4	0	1	10
	with	2	1	1	0	0	4
Swift	at	0	4	1	0	0	5
	with	3	0	1	0	0	4
Others	at	0	4	0	1	1	6
	with	0	0	0	2	2	4
Total	at	3	23	23	12	2	63
	with	5	2	5	23	3	38
	by	0	0	0	1	0	1

Note: 0 means that the verb is used but not in the passive and if used in the passive, with no preposition; – means that the verb is not used at all by the author

The verbs chiefly used in the earlier part of this period are *amaze*, *astonish* and *dismay*, with *alarm* and *perplex* trailing after them. *Amaze* is widely used by all the authors, while *astonish* is preferred in the Bible and *dismay* by Spenser.

---

6) *About* occurs with *perplexed* three times (the Bible, Defoe, Swift) and with *alarmed* once (Defoe).

Shock, *startle* and *stun* are each used only once or twice with a preposition, so they are also excluded from the table. *Appall*, *astound*, *baffle* and *bewilder* hardly occur at all during this period. These verbs are latecomers and when they made an entrance, they may have begun to occur with a newer preposition *by*, not bound by the yoke of older prepositions, *at* or *with*. This seems to be the presage of the usage of the forthcoming period.

At is the most frequently used preposition with these psych-passives. *Amaze* and *astonish* occur mostly with *at* and this seems to predict the later usage. *With* was not much used except for Spenser's unusual preference for it with *dismay*. *By* hardly appeared at this stage yet, except for one example in Spenser.

In terms of semantics, *at* may have been used to indicate the semantic role of 'stimulus' of the agentive noun phrase, as Leech and Svartvik (2002: 137) say, "An emotive reaction to something can be expressed by the preposition *at*" or "In <BrE>, *with* is often used instead of *at* when what causes the reaction is a person or object rather than an event." This description about Present-day English should be applicable to the English of this period as well.

It may be possible to interpret *at* to indicate 'instrument', as Mustanoja (1960: 363–64) says, "Cases of this kind illustrate the development of the original local use of *at* into an instrumental function." Other verbs must have followed suit and come to take *at* to show 'stimulus' or 'instrument'.

These verbs continued to be used with *at* till and during the Late ModE period. This continued use of *at* may be said to be due to the 'frequency' principle at work (or we may say the 'old-habits-die-hard' principle), as is suggested by the statements of Jespersen (1922: 267) or Baugh (1935: 65).[7]

Since *by* is virtually non-existent during this period except for one example of Spenser's, the ratio of *at* and *by* in the Early ModE period can be roughly calculated to be 1 : 0.02 and for the sake of convenience, it may be rounded to be 1 : 0.

---

7) Jespersen says, "Frequency of repetition would in itself tend to render the habitude firmly rooted, thus really capable of resisting change," Baugh states, "An examination of the words in an Old English dictionary shows that about eighty-five per cent of them are no longer in use. Those that survive, to be sure, are basic elements of our vocabulary, and by the frequency with which they recur make up a large part of any English sentence."

Chapter 3

III. Late Modern English

To collect data for Late Modern English, we mainly used the VLSA and to compare the results from the VLSA, the COHA was used as a supplementary corpus. From the VLSA, we selected some thirty-plus writers each from Britain and America. From the COHA, we gathered data from 1800 to 1900, the period equivalent to the latter half of the Late ModE period.

3.1 The VLSA

We have examined thirty-four writers from Britain and thirty-two from America. Writers of Britain are as follows:[8]

Henry Fielding (1707–54), Samuel Johnson (1709–84), Oliver Goldsmith (1728–74), Walter Scott (1771–1832), Jane Austen (1775–1817), Charles Lamb (1775–1834), Thomas Carlyle (1795–1881), Mary Shelly (1797–1851), Benjamin Disraeli (1804–81), W. H. Ainsworth (1805–82), Charles Darwin (1809–82), Thomas Peckett Prest (1810–59), Elizabeth Gaskell (1810–65), W. M. Thackeray (1811–63), Anthony Trollope (1815–82), Charlotte Brontë (1816–55), Emily Brontë (1818–48), George Eliot (1819–80), C. M. Yonge (1823–1901), Wilkie Collins (1824–89),[9] Lewis Carroll (1832–98), Samuel Butler (1835–1902), Thomas Hardy (1840–1928), Andrew Lang (1844–1912), Robert Louis Stevenson (1850–94), Oscar Wilde (1854–1900), George Bernard Shaw (1856–1950), George Gissing (1857–1903), Joseph Conrad (1857–1924), Arthur Conan Doyle (1859–1930), Rudyard Kipling (1865–1936), H. G. Wells (1866–1946), G. K. Chesterton (1874–1936) and W. S. Maugham (1874–1965).

American writers are:

---

[8] As Dickens will be treated in the next chapter to be compared to his contemporary writers, the novelist is not included here.

[9] The number of Collins' works contained in the VLSA is so large that the yielded data could disrupt the whole statistics. In fact, the total number of instances is 278, compared to the second largest Gaskell's data is 151, so I have decided to use twenty of his works from *Antonia* to *The Black Robe*. The size of the data (the total number) thus obtained is 175 instances, close to Gaskell's data. This reducing of the data does not seem to affect the overall ratio of *at* and *by*.

George Washington (1732–99), Washington Irving (1783–1859), James Fenimore Cooper (1789–1851), Catharine Sedgwick (1789–1867), William H. Prescott (1796–1859), Maria Lydia Child (1802–80), Ralph Waldo Emerson (1803–82), Nathaniel Hawthorne (1804–64), Robert Montgomery Bird (1806–54), Nathaniel Parker Willis (1806–67), William Gilmore Simms (1806–70), Henry Wadsworth Longfellow (1807–82), Edgar Allan Poe (1809–49), Harriet Beecher Stowe (1811–96), Henry David Thoreau (1817–62), Herman Melville (1819–91), George William Curtis (1824–92), Bayard Taylor (1825–78), Maria S. Cummins (1827–66), Luisa May Alcott (1832–88), Alger Horatio (1832–99), Mark Twain (1835–1910), W. D. Howells (1837–1920), Henry James (1843–1916), Edith Wharton (1862–1937), Frank Norris (1870–1902), Willa Cather (1873–1947), Ellen Glasgow (1873–1945), Jack London (1876–1916), Sherwood Anderson (1876–1941) and Scott Fitzgerald (1896–1940).

These writers are selected because they are popular and eminent writers in the literary history of the 18th and 19th centuries and many of them are prolific enough to provide sufficient data and meaningful results. Some of the writers produced their works in the early 20th century, but as their acquisition of English had taken place in the late 19th century and therefore they are assumed to have been using 19th-century English, they are also included.

The data of just over thirty writers from each country may not be representative of the linguistic situations of the period but they are assumed to be a close representation of them since the results (that is, the ratio of *at* and *by*) of Britain and America have proved to be quite similar to each other.

British writers and their American counterparts are examined separately because it may be possible that the two countries have different linguistic tendencies with their own characteristics. It has been claimed that America has preserved older features of English that Britain has lost. Markwardt (1958: 59–80) describes it as the "colonial lag." Nevalainen (2006: 146) seems to be in agreement to this idea and says that "this conservatism is called colonial lag." So it may be expected that American writers show an older tendency in their choice of preposition, but it has proved that the results from the two countries show quite a similarity in the ratio of *at* and *by*.

3.2 Some collected examples

Let us now provide a portion of examples of psych-passives occurring with *at* or *by* collected from the corpora. Samples with other prepositions such as *with* or *about* are retrieved, but they are not taken into consideration due to the much lower frequency of occurrence.

The following is a list of samples and they are presented in such a way as to represent a general tendency of each verb. 'Br.' at the head of the examples stands for Britain and 'Am.' for America. The numbers of occurrences are shown in the parentheses.

(11)
(a) *alarm* [Br. *at* 127, *by* 138; Am. *at* 85, *by* 58]
Br.: Somewhat **alarmed at** this account, Butler entered the orchard . . . (Scott, *The Heart of Mid-Lothian*); Dobbin said, rather **alarmed at** the fury of the old man, (Thackeray, *Vanity Fair*); She was so **alarmed at** having said this . . . she would have run quite away, (Yonge, *The Heir of Redclyffe*); Rowena, somewhat **alarmed by** the mention of outlaws in force, (Scott, *Ivanhoe*); when they were **alarmed by** the sudden and furious ringing of a bell overhead. (Ainsworth, *Auriol*); Mr. Donne . . . was too much **alarmed by** what he heard of the fever . . . (Gaskell, *Ruth*); etc.
Am.: I am . . . **alarmed at** dangerous spirit which has appeared in the troops . . . (Washington, *Writings*, Vol.15); "And why?" said I . . . more and more **alarmed at** his wildness, and fearful of the effects of his drinking . . . (Melville, *Redburn*); **Alarmed by** the rapid approach of the storm, (Sedgwick, *Hope Leslie*); I was a little **alarmed by** his energy. (Melville, *Moby Dick*); etc.

(b) *amaze* [Br. *at* 157, *by* 16; Am. *at* 58, *by* 8]
Br.: She was quite **amazed at** her own discomposure; (Austen, *Pride and Prejudice*); "Are they foreigners?" I inquired, **amazed at** hearing the French language. (Ch. Brontë, *Jane Eyre*); Grace was **amazed at** the mildness of the passion . . . (Hardy, *The Woodlanders*); Jack was **amazed at** the outburst of wrath . . . (Gissing, *Thyrza*); They listened and assented, **amazed by** the wonderful simplicity and the foolish hopefulness of the man, (Conrad, *Almayer's Folly*); etc.

Am: you are not **amazed at** your calamity . . . (Sedgwick, *Hope Leslie*); Much **amazed at** such active benevolence, he huddled himself . . . (Hawthorne, *Twice-Told Tales*); He was **amazed** also **at** the vehemence of her emotion. (Sinclair, *King Coal*); He . . . was . . . much **amazed by** the contradictions of voice, face, manner, (Alcott, *Little Women*); etc.

(c) *appall* [Br. *at* 21, *by* 26; Am. *at* 27, *by* 17]
Br.: Lord Kirkaldy . . . was **appalled at** my blunders . . . (Yonge, *Nuttie's Father*); he was **appalled at** the thought of bidding her . . . (Gissing, *The Whirlpool*); A man . . . should not be **appalled by** a breach of etiquette, (Stevenson, *New Arabian Nights*); Mr. Thumble started back, **appalled by** the energy of the words used to him. (Trollope, *The Last Chronicle of Barset*); etc.
Am.: **Appalled at** the dreadful fate that menaced me, I clutched frantically at the only large root . . . (Melville, *Typee*); Natty . . . was **appalled at** beholding his comrade on the ground, (Cooper, *The Pioneers*); He was **appalled at** the vast edifice of etiquette, (London, *Martin Eden*); How often was he **appalled by** some shrub covered with snow, (Irving, *The Sketch Book*); He was **appalled by** the selfishness he encountered, (London, *The Iron Heel*); etc.

(d) *astonish* [Br. *at* 248, *by* 39; Am. *at* 131, *by* 10]
Br.: "I am equally **astonished at** the goodness of your heart, and the quickness of your understanding." (Fielding, *Tom Jones*); "I am **astonished at** his intimacy with Mr. Bingley!" (Austen, *Pride and Prejudice*); His father and brothers were quite **astonished at** his magnificence, (Lang, *The Blue Fairy Book*); I am so **astonished at** what you tell me that I forget myself. (Gissing, *Workers in the Dawn*); I am more often **astonished by** the prudence of girls than by their recklessness. (Trollope, *The Belton Estate*); etc.
Am.: The rest of the savages . . . seemed grieved and **astonished at** the earnestness of my solicitations. (Melville, *Typee*); Mabel was **astonished at** his indifference to many of her favorites, (Cummins, *Mabel Vaughan*); Full-grown people . . . were often **astonished at** the wit and wisdom of his decisions. (Twain, *The Prince and the Pauper*); when we have left Rome . . . we are **astonished by** the discovery. (Hawthorne, *The Marble Faun*); etc.

(e) *astound* [Br. *at* 29, *by* 22; Am. *at* 12, *by* 13]

Br.: and he was **astounded**, and almost more than enraged, **at** such an indignity. (Thackeray, *Pendennis*); leaving the butler and the other servants perfectly **astounded at** his coolness. (Ainsworth, *Boscobel*); they were all **astounded by** the news that Georgiana had run away with Mr Batherbolt. (Trollope, *The Way We Live Now*); The butler was **astounded by** the manner of this advice, (Conrad, *Chance*); etc.

Am.: Even Ernest was **astounded at** the quickness with which it had been done. (London, *The Iron Heel*); Though **astounded**, at first, **by** the uproar, Heyward was soon enabled to find its solution . . . (Cooper, *The Last of the Mohicans*); etc.

(f) *baffle* [Br. *at* 0, *by* 22; Am. *at* 0, *by* 13]

Br.: I don't mean to be **baffled by** a little stiffness on your part; (Ch. Brontë, *Jane Ayre*); She was **baffled by** the same hopeless confusion of ideas. (Collins, *The New Magdalen*); with the usual sense of having been somehow **baffled by** this woman's disparagement of this reputation . . . (Conrad, *Nostromo*); etc.

Am.: Then he checked himself, **baffled by** the massive ignorance he confronted. (Glasgow, *The Voice of the People*); He lingered beside the lake . . . **baffled by** the question of the girl's sudden familiarities and caprices. (James, *Daisy Miller*); etc.

(g) *bewilder* [Br. *at* 9, *by* 71; Am. *at* 5, *by* 51]

Br.: when Julian, much **bewildered at** her superfluity of emotion, assisted her to a seat in sheer humanity. (Hardy, *The Hand of Ethelberta*); There were moments when I was **bewildered by** the terror he inspired. (Ch. Brontë, *Jane Ayre*); Silas, **bewildered by** the changes thirty years had brought over his native place, had stopped several persons . . . (Eliot, *Silas Marner*); poor Ethel was **bewildered by** a multiplicity of teachers, (Thackeray, *The Newcomes*); etc.

Am.: Page caught her breath, a little **bewildered at** her own vehemence and audacity. (Norris, *The Pit*); Cora and Alice had stood trembling and **bewildered by** this unexpected desertion; (Cooper, *The Last of the Mohicans*); The young man was **bewildered by** his rage and disappointment. (Simms, *Beauchampe*); She . . . clung to her friend as if she was a little **bewildered by** the sudden news. (Alcott, *Little Women*); etc.

Psychological Passives and the Agentive Prepositions in English

(h) *dismay* [Br. *at* 28, *by* 29; Am. *at* 13, *by* 7]
Br.: I was weakly **dismayed at** the ignorance, (Ch. Brontë, *Jane Eyre*); We are rather **dismayed at** their bringing two servants with them. (Gaskell, *Cranford*); Molly was rather **dismayed by** the offers of the maid . . . (Gaskell, *Wives and Daughters*); I was . . . so **dismayed by** the first waking impressions of my dream, (Collins, *The Woman in White*); etc.
Am.: Admiral Alpendam was . . . no way **dismayed at** the character of the enemy, (Irving, *A History of New York*); He was astonished and **dismayed at** his own emotion. (Stowe, *Agnes of Sorrento*); I cannot say that I had been much **dismayed by** their menaces. (Irving, *Tales of a Traveller*); etc.

(i) *perplex* [Br. *at* 13, *by* 52; Am. *at* 3, *by* 37]
Br.: "I must say I am often **perplexed at** the differences . . ." (Disraeli, *Lothair*); He was often so much **perplexed by** the problems of life . . . (Gaskell, *Ruth*); She was the only child of old Admiral Greystock, who . . . was much **perplexed by** the possession of a daughter. (Trollope, *The Eustace Diamonds*); etc.
Am.: I am extremely **perplexed** . . . **at** the uneasiness, (Washington, *Writings*, Vol. 9); he was **perplexed by** its prolonged secrecy, (Sedgwick, *Married or Single?*); the young Dinks was **perplexed by** a singular feeling of happiness. (Curtis, *Trumps*); etc.

(j) *shock* [Br. *at* 161, *by* 74; Am. *at* 66, *by* 37]
Br.: I was greatly **shocked at** the barbarity of the letter . . . (Fielding, *Amelia*); I suppose you are **shocked at** my character. (Scott, *The Heart of Mid-Lothian*); The Countess was **shocked at** the familiarity of General Tufto with the aide-de-camp's wife. (Thackeray, *Vanity Fair*); A stranger is **shocked by** a tone of defiance in every voice. (Gaskell, *The Life of Charlotte Brontë*); He was a little **shocked** at first **by** the language he heard . . . (Trollope, *The Three Clerks*); etc.
Am.: one of her aunts, **shocked at** the omission of . . . decorum . . . (Sedgwick, *A New-England Tale*); She looked **shocked at** such unchristian ignorance. (Wharton, *The Age of Innocence*); Fresh from his revolutionists he was **shocked by** the intellectual stupidity of the master class. (London, *The Iron Heel*); etc.

(k) *startle* [Br. *at* 63, *by* 263; Am. *at* 45, *by* 162]
Br.: He was . . . **startled at** his own audacity. (Gissing, *A Life's Morning*); Celia was really **startled at** the suspicion which had darted into her mind. (Eliot, *Middlemarch*); Doubtless you are **startled by** the suddenness of this discovery. (Eliot, *Middlemarch*); The major was **startled by** her eloquence, (Trollope, *The Last Chronicle of Barset*); She blew the candles out one by one . . . and was horribly **startled by** the darkness. (Conrad, *Tales of Unrest*); etc.
Am.: But Pearl, not a whit **startled at** her mother's threats . . . (Hawthorne, *The Scarlet Letter*); Robinson Crusoe could not have been more **startled at** the footprint in the sand than we were at this unwelcome discovery. (Melville, *Typee*); Isabella was . . . **startled by** a corresponding mental resemblance, (Sedgwick, *The Linwoods*); I was suddenly **startled by** a scream, (Melville, *Typee*); etc.

(l) *stun* [Br. *at* 0, *by* 50; Am. *at* 1, *by* 15]
Br.: She were just **stunned by** finding her mother was dying in her very arms . . . (Gaskell, *Sylvia's Lover*); he was partly **stunned by** the discovery he had made . . . (Conrad, *Lord Jim*); I was so **stunned by** this sudden shock that for a time I must have nearly lost my reason. (Doyle, *The Lost World*); etc.
Am.: The poor youth was actually **stunned**, not **by** what was said to him, but **by** the sudden consciousness of his own vehemence. (Simms, *Beauchampe*); But she was **stunned by** her own grief, (Curtis, *Trumps*); I was for the moment **stunned by** what they disclosed to me. (London, *The Sea Wolf*); etc.

3.3 Statistics

The collected data on each verb and each writer can be arranged as in the following tables. The tables show the occurrences of each author's use of psych-passives with *at* or *by*.[10] Table 2 shows the statistics of British writers and Table 3 shows those of American writers.

---

10) Although sufficient attention was paid in collecting data, there may be a chance that some figures are not perfectly exact because there are examples with ambiguous meanings whether they are psychological or pseudo-psychological. There may also be some human oversight in dealing with a large amount of data. This will be the case with the figures in Figure 7 in §4.2, where the division (by 4.5) may naturally lead to approximate numbers. Nevertheless, it does not seem to affect the general ratio of *at* and *by*.

Psychological Passives and the Agentive Prepositions in English

Table 2
British writers' use of psych-passives with *at* or *by*

author	year of birth & death	alarm at	alarm by	amaze at	amaze by	appall at	appall by	astonish at	astonish by	astound at	astound by	baffle at	baffle by	bewilder at	bewilder by	dismay at	dismay by	perplex at	perplex by	shock at	shock by	startle at	startle by	stun at	stun by	Total at	Total by
Fielding	1707–54	6	4	4	0	0	0	10	0	0	0	0	0	0	0	0	0	0	0	11	0	1	0	0	1	32	5
Johnson	1709–84	2	3	1	2	0	0	0	0	0	0	0	0	0	2	0	0	0	3	2	1	0	0	0	0	5	11
Goldsmith	1728–74	1	1	5	0	0	0	3	0	0	0	0	0	0	0	0	0	0	0	1	0	0	0	0	0	10	1
Scott	1771–1832	10	6	0	0	0	3	11	1	0	1	0	0	0	0	0	0	0	0	4	3	2	3	0	0	27	17
Austen	1775–1817	2	4	8	0	0	1	14	4	0	0	0	0	0	1	0	1	0	0	4	0	2	5	0	4	30	19
Lamb	1775–1834	0	0	4	0	0	0	4	0	0	0	0	0	0	0	0	0	0	0	0	0	2	0	0	0	11	0
Carlyle	1795–1881	0	0	2	0	0	0	2	0	0	0	0	0	0	2	0	0	0	0	1	0	2	0	0	0	5	2
Shelley	1797–1851	1	2	0	0	0	0	1	0	0	0	0	0	0	2	0	0	0	0	0	0	0	2	0	0	3	6
Disraeli	1804–81	12	5	2	0	0	2	11	1	0	4	0	0	0	0	0	0	5	6	4	2	1	3	0	0	38	24
Ainsworth	1805–82	13	37	1	0	2	5	7	3	3	1	0	0	0	3	0	1	0	1	4	4	2	15	0	3	32	73
Darwin	1809–82	4	0	0	1	0	0	7	1	0	0	0	0	0	1	0	0	0	2	0	0	3	1	0	0	14	5
Prest	1810–59	3	3	8	0	0	1	3	1	0	0	0	1	0	3	0	0	0	0	2	0	1	2	0	3	18	13
Gaskell	1810–65	12	9	1	0	4	1	10	1	0	2	0	0	1	4	5	6	3	13	20	6	14	32	0	12	66	85
Thackeray	1811–63	10	3	18	1	0	0	13	2	4	0	0	0	0	8	2	1	1	1	9	5	0	2	0	0	58	24
Trollope	1815–82	1	2	3	1	0	3	17	13	2	8	3	0	1	10	1	11	0	5	7	9	2	13	0	4	33	79
Ch. Brontë	1816–55	1	0	4	0	0	0	2	0	0	0	0	3	0	1	0	0	0	0	12	3	2	4	0	0	24	12
E. Brontë	1818–48	2	0	2	0	0	1	1	0	0	0	0	0	0	0	0	0	0	0	4	0	0	0	0	1	10	1
Eliot	1819–80	8	5	6	0	0	0	6	0	0	0	0	0	0	2	0	0	0	5	11	2	3	19	0	3	35	31
Yonge	1823–1901	13	3	11	0	4	1	4	1	1	0	0	0	1	2	8	1	5	4	16	6	5	17	0	4	63	39
Collins	1824–84	8	20	12	5	0	0	22	3	2	0	0	0	0	14	1	2	0	0	12	7	1	56	0	0	58	118
Carroll	1832–98	4	0	0	0	0	0	0	0	0	0	0	0	0	0	0	0	0	0	0	0	0	3	0	0	4	3
Butler	1835–1902	2	1	0	1	0	1	1	0	0	2	0	0	0	0	0	0	0	0	0	1	0	0	0	2	6	4
Hardy	1840–1928	1	1	12	0	2	2	7	0	4	5	0	0	2	5	0	2	3	3	6	0	0	11	0	0	39	25
Lang	1844–1912	0	2	3	0	1	0	19	2	2	1	0	0	1	0	0	0	0	0	0	0	0	4	0	0	26	8
Stevenson	1850–94	0	2	2	0	0	2	8	1	0	0	0	0	2	3	0	2	0	0	2	2	1	7	0	2	13	20
Wilde	1854–1900	0	1	5	0	0	0	0	0	0	1	0	0	0	0	0	0	0	0	0	0	1	0	0	0	6	2
Shaw	1856–1950	1	1	6	1	0	0	3	0	0	0	0	3	0	0	0	1	0	0	2	0	0	3	0	0	12	9
Gissing	1857–1903	6	11	8	1	3	1	27	2	0	2	0	3	0	5	0	0	2	2	8	2	7	18	0	3	60	44
Conrad	1857–1924	4	10	13	5	3	6	13	2	4	5	0	4	0	1	2	1	0	3	6	10	4	26	0	4	50	81
Doyle	1859–1930	3	0	6	0	1	0	7	2	2	1	0	3	2	0	0	0	0	2	4	4	3	6	0	6	26	23
Kipling	1865–1936	0	0	7	0	0	0	2	0	1	0	0	0	0	2	0	0	0	2	6	0	1	3	0	0	20	5
H.G. Wells	1866–1946	1	2	2	0	0	0	6	0	0	0	0	0	0	3	0	1	0	2	0	2	0	7	0	2	11	13
Chesterton	1874–1936	0	0	0	0	0	0	5	0	0	0	0	0	0	1	0	0	0	0	0	1	1	1	0	0	6	3
Maugham	1874–1965	0	0	0	0	1	0	4	0	0	0	0	0	0	0	0	1	0	0	1	5	4	0	0	0	10	6
Total		131	138	157	16	20	27	250	40	29	22	0	22	9	71	28	29	13	52	161	74	63	263	0	56	861	810

56

Table 3
American writers' use of psych-passives with *at* or *by*

author	year of birth & death	alarm at	alarm by	amaze at	amaze by	appall at	appall by	astonish at	astonish by	astound at	astound by	baffle at	baffle by	bewilder at	bewilder by	dismay at	dismay by	perplex at	perplex by	shock at	shock by	startle at	startle by	stun at	stun by	Total at	Total by
Washington	1732–99	24	6	3	0	0	0	7	0	0	0	0	0	0	0	1	0	2	4	1	0	0	0	0	0	38	10
Irving	1783–1859	1	3	0	1	0	1	4	0	1	1	0	0	0	2	2	2	0	5	1	0	3	7	0	0	12	22
Cooper	1789–1851	4	8	4	0	4	0	9	1	1	5	0	2	1	3	0	0	0	1	1	1	10	10	0	0	34	31
Sedgwick	1789–1867	8	15	9	0	1	2	4	0	0	2	0	4	0	3	1	0	0	5	8	5	1	35	0	0	32	71
Prescott	1796–1859	3	3	2	0	0	0	7	1	0	2	0	1	0	2	1	1	0	2	3	0	0	4	0	0	15	16
Child	1802–80	1	0	0	0	0	0	1	0	0	0	0	0	0	0	0	0	0	0	1	0	0	0	0	0	2	6
Emerson	1803–82	1	1	0	0	0	0	0	0	0	0	0	0	0	2	0	0	0	0	1	0	0	2	0	0	3	3
Hawthorne	1804–64	0	1	1	0	1	0	6	2	0	1	0	0	1	4	0	0	0	1	2	5	6	17	0	0	18	31
Bird	1806–54	2	1	3	0	0	0	3	0	0	0	0	0	0	0	0	0	0	0	4	2	3	0	0	0	17	5
Willis	1806–67	1	0	0	0	0	1	5	1	1	0	0	0	0	0	0	0	0	1	0	0	1	1	0	0	7	3
Simms	1806–70	2	1	0	0	0	0	1	0	1	1	0	2	0	3	0	0	0	0	2	0	1	5	0	5	7	17
Longfellow	1807–82	1	0	1	0	0	0	2	0	0	1	0	0	0	1	0	0	0	0	0	1	1	0	0	0	5	3
Poe	1809–49	4	2	2	0	0	1	12	1	0	1	0	0	0	0	0	0	0	1	0	0	3	1	0	1	21	8
Stowe	1811–96	2	0	1	0	0	1	6	0	0	0	0	0	0	0	0	1	0	2	3	0	0	0	0	0	15	7
Thoreau	1817–62	1	0	1	0	0	0	3	0	0	1	0	0	0	1	0	0	0	0	0	0	0	9	0	0	5	11
Melville	1819–91	5	1	4	1	4	0	7	0	0	0	0	0	0	0	0	0	0	1	3	0	2	11	0	0	25	14
Curtis	1824–92	4	0	0	0	0	1	0	0	0	0	0	0	0	2	0	0	0	2	1	0	0	3	0	1	5	9
Taylor	1825–78	1	0	1	0	0	0	2	0	0	0	0	0	0	6	0	0	0	0	3	0	3	2	0	1	10	9
Cummins	1827–66	1	1	2	0	2	0	16	0	1	0	0	0	1	6	0	0	0	0	3	1	0	16	0	0	29	18
Alcott	1832–88	5	1	3	2	1	0	1	1	0	0	0	1	0	4	2	1	0	2	1	0	1	2	0	0	14	13
Horatio	1832–99	5	1	3	0	0	0	4	0	0	0	0	2	0	2	1	0	0	0	3	1	3	3	0	0	18	6
Twain	1835–1910	0	1	5	0	3	0	11	0	0	1	0	0	0	2	0	0	0	0	2	1	2	4	0	0	24	8
Howells	1837–1920	1	2	3	0	0	0	1	0	0	4	0	1	1	2	0	1	0	0	2	0	0	1	0	2	10	8
H. James	1843–1916	1	0	2	0	2	0	3	0	0	0	0	2	0	3	1	0	0	0	5	4	0	4	0	0	14	14
Wharton	1862–1937	2	1	1	0	0	0	0	0	0	0	0	0	0	3	0	1	0	1	3	0	1	3	0	0	9	9
Norris	1870–1902	0	0	0	0	0	0	1	0	0	0	0	0	3	3	0	0	0	0	0	2	0	1	0	2	4	8
Dreiser	1871–1945	0	0	1	1	0	0	5	2	0	0	0	1	0	2	0	0	0	1	0	5	0	3	0	0	8	12
Cather	1873–1947	2	0	0	0	0	0	2	0	0	0	0	0	0	0	0	0	0	0	3	0	0	3	0	0	7	3
Glasgow	1873–1945	0	1	1	0	0	0	1	0	0	1	0	0	0	0	0	0	0	0	0	0	1	4	0	0	5	6
London	1876–1916	0	2	4	1	9	6	1	0	4	0	0	0	0	4	0	0	0	3	0	6	0	6	0	2	18	30
Anderson	1876–1941	1	1	1	2	0	0	1	1	0	0	0	1	0	0	0	1	0	3	0	0	1	1	0	0	4	10
Fitzgerald	1896–1940	1	1	0	0	1	3	1	0	0	0	0	0	0	1	1	0	0	0	3	1	2	2	0	0	9	8
Total		84	57	58	8	30	17	128	10	12	13	0	15	6	52	13	7	3	37	66	36	45	162	0	15	446	430

Chapter 3

57

3.4 The role of statistics in language studies

Before getting into the analysis of the data, some comments must be made on the role that statistics play in language studies. Statistics cannot be expected to make an exact representation of a linguistic phenomenon but can be utilized to show a general tendency of it. All we would like to show in this study is the approximate ratio of *at* and *by* occurring with psych-passives. The statistics obtained will be of assistance in understanding a behavioral pattern of the prepositions.

To collect data for any language analysis, the ideal way would be to collect the totality of sentences or utterances, written or spoken, in the whole society. But it would be impossible to achieve this. The next best thing we can do is to collect a certain kind of and certain amount of data within a certain microcosmic world, within a certain space of time. The microcosm here would be literary circles, Britain and America, during the 18th and 19th centuries. The statistics obtained in this way would be an approximate representation of the linguistic issue in question in that society within that period of time.

The figures from each verb or each author on the tables above show a great deal of variation. It is difficult to capture the characteristics of the behaviors of the agentive prepositions. To solve this shortcoming would be to add up the figures from each verb or each author, so that some bigger picture could be seen.

Simple adding of the figures, however, may not represent a real linguistic situation. Nevertheless, it can be expected that some tendencies can be seen at the very least. The final total, therefore, may be considered to be a condensed picture of this particular linguistic phenomenon in this microcosmic society.

The picture we get from the analysis of the data may be likened to a huge jigsaw puzzle in which some pieces may be missing here and there, but we can still see the whole picture and find out the overall pattern. And that would suffice for the purpose of the present study.

Chapter 3

3.5 Analysis of the Data
3.5.1 The statistics

Let us show the statistics in chart form so that we can capture a graphical idea of the frequencies of occurrence of *at* and *by* for each verb.

Figure 1
At and *by* with psych-passives in LModE (VLSA)

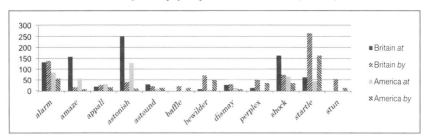

The general tendencies of occurrence of *at* and *by* seem to be quite similar between Britain and America. Their ratios for each verb also show similarities, despite the quantitative difference. The following figure shows the total frequencies of occurrence of *at* and *by* for each verb in the Late Modern English period.

Figure 2
Total frequencies of *at* and *by* with psych-passives in LModE

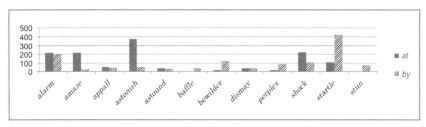

3.5.2 Some characteristics about verbs

Some characteristics of the verbs can be observed from the chart. The most frequently used verb is *startle* (*surprise* aside), followed by *astonish*,

59

alarm, shock, amaze and so on in the order of frequency of occurrence. The verbs may be classified into three groups depending on which preposition they tend to occur with. The three groups are:

(i) verbs which prefer to occur with *at*
(ii) verbs which tend to take *by*
(iii) verbs which accompany *at* and *by* more or less in similar numbers

Amaze and *astonish* have a very strong tendency to occur with *at*, with a small number of occurrences with *by*. *Shock* occurs with *at* more than *by*, but not to the extent of *amaze* and *astonish*. *Bewilder, perplex* and *startle*, on the other hand, show the opposite tendency, occurring mainly with *by*. *Baffle* and *stun* virtually occur only with *by*.

The verbs of the third group *alarm, appall, astound* and *dismay* show more or less similar frequencies of occurrence of *at* and *by*. There is a fluctuation of occurrence, however, between the two countries. *Alarm*, for instance, tends to occur with *at* more than *by* in America, while *by* is more prevalent than *at* in Britain. This kind of discrepancy is also true of other verbs as well.

It seems to be generally thought that typical psych-verbs are such verbs as *surprise, amaze* or *astonish* as they are often employed as sample sentences in grammar or usage books. In actuality, however, other psych-verbs like *startle, shock* or *alarm* occur as often as or maybe more than these verbs.

Considering the number of these verbs and the number of their total occurrences, these verbs may be exerting such an influence on other verbs as to make them behave in a similar way and move toward the tendency to use *by*. This kind of influence may be accelerated by the force inherent in English, where the agentive *by* expelled other prepositions to become the chief agentive preposition occurring with regular passives in English.

3.5.3 Some characteristics about writers

From Tables 2 and 3 above, we can see that the writers show unique characteristics. It may be possible to make the following observations about the writers depending on their preference for the preposition, whether *at* or *by*. Some writers seem to prefer to use *at*, while others have a tendency to use *by* and some others use both *at* and *by* more or less similarly.

In Britain, the writers who seem to prefer to use *at* are Fielding, Goldsmith, Scott, Thackeray, Yonge, Lang, Gissing and Kipling, whereas the writers who tend to use *by* more than *at* are Johnson, Ainsworth, Gaskell, Trollope, Collins, Stevenson and Conrad.

In America, the writers who like to use *at* better than *by* are Washington, Poe, Stowe, Melville, Cummins, Horatio and Twain, while those who like to use *by* are Irving, Sedgwick, Hawthorne, Simms, Dreiser and London. This does not mean, of course, that the writers do not refrain themselves from using the rival preposition.

It may be said that the writers of the first group are more or less conservative writers, preferring to use the 'older' preposition *at*, whereas the writers of the latter group are rather progressive and free from traditional norm by adopting the 'newer' preposition *by*.

There seems to be another tendency: a particular writer seems to prefer to use a certain verb (aside from *surprise*, the most widely-used verb of this group). In Britain, Gaskell, for instance, makes great use of *perplex*, *shock* and *startle*. Ainsworth uses *alarm*, Thackeray *amaze*, Trollope *astonish*, *bewilder* and *dismay*. Collins utilizes *alarm*, *bewilder* and *startle*, Gissing *astonish*, Conrad *amaze* and *startle* and so on. In America, Sedgwick makes good use of *alarm* and *startle*, Hawthorne *startle*, Poe *astonish*, Melville and Cummins *astonish* and *startle*, London *appall* and so forth.

The writers who prefer to use *by* tend to make much use of *startle*, the verb mainly occurring with *by*. Gaskell, Trollope, Conrad, Sedgwick and Hawthorne are such writers. Furthermore, Trollope uses *by* many times with *astonish* and Conrad with *amaze*, seemingly challenging the norm of the day. Ainsworth, Collins and Sedgwick use *alarm* with *by* much more frequently than *at*, although the verb occurs with both *at* and *by* almost equally. Gissing and Yonge are the writers who prefer to use *at* and they use *at* with *startle*, much more frequently than the average. Thackeray tends to use *at* and he makes much use of *amaze* and *astonish* and uses *startle* less frequently.

Each writer may have had their own favorite verb or verbs and they may have decided that it would be the better word(s) for expressing 'amazement' or 'astonishment' in a particular context and may have used them with some significant meanings intended.

Furthermore, a conscious distinction between *at* and *by* seems to have been made on a writer's part, as in (12), where three psych-passives are used in proximity and the choice of preposition seems to be dependent on a writer's preference.

(12) He was **surprised at** the commonness of the clay. Life proved not to be fine and gracious. He was **appalled by** the selfishness he encountered, and what had surprised him even more than that was the absence of intellectual life. Fresh from his revolutionists, he was **shocked by** intellectual stupidity of the master class. (London, *The Iron Heel*)

In (12), London uses the passives of *surprise*, *appall* and *shock* in a four-line space and seems to make an intentional distinction which preposition to use depending on the verb. The passive of *surprise* usually comes with *at*, so London's use is a normal usage, but the passives of *appall* and *shock* generally comes with *at*, not *by* in American English. This use of London's seems to reflect his overall preference for *by* with psych-passives (*at* 18 times vs. *by* 30 times).

3.6 The ratios of *at* and *by*

The frequencies of occurrence of *at* and *by* for Britain, America and their total are shown in Figure 3.

Figure 3
At and *by* with psych-passives in LModE (VLSA)

It shows that *at* and *by* occur more or less in similar rates between Britain and America, with *at* slightly more preferred to *by*. The overall ratio of *at* and *by* in Late Modern English is approximately 1 : 0.94, which I will round off to one decimal place and use the simpler rate of 1 : 0.9 for easier comparison hereafter.

3.7 The statistics from the COHA

The COHA is a corpus of 400 million words containing texts from 1810 to 2009. To compare the results with those obtained from the VLSA, I have collected data from 1810 to 1900, the period equivalent to the latter half of the Late ModE period. The statistics for each verb are shown in Figure 4.

Figure 4
At and *by* with psych-passives in LModE (COHA 1810–1900)

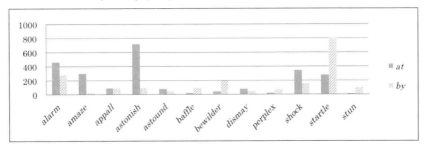

The tendency for each verb to occur with *at* or *by* seems to be quite similar to the data from the VLSA. The total occurrences of *at* and *by* in the two corpora are shown in Figure 5.

Figure 5
At and *by* with psych-passives in LModE

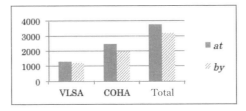

The ratio of *at* and *by* of the COHA has turned out to be approximately 1 : 0.7, showing that *at* is used slightly more often in this corpus than in the data of the VLSA, whose ratio is 1 : 0.9. The difference of the ratios may be attributed to the difference of genres of the texts contained: the texts of the VLSA are mostly literary works, while the COHA contains fiction, non-fiction, magazines and newspapers. If we combine the statistics of the two corpora, the ratio of *at* and *by* becomes approximately 1 : 0.8.

IV. Present-day English

We have seen a developmental history of psych-passives with agentive prepositions from Early Modern English to Late Modern English. Now let us examine their behavior in Present-day English. To collect data, we used the BNC and the Wordbanks[11] for British English and the COCA and the COHA for American English.

4.1 The British corpora

The search of the two corpora yields the results on the following chart. The frequencies of occurrence of *at* and *by* with each psych-verb are shown.

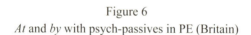

Figure 6
At and *by* with psych-passives in PE (Britain)

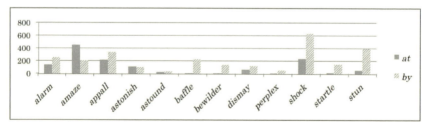

---

11) The Wordbanks contain the texts of English-speaking countries and the text of British English constitute 74 percent of all the texts, so I include this corpus as the British corpus for convenience' sake.

4.2 American corpora

The COCA is a corpus of 450 million words (as of 2015)[12] and it is supposedly 4.5 times larger than the other corpora. In order to make an easier and clearer comparison and contrast of the data, adjustments were made by dividing the data from the COCA by 4.5.

From the COHA, the data from 1970 to 2000 are obtained. The period is almost equivalent to that of the BNC and its size is very similar. The following chart shows the results obtained from the combined statistics of the COCA and the COHA.

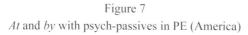

Figure 7
At and *by* with psych-passives in PE (America)

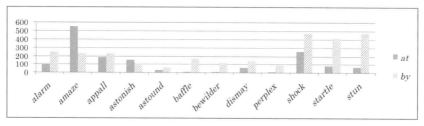

It is quite similar to those of the British corpora, but there are some differences. Similarities include the ratios of *at* and *by* for each verb and the number of occurrences. Differences are that the verbs *amaze* and *startle* occur more frequently in America than in Britain, while the verb *shock* is the other way around.

There seem to be regional differences in popularity between Britain and America. We can observe that *shock* with *by* is more popular in Britain than in America and *amaze* with *at* shows the opposite behavior. *Startle* with *by* used to be in such a vogue in Britain but it has surprisingly lost its popularity, which America still retains.

Let us combine the data of the two statistics to present the total statistics of Present-day English.

---

12) The COCA is constantly updated and the data for this chapter was collected in the early part of 2015.

65

Figure 8
At and *by* with psych-passives in PE

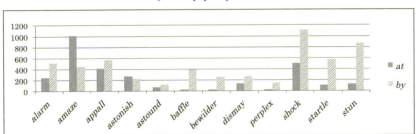

It may be interesting to note that there is a rise and fall of popularity among the verbs. The most frequently used verb is *shock*, followed by *amaze*, *appall*, *stun*, *alarm*, *startle* and so on, in the order of frequency. The order has changed from that of Late Modern English: less popular verbs like *shock* or *appall* have gained more popularity and more popular verbs like *astonish*, *alarm* and *startle* have lost favor.

As far as the agentive prepositions are concerned, Present-day English has seen a totally different picture: the overall increase of *by* and the decline of *at*. All the psych-verbs except *amaze* and *astonish* are now occurring with *by* more frequently than *at*. This is different from the situation in the Late ModE period where several verbs in the passive occurred with *at* more frequently than *by*.

The following chart shows the frequencies of occurrence of *at* and *by* in each corpus.

Figure 9
At and *by* with psych-passives in each PE corpus

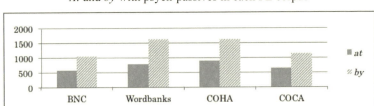

The ratio of *at* and *by* in each corpus becomes as follows: the BNC 1 : 1.8, the Wordbanks 1 : 2, the COHA 1 : 1.8, and the COCA 1 : 1.8, with the value of one given to *at*. It is surprising that three corpora show exactly the same ratio. The total ratio of four corpora becomes 1 : 1.9.

4.3 The comparison of Early ModE, Late ModE and PE

The outcome of the investigation into the corpora of Late Modern English and Present-day English, together with the result of Early Modern English will show the ratio for each period in Figure 10.

Figure 10
The shift of the ratio of *at* and *by* from EModE to PE

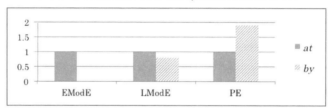

The general decline of *at* and the overall increase of *by* is obvious. It seems to suggest that *by* has been increasing its strength and is steadily ousting *at* in the history of psych-passives synonymous to *surprise*.

4.4 A developmental history of English passives + *by*

Considering the increase of *by* and the decline of *at* as an agentive preposition, psych-passives seem to have been treading the same developmental path that the passives in English had trodden. In the history of the English passives, *by* became so dominant since the ME period that it replaced other agentive prepositions such as *of, from, through, at* and so forth, which had been used since the OE period.

The same kind of shift may have been happening to the passives of *surprise* and its synonymous psych-verbs, albeit with a few centuries delay. It may be possible to assume that an increasing number of psych-passives have been forsaking *at, with* or *about* (which had been used during the Early

ModE and Late ModE periods) and have begun to adopt *by* more frequently. This has resulted in a dramatic increase in the use of *by* with psych-passives synonymous to *surprise* in Present-day English. It may be possible to assume that dominance of *by* over other prepositions with psych-passives will take place in the future.

V. Summary

This chapter attempts to discover how the passives of psych-verbs synonymous to *surprise* have occurred with agentive prepositions and how the shift from *at* or *with* to *by* has taken place from Early Modern English through Late Modern English to Present-day English.

The examination of the usages of the writers of the Early ModE period shows that *amaze, astonish* and *dismay* are the main verbs used in the passive and occurred mostly with *at* or *with*. *At* has continued to be used till present-day, while *with* has declined to fall into gradual disuse.

There is a single example in which *by* is used with the passive of *dismay* in Spenser's *The Faerie Queene* (1590). This may be one of the earliest examples of *by* being used with a psych-passive and may be the forerunner of the later development.

In Late Modern English, after examining the data of some thirty writers each from Britain and America using the VLSA, we obtain the overall ratio of *at* and *by*, which is approximately 1 : 0.9, a drastic increase of *by* from the previous period.

We have found that the verbs can be classified into three groups depending on which preposition they tend to occur with. *Amaze, astonish* and *shock* occur predominantly with *at*, whereas the verbs like *baffle, bewilder, perplex, startle* and *stun* show the opposite tendency, occurring mostly with *by*. There is another group of verbs such as *alarm, appall, astound* and *dismay*, which show the occurrences of *at* and *by* in more or less similar numbers.

Writers also show interesting features. Some writers exhibit a preference for *at* and others for *by*, and there are writers who use both *at* and *by* in rather similar numbers. The writers who prefer to use *by* show a tendency to use the verbs which are likely to occur with *by*. They may also have a tendency to use *by* with verbs which normally occur with *at*. The opposite tendency can be seen for the writers who prefer to use *at*.

Furthermore, a particular writer is observed to prefer to use a certain verb. Thackeray utilizes *amaze* and *astonish*, Collins *alarm, bewilder* and *startle*, Trollope *astonish, bewilder* and *dismay*, Conrad *amaze* and *startle*, Hawthorne *startle* and London *appall* and so on.

The search into the COHA (1800–1900) yields the results fairly similar to those obtained from the VLSA, with a slight difference of the ratio of *at* and *by*, which is 1 : 0.7. *At* is used in higher frequency in this corpus than in the VLSA and this difference may come from the different genres. The total ratio of the Late ModE period has turned out to be 1 : 0.8.

In Present-day English, however, *by* has become so dominant for most of the verbs except for *amaze* and *astonish* that the ratio of *at* and *by* has become 1 : 1.8. Some of the verbs have changed their behavioral patterns to occur with *by* more than *at* and some others have made the bond with *by* stronger. *Amaze* is the verb that shows an obstinate affection for *at* maybe because of the long history of the friendly rapport of the verb and the preposition. It is obvious that the chief agentive preposition with psych-passives has been shifting from *at* or *with* to *by*.

In the history of English passives in general, *by* became the chief agentive preposition, expelling other prepositions such as *of, from, through* and so forth. The psych-verbs synonymous to *surprise* in the passive may be following the same path with a few centuries' delay that the English passives had trodden a few centuries earlier.

Chapter 4
How Dickens used psych-passives with *at* or *by*

In Dickens' novels, the socially weak or abused people of the lower class are portrayed: Oliver Twist, David Copperfield, Nicholas Nickleby's pupils, to name a few. The same sentiment of Dickens to the ill-treated populace may have been directed to non- or sub-standard usages of English, which may be equivalent to the weak and the abused in society. I cannot help feeling that the English usages considered to be socially bad or inadequate may have been rescued and saved by the novelist and saw the light of day.

I. Introduction

We have examined the behaviors of the agentive prepositions with the passives of *surprise* and its synonymous verbs. There has been an increase of *by* and a decrease of *at* with the passive of *surprise*: the ratio of *at* and *by* was roughly 1 : 0.3 in Late Modern English, while in Present-day English, the ratio has risen to 1 : 1 or even to 1 : 1.9 in the most recent decade.

In doing research, it was brought to my notice that a number of famous and popular writers of Late Modern English favored to use *by* with the passive of *surprise* when there were writers who adhered to *at* and hardly used *by* at all. Charles Dickens (1812–70) seems to be one of the writers who showed a particular preference for *by*. Dickens' unusual usage stirred my curiosity and made me launch the investigation into how the novelist actually used *at* or *by* with the predicate. In this chapter, we will inquire into how Dickens used the agentive prepositions with the passives of *surprise* and synonymous verbs and why he came to favor the agentive *by*.

Chapter 4

II. The passive of *surprise* with *at* or *by*

2.1 Data collection

I used the computer concordance of Dickens to write my 2002 article, and the VLSA to write my 2015(a) article. This chapter is based on these articles. In addition to these corpora, I also used CLiC Dickens as a supplementary corpus to confirm the data.

Although it would be essential to read texts carefully to collect data in a philological study, computer corpora are extremely useful and may be indispensable in searching for words or phrases which appear only a few times in one volume. It does not mean of course that careful reading of texts is not necessary. To compensate this drawback and to confirm the data obtained is authentic, I make it a rule to read the chapter containing sample quotations to see how they are actually used in a particular context.

2.2 Novels examined

The following novels of Dickens, arranged in chronological order of publication, were examined. Abbreviations for titles, mostly based on Brook (1970), are in parentheses, followed by the dates of publication. Other works were also examined but as the obtained results are very few, they are not included.[1)]

Sketches by Boz (*SB*)	1833–36
Pickwick Papers (*PP*)	1836–37
Oliver Twist (*OT*)	1837–39
Nicholas Nickleby (*NN*)	1838–39
The Old Curiosity Shop (*OCS*)	1840–41
Barnaby Rudge (*BR*)	1841
Martin Chuzzlewit (*MC*)	1843–44
Dombey and Son (*DS*)	1846–48
David Copperfield (*DC*)	1849–50
Bleak House (*BH*)	1852–53

---

1) The works examined and the obtained data are as follows: *Master Humphrey's Clock* (*at* 0, *by* 0), *American Notes* (*at* 0, *by* 1), *Christmas Books* (*at* 1, *by* 1), *A Child's History of England* (*at* 0, *by* 1), *The Uncommercial Traveller* (*at* 0, *by* 1).

Hard Times (*HT*)	1854
Little Dorrit (*LD*)	1855–57
A Tale of Two Cities (*TTC*)	1859
Great Expectations (*GE*)	1860–61
Our Mutual Friend (*OMF*)	1864–65
The Mystery of Edwin Drood (*ED*)	1870

2.3 The occurrence of *at* and *by* and the types of complement

The search of the Dickens' corpora retrieves 39 occurrences of *at* and 38 occurrences of *by* with the passive of *surprise*, as in Table 1. (All the examples are listed in Appendix).

Table 1
The occurrence of *at* and *by* in Dickens' novels

at	*by*
39	38

Dickens's ratio of *at* and *by* is quite similar to the ratio of the last couple of decades of the 20th century. It means that his ratio is totally different from those of his contemporary writers. (Compare Dickens' ratio with those of other writers in Appendix in Chapter 1.)

As Harry Stone (1959) says, "It is only after reading Dickens' contemporaries that one is able to understand how fresh and impressive his experiments were" (quoted in Sørensen 1985:12), Dickens has often been referred to as a writer who is ahead of his time and whose English reveals characteristics common in Present-day English.[2] The occurrence rate of *at* and *by* seems to confirm such characterization of Dickens' English, which exhibits features of Present-day English.

The classification of the quotations in accordance with the type of prepositional complement yields the results in Figure 1.

---

2) Sørensen (1985:12) says, "many—if not most—of the constructions, idioms, lexical items, and special uses of words that he introduced are current today . . ."

Chapter 4

Figure 1
The types of complement occurring with *at* and *by*

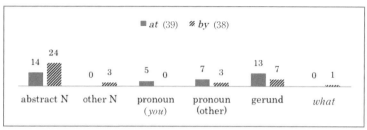

Abstract nouns have a tendency to occur with *by*, just like Present-day English, as in (1).

(1) "Oh, you're here, are you, sir?" said John, rather **surprised by** *the quickness* with which he appeared. (*BR*, ch.29); Miss Tox . . . was so **surprised by** *the amount of expression* Mrs. Chick had conveyed into her face, (*DS*, ch.29); etc.

Pronouns occur with *at* much more frequently than with *by*, especially with *you*, as in a near-idiomatic expression *I am surprised at you!*, which occurs as many as five times.

Gerunds with *surprised*, which seems to be decreasing in Present-day English, are abundant in Dickens' English. Not only quantitatively, but qualitatively, Dickens' gerunds take such complex forms as are rarely seen in Present-day English, as in (2).

(2) He was not so much **surprised at** *the man's being* there, as **at** *his having got* close to him so quietly and swiftly; (*MC*, ch.40); I believe nobody will be **surprised**, either **at** *its being required* from you, or **at** *your making* it. (*DS*, ch.40); "You will not be **surprised at** *my coming* alone, or **at** *John's not having told* you I was coming," said Harriet; (*DS*, ch.58); etc.

In Dickens' English, however, there is no *how*-clause after the preposition, as in (3), which was rarely seen to occur in Late Modern English but has seen a drastic increase in Present-day English.

(3) "I suppose you are **surprised at** me." "**Surprised**?" "**At how** determined I was. To get in here tonight." (Kazuo Ishiguro, *When We Were Orphans*, 2000, p.46)[3]

Although the ratio of *at* and *by* is similar to that of Present-day English, the types of prepositional complement are somewhat dissimilar and seem to retain the characteristics of 19th-century English. Dickens' use of *surprised* with *at* or *by* partly shows the characteristics of the English of his day in terms of the types of prepositional complement (i.e. qualitative dissimilarity to PE) and partly envisages the characteristics of current English in terms of the ratio of *at* and *by* (i.e. quantitative similarity to PE).

2.4 The shift from *at* to *by*

The frequencies of occurrence of *at* and *by* with *surprised* in each novel of Dickens are shown in Figure 2 below.

Figure 2
The occurrence of *at* and *by* in each novel

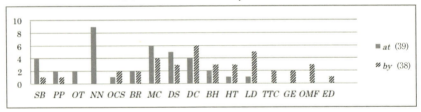

What is most striking is the gradual shift in the use of the preposition from *at* to *by* with the passage of time. The chart exhibits that Dickens used *at* fairly frequently in his earlier novels, but gradually seems to have forsaken it in later works. The novelist, on the other hand, put *by* into only scanty use in earlier works but gave preference to it in his later novels.

The occurrence rate between *at* and *by* is reversed in *David Copperfield*

---

3) Ishiguro, like Follett we have seen in Chapter 1, seems to make a distinction in the choice of *at* or *by*, using *by* with an abstract noun as follows: *I remember too being surprised by the way Mr. Anderson himself... behaved towards me as though we were old friends.* (*When We Were Orphans*, p.24)

and *by* became the predominant preposition thereafter. In fact, Dickens never used *at* after *Little Dorrit*, giving the impression that *at* was totally replaced with *by*. The contrast seems to be too striking to be accidental.

Now the question will arise as to how Dickens chose *at* or *by* with *surprised* and why the shift from *at* to *by* took place in the middle of his writing career. We will try to answer these questions in the following sections.

2.5 Stylistic variation

How the choice of *at* or *by* was made seems to involve the possible stylistic differentiation on Dickens' part. My previous investigation into the COBUILD in Chapter 2 indicates that 'UK Spoken English' contains more occurrences of *at* (24 examples) than those of *by* (9 examples). This suggests that *at* is more likely to be used in spoken English. In the same vein, in Dickens' English, more occurrences of *at* (18 instances) are observed than *by* (3 instances) in speech. Five instances of *I am surprised at you!* particularly contributes to this tendency.

Figure 3 below illustrates how Dickens may have made a distinction between *at* and *by*, depending on the style.

Figure 3
At and *by* in speech and narrative

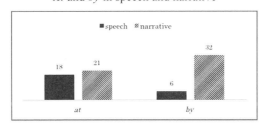

At occurs both in speech and in narrative in almost equal numbers, whereas the majority of *by* tend to appear in narrative. It may be said that Dickens differentiated the use of *at* and *by* to a certain degree, depending on whether they are used in spoken or written English.

Another factor for the differentiation may have to do with the comments made by Bolinger and Ilson, already seen in Chapter 2.[4] The following passage in *Hard Times* illustrates the distinction Dickens may have made in the use of the two prepositions.

(4) "I always come to a decision," said Bounderby, tossing his hat on: "and whatever I do, I do at once. I should be **surprised at** Tom Gradgrind's addressing such a remark to Josiah Bounderby of Coketown, knowing what he knows of him, if I could be **surprised by** anything Tom Gradgrind did, after his making himself a party to sentimental humbug. I have given you my decision, and I have got no more to say. Good night!" (*Hard Times*, Book III, ch. 3)

In this passage, the sentence containing *surprised at* conveys a strong sense of emotion, while the sentence with *surprised by* seems to simply make a statement of assumption, which may be said to be a neutral or suppressed feeling.

Allowing for these stylistic variations, the reason for the shift from *at* to *by* remains a puzzle. How could the gradual shift of the prepositions be explained?

2.6 The 'passive of *surprise* + *by*' construction gaining currency

In terms of the history of constructional change, it may be that the 'passive of *surprise* + *by*' construction was gaining currency at the time when Dickens was writing his novels. The first citation of the construction in the *OED* is a 1786 quotation (s.v. *stay* v.17). It is antedated, however, some 30 years by Dr. Johnson's use of the construction in *the Rambler* (1750–52). It is also utilized by Jane Austen (1775–1817), a novelist a generation earlier than Dickens.

Not only Dickens' contemporaries such as Ainsworth (1805–82), Trollope (1815–82) and Collins (1824–89), but Hardy (1840–1928), Gissing (1857–1903) and Conrad (1857–1924), novelists a generation later, also favored it against the norm of the day. It may be assumed that the construc-

---

4) The following comment is made in *Luminous E-J Dictionary*: "*by* is a colorless preposition used to mention a fact, whereas when *at* is used, a strong shock or an emotional response or reaction can be felt."

tion was taking root and was establishing itself throughout the 19th century.

Around the middle of the century when Dickens was in the prime of his writing career, the novelist must have accepted the construction to be legitimate, while there were a number of writers who seem to have deemed it as non- or sub-standard. Dickens' decision to use the construction may partly come from his inclination for linguistic innovation, to be discussed in §4.

2.7 Dickens' recognition of the construction as a passive

Syntactically, it may be speculated that Dickens began to recognize the past-participle form of *surprise* to be a passive and so he began to make a rather frequent use of *by*, the typical preposition of the passive, in his later novels.

The following sentences in (5) suggest that Dickens must have been conscious in using the predicates as passives.

(5) a. In his secret heart, Daniel Quilp was both **surprised** and **troubled by** the flight which had been made. (*OCS*, ch.13)
b. Scarcely less **moved** and **surprised by** the sight of the child than she had been on recognizing him, (*OCS*, ch.46)

The past-participle forms of *trouble* and *move*, both of which are not typical psychological verbs, are used here as passives. The past participles of *surprise* used in coordination with these predicates are also to be interpreted to be passives and Dickens must have been aware of it.

The following passage may also hint at Dickens' recognizing the construction to be a passive.

(6) He was not **surprised by** the attentions he received from Mr Chivery when that officer was on the lock, for he made little distinction between Mr Chivery's politeness and that of the other turnkeys. It was on one particular afternoon that Mr Chivery **surprised** him all at once, and stood forth from his companions in bold relief. (*Little Dorrit*, ch.22)

The past-participle form of *surprise* on the first line followed by its active counterpart in the next sentence seems to suggest that they were recognizably used as active and passive pairs. Dickens may have been aware of his using the first *surprise* in the past-participle form as a passive. Dickens' recognition of the construction as a passive may have led to his profuse use of *by* with the predicate. This awareness of Dickens may partly come from the constructional change that may have been taking place in his day, just seen in the previous section.

We will further deal with this issue after we examine Dickens' use of *at* and *by* with the synonymous psych-passives in the next section.

III. Psych-passives with *by*

We have discovered that *at* and *by* are used with the passive of *surprise* almost in equal numbers in Dickens' major novels. This is quite anomalous from the norm of the day, considering the ratio of *at* and *by* in his day being 1 : 0.3. Moreover, the shift in the use of preposition from *at* to *by* apparently took place.

We will examine in this section how Dickens used *at* and *by* with the passives of synonymous verbs and also examine how different Dickens' use is from the usage of his contemporary writers and that of Present-day English.

3.1 Synonymous verbs

The synonymous verbs to be treated are: *alarm*, *amaze*, *appall*, *astonish*, *astound*, *baffle*, *bewilder*, *dismay*, *perplex*, *shock*, *startle* and *stun*. How Dickens used these verbs synonymously can be illustrated by the coordinated use of the two predicates, as shown in (7).

(7) Mr. Pickwick felt, with some astonishment, that Sam's fingers were trembling at the gaiters, as if he were rather **surprised** or **startled**. (*PP*, ch.44); the two poor strangers, **stunned** and **bewildered** by the hurry they beheld ... (*OCS*, ch.44); "I am **astonished**—I am **amazed**—at her

audacity." (*BR*, ch.80); etc.[5]

It shows that they are so synonymous that they tend to co-occur with each other. Synonymous as they may be, these verbs are likely to have some slightly different shades of meaning from each other, as in (8).

(8) He was **astonished**, but by no means **dismayed**. (*PP*, ch.2); Arthur was more **shocked** than **surprised** to hear it. (*LD*, ch.70); etc.

Dickens, with these differences of meaning in mind, must have used the verbs in a proper way in a suitable context, but basically they seem to possess such identical or similar meanings as to be included in a group of synonymous words.

3.2 Data collection

Using the VLSA, the data was collected from the same novels examined in §2, plus such other works as *Master Humphrey's Clock* (1840–41), *American Notes* (1842), *Christmas Books* (1843–48), *A Child's History of England* (1851) and *The Uncommercial Traveller* (1860). The same procedure of searching and screening was followed and the samples were collected.

Let us present some examples in (9) below. The samples are presented in such a way as are likely to represent Dickens' use. The figures in the parentheses after each verb are the frequencies of occurrence of the prepositions.

(9)
(a) *alarm* [*at* 18, *by* 30]
"Oh, don't tell me you are going to send me away, sir, pray!" exclaimed Oliver, **alarmed at** the serious tone of the old gentleman's commencement! (*OT*, ch.14); He entreated him not to be **alarmed at** what he was about to say; (*NN*, ch.29); Quite **alarmed at** being the only recipient of this

---

5) More examples are found: 'bewildered and amazed' (*PP*, ch.16), 'surprised and astonished' (*NN*, ch.37), 'startled and bewildered' (*OCS*, ch.15), 'astounded and bewildered' (*BR*, ch.65), 'stunned and shocked' (*BR*, ch.68), 'startled or shocked' (*DS*, ch.1), 'dismayed and shocked' (*DS*, ch.8), 'astonished and dismayed' (*DS*, ch.46), 'perplexed and dismayed' (*GE*, ch.41); 'startled or surprised' (*GE*, ch.11); etc.

untimely visit . . . I exclaimed again, (*DC*, ch.32); etc.
Oliver, who watched the old lady anxiously, observed that she was **alarmed by** these appearances. (*OT*, ch.33); Paul was quite **alarmed by** Mr Feeder's yawning; it was done on such a grand scale, (*DS*, ch.12); Mr. Chillip was so **alarmed by** her abruptness . . . (*DC*, ch.1); "Do not be **alarmed by** what I say, Agnes," (*DC*, ch.19); etc.

(b) *amaze* [*at* 16, *by* 15]
Nicholas looked on, quite **amazed at** the introduction of this new theme. (*NN*, ch.37); But Withers, meeting him on the stairs, stood **amazed at** the beauty of his teeth, (*DS*, ch.37); Miss Abbey was **amazed at** her demeanour. (*OMF*, ch.6); etc.
John Willet was so **amazed by** the exasperation and boldness of his hopeful son, (*BR*, ch.3); Mr. Jonas was so very much **amazed by** these proceedings that he could do nothing but stare at the two old men, (*MC*, ch.18); I sat all the while, **amazed by** Mr. Micawber's disclosure, and wondering what it meant; (*DC*, ch.36); etc.

(c) *appall* [*at* 0, *by* 5]
"Oh dear, dear, I shall never try it," said Arthur Gride, **appalled by** the mention of the word, (*NN*, ch.51); Master Charles Bates, **appalled by** Sike's crime, fell into a train of reflection . . . (*OT*, ch.53); The first four days of his endurance were days so long and heavy, that he began to be **appalled by** the prospect before him. (*HT*, ch.20); etc.

(d) *astonish* [*at* 26, *by* 13]
for Mr. Winkle was so very much **astonished at** the extraordinary behaviour of the medical gentleman, (*PP*, ch.38); "How dare you, Dolly? I'm **astonished at** you." (*BR*, ch.27) "Oh! I am not at all **astonished at** your speaking thus openly when my country is in question," (*MC*, ch.17); "I'm **astonished at** that, Master Copperfield, you being usually so quick!" (*DC*, ch.42); etc.
"Sir!" said the spinster aunt, rather **astonished by** the unexpected apparition and somewhat doubtful of Mr. Jingle's sanity. (*PP*, ch.8); "Is the gentleman at home?" said Kit, rather **astonished by** this uncommon reception. (*OCS*, ch.56); etc.

(e) *astound* [*at* 1, *by* 7]

The linen-drapers of Hammersmith were **astounded at** the sudden demand for blue sarsenet ribbon, and long white gloves. (*SB*, ch.3); Oliver was rather **astounded by** this intelligence, and was not quite certain whether he ought to laugh or cry. (*OT*, ch.2); But, **astounded** as he was **by** the apparition of the dwarf among the Little Bethelites. (*OCS*, ch.41); So immensely **astounded** was Mr. Merdle **by** the entrance of Bar with such a reference in his mouth, (*LD*, ch.48); etc.

(f) *baffle* [*at* 0, *by* 5]

The little man seemed rather **baffled by** these several repulses, (*PP*, ch.10); Dennis, who was very much **baffled by** the cool matter-of-course manner of this reply, recovered his self-possession . . . (*BR*, ch.53); etc.

(g) *bewilder* [*at* 0, *by* 17]

Richard Swiveller, who being **bewildered by** the rapidity with which his cards were told, (*OCS*, ch.23); The single gentleman, rather **bewildered by** finding himself the centre of this noisy throng, (*OCS*, ch.47); UNCERTAIN where to go next, and **bewildered by** the crowd of people who were already astir, (*BR*, ch.48); the good Captain was so **bewildered by** her attention that he held it as if he had never held a pipe, in all his life. (*DS*, ch.49); etc.

(h) *dismay* [*at* 0, *by* 8]

Mr. Pinch was not so **dismayed by** this terrible threat, (*MC*, ch.7); Edith . . . never seemed **dismayed by** anything her mother said or did. (*DS*, ch.40); Here Mr. George is much **dismayed by** the graces and accomplishments of his nieces. . . (*BH*, ch.63); etc.

(i) *perplex* [*at* 0, *by* 12]

Very much **perplexed by** this summary disposition of this person, Mr. Pickwick walked back into the prison, (*PP*, ch.42); Captain Cuttle, **perplexed by** no such meditations, guarded Florence to her room, (*DS*, ch.49); If Little Dorritt were beyond measure **perplexed by** this curious conduct on the part of her new acquaintance, (*LD*, ch.24); etc.

(j) *shock* [*at* 6, *by* 11]
"He's **shocked at** the way your father goes on in," replied Mrs. Weller. (*PP*, ch.27); "Ugh!" cried Mr. Lorry, rather relenting, nevertheless, "I am **shocked at** the sight of you." (*TTC*, III, ch.9); etc.
If Miss Miggs had had her hearing, no doubt she would have been greatly **shocked by** the indelicacy of a young female's going away with a stranger by night. (*BR*, ch.70); I was **shocked by** the mere thought of her having lived, an hour, within sight of such a man. (*DC*, ch.52); She was so very earnest and injured, that Mr. Gradgrind, **shocked by** the possibility which dawned upon him, (*HT*, ch.33); etc.

(k) *startle* [*at* 0, *by* 44]
for he was considerably **startled by** this tragical termination of the narrative. (*PP*, ch.64); when Mrs. Mann, the good lady of the house, was unexpectedly **startled by** the apparition of Mr. Bumble . . . (*OT*, ch.2); He was **startled by** the mention of his sister's name. (*NN*, ch.32); The solitary passenger was **startled by** the chairmen's cry of "By your leave there!" (*BR*, ch.16); At first I was **startled by** so abrupt a departure, and almost feared I had displeased her; (*DC*, ch.15); etc.

(l) *stun* [*at* 0, *by* 18]
Solomon Gills was at first **stunned by** the communication, which fell upon the little back-parlour like a thunderbolt, (*DS*, ch.17); Oliver felt **stunned** and stupefied **by** the unexpected intelligence; he could not weep, or speak, or rest. (*OT*, ch.34); I was not **stunned by** the praise which sounded in my ears, (*DC*, ch.48); etc.

3.3 Statistical results

From the data we obtain the results on the following table. Verbs are horizontally arranged and each work of Dickens is vertically listed with the year of publication. The frequencies of occurrence of *at* and *by* are shown under each verb. The total numbers from each verb and from each work are shown at the bottom and at the right of the table, respectively.

Table 3
Dickens' use of psych-passives with *at* or *by*

Works	Year of publication	alarm at	alarm by	amaze at	amaze by	appall at	appall by	astonish at	astonish by	astound at	astound by	baffle at	baffle by	bewilder at	bewilder by	dismay at	dismay by	perplex at	perplex by	shock at	shock by	startle at	startle by	stun at	stun by	Total at	Total by
Sketches by Boz	1833-36	2	2	0	0	0	1	4	0	1	0	0	0	0	0	0	0	0	0	0	0	0	1	0	0	7	4
Pickwick Papers	1836-37	4	0	0	0	0	0	2	2	0	0	0	1	0	1	0	0	0	2	1	0	0	5	0	0	7	11
Oliver Twist	1837-39	3	1	0	1	0	1	0	0	0	1	0	0	0	1	0	0	0	0	0	0	0	3	0	1	3	9
Nicholas Nickleby	1838-39	3	2	1	1	0	1	4	1	0	0	0	0	0	1	0	1	0	0	0	0	0	5	0	1	8	13
Old Curiosity Shop	1840-41	0	3	2	0	0	0	0	1	0	1	0	0	0	5	0	0	0	1	0	0	0	1	0	2	2	13
Master Humphrey's Clock	1840-41	0	1	2	0	0	0	0	0	0	0	0	0	0	0	0	0	0	0	0	0	0	0	0	0	2	1
Barnaby Rudge	1841	1	3	1	1	0	0	3	1	0	0	0	1	0	0	0	0	0	0	2	1	0	4	0	0	7	14
American Notes	1842	0	0	2	0	0	0	0	0	0	1	0	0	0	2	0	0	0	0	0	0	0	2	0	0	2	3
Martin Chuzzlewit	1843-44	1	0	0	4	0	0	1	3	0	1	0	0	0	0	0	1	0	0	0	2	0	4	0	2	2	17
Christmas Books	1843-48	0	0	0	0	0	0	2	0	0	1	0	0	0	0	0	0	0	0	0	1	0	2	0	0	2	5
Dombey and Son	1846-48	0	2	3	0	0	0	1	0	0	0	0	0	0	0	0	2	0	2	0	1	0	2	0	4	4	17
David Copperfield	1849-50	1	3	2	1	0	0	1	0	0	0	0	0	0	3	0	2	0	0	1	2	0	3	0	1	5	13
Child's History of England	1851	1	1	0	0	0	0	0	0	0	0	0	0	0	0	0	1	0	0	0	0	0	0	0	1	1	3
Bleak House	1852-53	0	2	1	1	0	1	3	1	0	0	0	1	0	0	0	1	0	2	0	1	0	2	0	1	4	12
Hard Times	1854	0	0	0	0	0	1	1	1	0	0	0	0	0	0	0	0	0	0	0	2	0	0	0	2	1	6
Little Dorrit	1855-57	0	1	0	2	0	0	3	0	0	1	0	0	0	1	0	0	0	3	1	1	0	2	0	1	5	12
Tale of Two Cities	1859	0	0	0	0	0	0	0	0	0	0	0	0	0	0	0	0	0	0	1	0	0	1	0	0	1	1
Uncommercial Traveller	1860	0	2	0	3	0	0	1	1	0	0	0	1	0	0	0	0	0	1	0	0	0	2	0	1	1	11
Great Expectations	1860-61		0	3	0	0	0	0	0	1	0	0	0	0	0	1	0	0	0	0	0	0	0	1	0	0	06
Our Mutual Friend	1864-65	2	4	1	1	0	1	0	1	0	1	0	0	0	0	0	0	0	1	0	0	0	2	0	1	3	12
Mystery of Edwin	1870	0	0	0	0	0	0	0	0	0	0	0	0	0	0	0	0	0	0	0	0	0	2	0	0	0	2
Total		18	30	16	15	0	5	26	13	1	7	0	5	0	17	0	8	0	12	6	11	0	44	0	18	67	185

83

3.4 The role of statistics in language studies

I made some comments on the role that statistics play in language studies in the previous chapter. Let us reiterate part of it. All I would like to show in this study is the approximate ratio of *at* and *by* with psych-passives. The statistics we obtained, however, may not be helpful in understanding the occurrence rate of *at* and *by* in Dickens' works as the figures from each item (that is, each verb or each book) are not large enough. Moreover, the occurrence rates are quite different from each other. The solution to this drawback would be to add up the figures from each verb or each novel.

The simple addition of the figures, however, may not constitute a true representation of any linguistic phenomenon. Nevertheless, we get a rough but a reasonably accurate picture at the very least. The picture we get from the analysis of the data may be compared to a huge jigsaw puzzle, in which some pieces are missing here and there but we can still see the whole picture and determine the general pattern. That should be sufficient in a language study like this.

3.5 Analysis of the data
3.5.1 Classification of the verbs

Let us now take a look at the characteristics of the verbs. The most frequently used verb is *alarm* (*surprise* aside), followed by *startle, astonish, amaze, shock, stun, bewilder* and so on. The order is slightly different from that of the Late ModE period.

Most of the verbs except for *amaze* and *astonish* have a tendency to occur with *by*; some verbs like *bewilder, startle, stun,* etc. only occur with *by*. It shows how Dickens preferred to use *by*, just as he did with the passive of *surprise*.

Although each verb has its own characteristics, it is possible to classify the verbs into three groups as follows, depending on which preposition they chiefly occur with:

Group 1: *Amaze* and *astonish* occur with *at* and *by*, with more occurrences of *at*

Group 2: *Alarm, astound* and *shock* occur mainly with *by*, with fewer occurrences of *at*

Group 3: *Appall, baffle, bewilder, dismay, perplex, startle* and *stun* only occur with *by*

There are verbs whose passives occur with both *at* and *by*. *Alarm, amaze, astonish, astound, shock* are such verbs. *Astonish*, for instance, occurs with *at* and *by* in *Pickwick Papers* (illustrated in the examples presented above) and there seems to be no explaining how and why the choice was made. Did Dickens try to make a meaningful distinction by using a different preposition? Did he choose a preposition in a haphazard way?

We are not certain if there is any intention in the choice on Dickens' part but there may be some factors involved in his choosing the preposition. This may be an interesting theme to pursue but we will not get into this here and confine our analysis to the quantitative one.

3.5.2 The dominance of *by*

Now let us take a look at the total statistics. Psych-passives occur with *at* 67 times and with *by* 185 times, as in the following table.

Table 3
The occurrence of *at* and *by* with psych-passives

at	*by*
67	185

The ratio of *at* and *by* is approximately 1 : 2.8 and it means that *by* occurs nearly three times more frequently than *at*. Let us make a comparison of the ratios of Late Modern English, Present-day English and Dickens in Table 4 on the next page.

Dickens' ratio is much higher than that of his contemporaries. It is even higher than that of Present-day English. Dickens' English may even be said to look further ahead into the future English.

Table 4
The comparison of the ratios

	at	by
LModE	1	0.9
PE	1	1.8
Dickens	1	2.8

IV. Dickens: Linguistic Innovator

As the title of Sørensen's book (*Charles Dickens: Linguistic Innovator*, 1985) aptly describes, Dickens has been said to be "linguistically ahead of his time" and "innovative" and even "revolutionary" in his day (pp. 12, 63).

Brook (1970: 223–48) allocates as many as twenty-five pages in his book *The Language of Dickens* to enumerate Dickens' "substandard grammar." Blake (1981: 157) refers to Dickens as a writer who "introduced many varieties of non-standard language into his writings." Blake claims that this is probably due to "his experience as a [court] reporter and shorthand writer" and "the continual recording of actual speech made him sensitive to the different varieties of English in use."[6] (see §3.8 in chapter 2.)

Crystal (1995: 191) states "Charles Dickens pulls no punches when he finds an opportunity to satirize the grammatical tradition which held such power in British schools during the early 19th century." This comment may summarize Dickens' philosophy toward traditional grammar.

Tieken-Boon (2009: 18) also says, "Dickens is perhaps most famous for the representation of non-standard speech in his novels," and elaborates the novelist's use of non-standard English (pp. 27, 80–81, 87–88).

It is apparent that Dickens did not pay as much respect to traditional grammar as had been exhibited by conservative writers of his day or later. Dickens, with an innovative and experimental mind, must have exploited sub-standard or unconventional language.[7]

---

6) Bailey (1996: 68) quotes Dickens' letter of 1856, which goes, "I left the reputation behind me of being the best and most rapid reporter ever."

7) Sørensen (1985: 63), however, has mentioned that "[Dickens] is not a syntactic

Dickens' employment of unconventional English may include his preference for *by* with the passives of *surprise* and its synonymous verbs. It may have resulted in the unusually frequent occurrence of the agentive *by*, compared to his contemporary writers.

V. The possible influence by Johnson and Austen

We will examine the two British writers who may have influenced Dickens in his preference for *by* with the passives of *surprise* and synonymous verbs. The writer who practically used this construction for the first time may have been Samuel Johnson, followed by Jane Austen, who also preferred to utilize this usage. They are eminent and popular writers in the history of British literature and their writings may be assumed to have had some influence on the dispersion of this usage and also on Dickens' use of unconventional English.

5.1 Samuel Johnson (1709–84)

Samuel Johnson was a writer and lexicographer during the latter part of the 18th century. Dr. Johnson, as he was familiarly called, established a literary magazine called *The Rambler* (1750–52),[8] and he contributed articles himself. Johnson is observed to use the construction six times in volumes of this magazine.[9] The following sentences are examples of psychological use.

---

innovator in the sense that he introduces a lot of new constructions. What he does in a number of cases is to exploit—and occasionally to over-exploit—the syntactic potential of English."

8) *The Rambler* was an essay magazine published twice a week from 1750 for two years. Johnson himself contributed to it. Nearly 500 copies were published for each issue and read around at coffee shops. Some articles were carried without permission in local newspapers including America. They were widely read, considering its being morality magazines. (Etoh et al., 2009: 31).

Boswell (1791: 94), Johnson's admirer and the author of his biography, says, "As the time passes, the popularity increased . . . the author saw the publication of ten different versions of the magazine."

9) *The Rambler* was contained in the MEC and *at* was used once. VLSA contains another work of Johnson, *The History of Rasselas*, and *at* alone is used twice.

(10) he is **surprised by** sudden alterations of the state of things ... (No. 14, 1750); Dryden ... never confessed that he had been **surprised by** an ambiguity. (No. 31, 1750); I turned about, and was **surprized by** the sight of the loveliest object I had ever beheld. (No. 44, 1750); etc.

Agentive nouns used in these sentences are all abstract nouns and this reminds us of the usage of Present-day English. Johnson's preference for *by* with the passive of *surprise* may be true of the passives of other synonymous verbs. Table 2 in Chapter 3 shows that Johnson preferred to use *by* more than *at* (*by* 11 times and *at* 5 times).

Where does this peculiarity of Johnson's come from? In compiling his renowned dictionary, Dr. Johnson wrote very unusual and even singular definitions.[10] As for those definitions, Hitchings (2005: 123) says that "he intended them to spark controversy" or "he hopes to awaken debate." Johnson's stance to use these unconventional and even provocative definitions suggests that Johnson may have possessed the inclination to use unusual usage of the day. Gordon (1966: 144) depicts Johnson's style as follows: "Johnson had established the manner of writing which ran counter to the prose of his contemporaries." These characteristics of Johnson's may be attributed to his preference for *by* with the psych-passives.

5.2 Jane Austen (1775–1817)

Jane Austen is another writer who preferred to use *by* with the passive of *surprise*. She uses *by* thirteen times altogether (*at* 26 times) in her letters and novels, as in (11).

(11) a. I was rather **surprised** on Monday **by** the arrival of a letter for you, from your Winchester correspondent, (*Letters*, 1808); We were agreeably **surprised** the other day **by** a visit from your beauty and mine ... (*Letters*, 1809)

b. I should have been much **surprised**, and much hurt, **by** such a proceeding. (*Mansfield Park*, 1814); she rose ... and was then most

---

10) 'Oats', for instance, is defined as "A grain, which in England is generally given to horses, but in Scotland supports the people."

agreeably **surprised by** General Tilney's asking her if... (*Northanger Abbey*, 1817); etc.

The sentences in (11a) are in Austen's personal letters[11] and the sentences in (11b) are in her novels.[12] It may be possible to think that the construction was inbuilt in her mental grammar, considering as many as six examples are used in the letters she wrote herself.

During the period from the late 18th century to the early 19th century when Austen was engaged in writing her novels, the 'passive of *surprise* + *by*' construction in a psychological sense is assumed to have been one of the non- or sub-standard usages. Austen has been dubbed as an "innovator" as Page (1972: 187) says, "her syntax is more experimental and adventurous." And so it is little wonder if she dared to use the construction, which may have been unconventional in her day.

Considering Austen's popularity among the general readers and her influence on later writers, she may have played some role in contributing to the spread of this anomalous construction among the English population.

It is possible to assume that Dickens, who may have read Johnson or Austen, was influenced by their writings in the use of *by* with psych-passives. Dickens is far more influential than Samuel Johnson or Jane Austen and he may have exerted much more influence on the writers and readers in later period. His unusually frequent use of *by* with the passives of *surprise* and synonymous verbs in his novels may have become a model and have been reproduced by later writers and readers.

It is therefore reasonable to suggest that the recognition and production of newly-coined usages by great and popular writers may have given legitimacy and even authority to them and that the new expressions may eventually become part of the English language.

---

11) *Jane Austen's Letters: to Her Sister Casandra and Others*. (R. W. Chapman ed., Oxford University Press, 1964)
12) The novels examined are: *Sense and Sensibility* (1811), *Pride and Prejudice* (1813), *Mansfield Park* (1814), *Emma* (1816), *Northanger Abbey* (1817) and *Persuasion* (1818).

VI. Summary

Charles Dickens is a writer who put the 'passive of *surprise* + *by*' construction, an unconventional usage in the 19th century, into far more frequent use than his contemporaries. We found 39 occurrences of *at* and 38 occurrences of *by* in his major novels. The ratio of *at* and *by* is very similar to that of Present-day English.

What is striking is the gradual shift from *at* to *by* taking place as the time progressed. Dickens used *at* fairly frequently in his earlier works but seems to have gradually abandoned it, and began to favor *by* in the middle of his writing career. He used *by* exclusively in his last four novels and it gives us an impression that Dickens replaced *at* with *by* as an agentive preposition.

Dickens' choice of *at* or *by* seems to involve stylistic issues. The novelist seems to have made a distinction between the two prepositions depending on the style: basically, *at* in speech and *by* in narrative. This may have to do with the fact that *at* was likely to be used to express an emotion, while *by* was used to state a fact, reminiscent of PE's usage.

There may be a couple of reasons for the increase of *by* during his writing career. One is that the construction may have been gaining popularity while Dickens was engaged in writing. Another reason is that Dickens may have become conscious that the predicate was a passive and therefore used *by*, the main preposition for the passive.

We have also examined Dickens' use of *at* and *by* with the passives of synonymous verbs. Dickens preferred to use *by* for most of the verbs except for *amaze* and *astonish*. He never used *at* with such verbs as *bewilder*, *startle*, *stun*, etc. The total occurrences of *at* and *by* are 67 times and 185 times respectively. The ratio is 1 : 2.8 and this is very striking because the ratio of his contemporary writers is 1 : 0.9. Since Dickens' ratio is even higher than that of Present-day English, which is 1 : 1.8, Dickens' usage is very peculiar and may be said to show a possible sign of future English.

This peculiarity of Dickens may come from his innovative mind as a writer as he has been referred to as a "linguistic innovator", who exploited unconventional usages. Dickens' employment of *by* with psych-passives may have to do with his being an innovator in writing.

Chapter 4

Finally, I argued that Dickens may have been influenced in the use of agentive prepositions by his predecessors like Johnson or Austen. Popular and great writers' use of unconventional usages may have given legitimacy or even authority to them, helping to establish them in society and to become part of the English language.

Appendix

The following are the sentences containing the 'passive of *surprise*' construction occurring with *at* or *by* in Dickens' works in chronological order. The quotation marks are placed, even if they are not there originally, for some utterances such as 2, 17, 20, etc. to show that they are used in dialogue.

AT

1. "Naughty boy!" said his mamma, who appeared more **surprised at** his taking the liberty of falling down, than at anything else; (*SB*, Part IV, ch.3)
2. "for I have known you, long enough, not to be **surprised at** anything you do, and you might extend equal courtesy to me." (*SB*, Part IV, ch.8)
3. We were not much **surprised at** the discovery that it was our friend, the military young gentleman, (*SB*, Part IV, ch.12)
4. and that they were **surprised at** Mrs. Brown's allowing it, (*SB*, Part IV, ch.12)
5. "Stay! No! The next day. You are **surprised at** my wishing to postpone it," (*PP*, ch.21)
6. "What business?" inquired Mr. Pickwick, **surprised at** Sam's confused manner. (*PP*, ch.43)
7. and a few made head upon her, and looked back, **surprised at** her undiminished speed, but they fell off one by one; (*OT*, ch.34)
8. Oliver walked into the window-recess to which Mr. Maylie beckoned him; much **surprised at** the mixture of sadness and boisterous spirits, which his whole behaviour displayed. (*OT*, ch.36)
9. Some considerable experience prevented the girl from being at all **surprised at** any outbreak of ill-temper on the part of Miss Squeers. (*NN*, ch.12)
10. "Kenwigs, my dear," returned his wife, "I'm **surprised at** you. Would you begin without my uncle?" (*NN*, ch.14)
11. "Kenwigs!' said Mr Lillyvick, in a loud voice, "I'm **surprised at** you." (*NN*, ch.15)
12. If she had been **surprised at** the apparition of the footman, she was perfectly absorbed in amazement at the richness and splendour of the furniture. (*NN*, ch.19)
13. "I'm not **surprised at** that," said Nicholas; "she must be quite a natural

genius." (*NN*, ch.23)

14. "Ah!" said Nicholas, a little **surprised at** these symptoms of ecstatic approbation. (*NN*, ch.25)
15. "Kate," interposed Mrs Nickleby with severe diginity, "I'm **surprised at** you." (*NN*, ch.49)
16. "I am **surprised at** you," repeated Mrs Nickleby; "upon my word, Kate, I'm quite astonished that . . . " (*NN*, ch.49)
17. "You never seem to me to be talking about anything else, Kate, and upon my word I am quite **surprised at** your being so very thoughtless". (*NN*, ch.55)
18. This made him doubt whether he had locked his door last night, and feel a little **surprised at** having a companion in the room. (*OCS*, ch.64)
19. John was not at all **surprised at** this, either. (*BR*, ch.55)
20. "you'd be **surprised at** the total—quite amazed, you would." (*BR*, ch.59)
21. "I am not **surprised**, sir, **at** anything you have told me tonight." (*MC*, ch.3)
22. "You're not **surprised at** my having two names, I suppose?" (*MC*, ch.5)
23. Is any one **surprised at** Mr. Jonas making such a preference to such a book for such a purpose? (*MC*, ch.11)
24. Mr. Tapley was very much **surprised at** this admission, but protested, with great vehemence, (*MC*, ch.33)
25. He was not so much **surprised at** the man's being there, as at his having got close to him so quietly and swiftly; (*MC*, ch.40)
26. You . . . were always so fond of him . . . that I am not **surprised at** your being attached to the place. (*MC*, ch.51)
27. "Really I'm **surprised at** them." (*DS*, ch.1)
28. The young woman seemed **surprised at** his appearance, and asked him where his mother was. (*DS*, ch.12)
29. I believe nobody will be **surprised**, either **at** its being required from you, or at your making it. (*DS*, ch.40)
30. "I'm **surprised at** you! Where's your feminine tenderness?" (*DS*, ch.52)
31. "You will not be **surprised at** my coming alone, or at John's not having told you I was coming," said Harriet; (*DS*, ch.58)
32. He appeared **surprised at** this. (*DC*, ch.5)
33. All about it was so very quiet, that I said to Mr. Mell I supposed the boys were out; but he seemed **surprised at** my not knowing that it was holiday-time. (*DC*, ch.5)
34. I am not **surprised** . . . **at** this peculiarity striking me as his chief one. (*DC*,

ch.6)
35. "You'd be **surprised at** the number of people that looks in of a day to have a chat." (*DC*, ch.51)
36. "I'm sure I'm **surprised at** that I wonder you don't starve in your own way also." (*BH*, ch.52)
37. "I'm **surprised at** the indiscreetness you commit." (*BH*, 54)
38. "I should be **surprised at** Tom Gradgrind's addressing such a remark to Josiah Bounderby of Coketown," (*HT*, ch.3)
39. Both gentlemen glanced at him, and seemed **surprised at** his assurance. (*LD*, Bk I, ch.10)

BY

1. "we were rather **surprised by** the sudden appearance of thirty-four of his Kit-ma-gars." (*SB*, Part IV, ch.7)
2. when he was very much **surprised by** observing a most brilliant light glide through the air . . . and almost instantaneously vanish. (*PP*, ch.39)
3. In his secret heart, Daniel Quilp was both **surprised** and troubled **by** the flight which had been made. (*OCS*, ch.13)
4. Scarcely less moved and **surprised by** the sight of the child than she had been on recognizing him, (*OCS*, ch.46)
5. Mr. Haredale paused for a moment, and looked at her as if **surprised by** the energy of her manner. (*BR*, ch.25)
6. "Oh, you're here, are you, sir?" said John, rather **surprised by** the quickness with which he appeared. (*BR*, ch.29)
7. Indeed, I have, now and again, been more **surprised by** printed news that I have read of myself, (*MC*)
8. "Most strangers—and partick'larly Britishers—are much **surprised by** what they see in the United States," remarked Mrs Hominy. (*MC*, ch.22)
9. The man appeared **surprised by** his unexpected irritability, and saying no more, smoked his pipe in silence. (*MC*, ch.47)
10. everybody present was so much **surprised** and embarrassed **by** the sight of everybody else, that nobody ventured to speak. (*MC*, ch.52)
11. The man who had been strolling carelessly towards her, seemed **surprised by** this reply, and looking attentively in her face, rejoined. (*DS*, ch.6)
12. she turned her head, and was **surprised by** the reflection of her thoughtful image in the chimney-glass. (*DS*, ch.29)

Chapter 4

13. Miss Tox ... was so **surprised by** the amount of expression Mrs. Chick had conveyed into her face, (*DS*, ch.29)
14. I recollect being very much **surprised by** the feint everybody made, (*DC*, ch.5)
15. I might have been **surprised by** the feeling tone in which he spoke, if I had given it a thought; (*DC*, ch.9)
16. I know enough of the world now, to have almost lost the capacity of being much **surprised by** anything; (*DC*, ch.11)
17. I was very much **surprised by** the inquiry; but could give no information on this point. (*DS*, ch.14)
18. I was not **surprised by** the suddenness of the proposal, and said: "Yes." (*DC*, ch.15)
19. "I should be an affected woman if I made any pretence of being **surprised by** my son's inspiring such emotions;" (*DC*, ch.20)
20. Mr.Tulkinghorn stops short, **surprised by** my Lady's animation and her unusual tone. (*BH*, 2)
21. I was not **surprised by** Caddy's being in low spirits when we went downstairs, (*BH*, ch.23)
22. "I am rather **surprised by** the course you have taken." (*BH*, 48)
23. She was not **surprised by** the result, . . . and her face beamed brightly. (*HT*, ch.2)
24. "You have missed my letter!' exclaimed Mr. Gradgrind, **surprised by** the apparition. (*HT*, ch.3)
25. "if I could be **surprised by** anything Tom Gradgrind did," (*HT*, ch.3)
26. nor was he at all **surprised by** the presence of two nieces instead of one, (*LD*, Bk. I, ch.20)
27. He was not **surprised by** the attentions he received from Mr. Chivery when that officer was on the look, (*LD*, Bk. I, ch.22)
28. 29. His glasses were in his hand, and he had just looked round; **surprised** at first, no doubt, **by** her step upon the stairs, not expecting her until night; **surprised** again, **by** seeing Arthur Clennam in her company. (*LD*, Bk. I, ch.35)
30. Little Dorrit was rather **surprised by** Fanny's being at home at that hour, (*LD*, Bk. II, ch.14)
31. it never occurred to him to be **surprised by** their appearance until a long time afterwards, (*TTC*, Part III, ch.2)

32. "The usual noises," Mr. Cruncher replied; and looked **surprised by** the question and by her aspect. (*TTC*, Part III, ch.14)
33. I then rejoined Mr. Wemmick, and affecting to consult my watch and to be **surprised by** the information I had received, accepted his offer. (*GE*, ch.32)
34. Much **surprised by** the request, I took the note. (*GE*, ch.44)
35. His pupil was a little **surprised by** this striking in with so sudden and decided and emotional an objection, (*OMF*, Bk. II, ch.1)
36. Lady Tippins is so **surprised by** seeing her dear Mrs. Veneering so early—in the middle of the night, (*OMF*, Bk. II. ch.3)
37. This repudiation was not only an act of deliberate policy on Fledgeby's part, in case of his being **surprised by** any other caller, (*OMF*, Bk. III, ch.13)
38. "You would not be **surprised by** this, Mr. Dean, if you had seen Mr. Sapsea deal with him in his parlour, as I did." (*ED*, ch.12)

Chapter 5
The semantic shift of psych-passives + *by*

Readers are invited to embark on a brief journey back in time to the Heian Era (794–1192) of medieval Japan. During this literally 'peaceful' period, the world-renowned *The Tale of Genji* was written by Lady Murasaki. This is a love romance centering around Prince Genji, the young shining prince of the aristocratic society twelve hundred years ago. In *Kiritsubo*, the first tale of *Genji*, the young prince is being examined by a physiognomist, who is astonished by his physical features.

I. Introduction

1.1 Arthur Waley's use of *astonished* + *by*
We find the following sentence in *The Tale of Genji*, translated in English by Arthur Waley.

(1) The fortune-teller was **astonished by** the boy's lineaments and expressed his surprise by continually nodding his head.[1]

(*Kiritsubo* in *The Tale of Genji*)

The psych-verb *astonish* is used here in the passive and followed by the agentive preposition *by* instead of *at*, a preposition usually occurring with this construction. Why did Waley prefer to use *by* here instead of *at*, which seemingly had been a standard usage?[2] It may be that *by* is used here to emphasize the force of the prepositional complement (*the boy's lineaments*);

---

1) The original Japanese sentence with a word-for-word translation is as follows: Soubito odorokite amatatabi ayasibi katabuku. [the fortune-teller / was astonished / many times / wondering / shook his head]

2) The ratio of *at* and *by* with the passive form of *astonish* during the period from the 1890s to the 1920s when Arthur Waley acquired English and began to translate *Genji* is assumed to have been roughly 5 : 1 from the analysis of the data from the COHA.

97

an 'astonishment' just does not come from the complement as a stimulus, but in this example the complement exerts an influence on the subject of the sentence (*the fortune-teller*). Waley may have decided that the sentence needs to be a passive, not just an adjectival construction, which would have required *at* here.

1.2 The etymology of psych-verbs

The verb *astonish*, just as *surprise*, used to occur mainly with the agentive *at* but now it is occurring with both *at* and *by*, with *by* becoming more predominant.[3] What is also common with these two verbs is that they used to have meanings different from the currently prevalent psychological meanings. *Astonish*, for instance, had the following meanings, which are now obsolete.

†1. To deprive of sensation, as by a blow; to stun, paralyze, deaden, stupefy. *Obs.*

The same is true of *surprise* and it carried such meanings as follows:

1. Chiefly *pass* To be seized *with* (or *of*) a desire, emotion, etc., a disease or illness. *Obs.* 2a. *Mil.* etc. To assail or attack suddenly and without warning; to make an unexpected assault upon (a place, body of troops, person, etc. that is unprepared); † to take or capture in this way. b. to capture, seize; to take possession of by force; to take prisoner. *Obs.* †c. to hold in one's power, to occupy. *Obs.*

These meanings of older times may be said to be 'physical', as opposed to the current psychological use. Some of these physical meanings are obsolete now except for the definition 2a above. The sentences with physical meanings are seen to have been occurring in earlier English, as in (2).

(2) Their encampments, too, are always subject to be **surprised by** wandering war parties ... (Irving, *A Tour on the Prairies*, 1835); At any moment we

---

3) The ratio of *at* and *by* with *astonished* in PE is approximately 1 : 1.2, whereas the ratio of Late ModE was 8 : 1.

might be **surprised by** a body of savages . . . (Melville, *Typee*, 1846); etc.

1.3 Psychological use and agentive prepositions

The verb *surprise* gradually acquired psychological meanings, retaining the physical meanings as well. In Chapter 1, we have seen the definitions and illustrative quotations of the psychological use of *surprise*. The verb is shown to be used often in the passive and to occur with such prepositions as *with* or *at*. Gradually *at* has become more dominant and furthermore, the agentive *by* appeared in the 18th century.

The agentive *by* has seen such an increase and become so prevalent in Present-day English that it has surpassed the occurrence rate of *at*, with the most recent ratio of *at* and *by* being 1 : 1.9.

In this chapter, we will analyze the process of the semantic shift in which the verb *surprise* and its synonymous verbs, *startle* and *stun*, have developed psychological meanings from their original physical meanings. I will demonstrate that what I call the 'intermediate' stage has taken place during the process of the semantic shift.

We will also consider the reasons why their passives are more likely to occur with *by* in Present-day English. I will argue that the preference for *by* may have to do with the 'intermediate' use, where *by* was chosen presumably on the analogy of the physical use and this use of *by* may have been extended to the psychological use as well.

II. The shift in meaning

2.1 The decline of the physical use

The verb *surprise* was originally used in such a physical meaning as "to attack suddenly and unexpectedly." The physical use, however, seems to have been declining in Present-day English. The decline can be shown by the search into the *OED* on CD-ROM. After the retrieved samples are sorted according to the meaning and the century of their appearance, the following results are obtained.

Figure 1
The century-by-century distribution of *surprised* + *by*

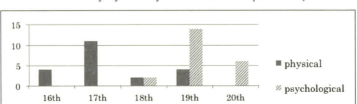

From the chart it is evident that the physical use has been declining, whereas the psychological use has been on the relative increase with each century.

The decline of the physical use can be confirmed by the search into the COHA. The data from the period between 1810 and 1900 (part of Late ModE) shows the occurrence rate of the physical use to be twenty percent, while the data from the period between 1970 and 2000 (PE) shows it to be six percent.[4] A search into the MEC and the BNC also reveals the decline: fifteen percent in Late ModE and 0.5 percent in PE. It seems evident that the decline has been taking place.

This is probably because the increase of the psychological use has caused the physical use to be replaced by some other forms of expression, possibly to avoid the confusion of meaning. Ikegami (1978: 130) aptly describes this kind of transition of meaning as follows: "When the meaning of a certain word changes from A to B, what will be at issue is in what way the meaning of A will be expressed."

2.2. The development of the intermediate stage
2.2.1 Psychological plus physiological meanings

The verb *surprise* underwent what I call the 'intermediate' stage before developing purely psychological meanings. By 'intermediate', I mean the stage at which a psych-verb has basically psychological meanings but it also contains a shade of physiological or physical meaning. The intermediate use

---

4) The physical use occurred 65 times out of a total of 325 occurrences of *surprised by* in Late ModE, while in PE, it occurs 23 times out of a total of 375 occurrences.

may be illustrated by the following sentences.

> (3) a. Well, we had not time to haul out a little before we were **surprised by** *a tremendous clap of thunder and lightning*.
> (Prest, *Varney the Vampire*, Vol. 3, 1847)
> b. She resembles an enormous and aquatic blackbeetle, **surprised by** *the light*, overwhelmed by the sunshine . . .
> (Conrad, *The Nigger of the Narcissus*, 1897)

In (3a), "we" had a terrifying experience of a deafening thunder and glaring lightning, which may have caused a mental astonishment and also exerted an influence on sensory organs, that is, eyes and ears. The influence may have caused such physiological reactions as a heart palpitation, a cold perspiration or the trembling of the body.

In (3b), the insect is affected by the light and sunshine, which seem to cause a sensory influence on eyes as well as a psychological effect. It may have triggered a physiological response like a secretion. I refer to the process as the 'intermediate' stage, in that physical or physiological influence as well as psychological effects may be exerted. Let us provide some more examples.

> (4) Joan [of Arc] told her father that she had one day been **surprised by** *a great unearthly light*, and had afterwards heard a solemn voice . . . (Dickens, *A Child's History of England*, 1851); I was just thinking how busy drink and the devil were at that very moment in the cabin of the *Hispaniola*, when I was **surprised by** *a sudden lurch of the coracle*. (Stevenson, *Treasure Island*, 1883); What thoughts passed through their minds . . . can only be guessed, for they were **surprised by** *the sharp rattle of a lock* . . . (Davis, *King's Jackal*, 1898)

Agentive nouns in these sentences are such dynamic nouns in meaning as a 'light', a 'sound' or a sort of a 'move' or 'motion', and they are perceived to be affecting mentally, possibly giving a physiological or physical influence at the same time.

2.2.2 'Appearance/entrance' as agentive nouns

Let us introduce another intermediate stage. The 'passive of *surprise* + *by*' construction is observed to have occurred with such agentive nouns as *appearance, entrance, visit, return, arrival* and the like, as in (5).

(5) We were suddenly **surprized by** the unexpected *return* of her husband, who, coming directly into his wife's apartment, just allowed me time to creep under the bed. (Fielding, *A Journey from This World to the Next*, 1749); On the morning following this event, the camp was **surprised by** the *appearance* of a small body of Tlascalans, decorated with badges, the white color of which intimated peace. (Prescott, *History of the Conquest of Mexico*, 1843); when the artist had returned from a customary ramble . . . he was **surprised by** the *entrance* of old Peter Hovenden. Owen never met this man without a shrinking of the heart. (Hawthorne, *The Artist of the Beautiful*, 1846); etc.

These examples have a connotation that an affected person or entity is not simply astonished mentally but the effect is such that it could cause a physical movement or physiological reaction (the pounding of a heart or body shaking) on the part of the 'surprised' with the sudden and unexpected *appearance, entrance* or *return* of a 'surpriser'. In this sense, the meaning involved here seems to have been derived from the original physical use and therefore the construction may be said to be at the intermediate stage. I refer to these nouns as nouns of 'appearance/entrance'.

The sentence of Fielding 1749 seems particularly to preserve the very physical meaning of *surprise*. In this sentence, a man, having an affair with a married woman, was caught by surprise and barely went under the bed in panic when her husband unexpectedly returned home. It may be possible to assume that the man experienced such physiological reactions as a throbbing of the heart, cold sweats and trembling of the body. This use of *surprise* seems to be suggestive of the original physical meaning of "to attack suddenly in a sneak and unexpected way." These agentive nouns seem to

---

5) Nouns like *entry, apparition, re-appearance, visitant*, etc. may be included in this group.

have had a tendency to occur with *by* probably on the analogy of the physical use and this use of *by* may have been extended later to the psychological use as well.

Another interesting instance containing the construction of the same type can be found as an illustrative quotation in a dictionary.

> APPEARACNE *n.s.* [from *To appear*] 1. The act of coming into sight; as, they were surprised by the sudden appearance of the enemy.

This is cited from Samuel Johnson's *A Dictionary of the English Language* (1755, 1773[4]). Dr. Johnson may have decided that the sentence *they were surprised by the sudden appearance of the enemy* was most appropriate to illustrate the word 'appearance'. The collocation of 'surprised by' and 'appearance' may have been very compatible to the lexicographer.

The time when Johnson made use of this expression coincided with the time when Fielding used it and it may suggest that this type of expression was put into fairly frequent use in their day. Furthermore, Johnson's dictionary had such authority and prestige that it may have given recognition to the expression and helped to spread the usage into wider use.

In Late Modern English, nouns of this type show a fairly frequent occurrence and they seem to have formed a significant lexical group during the period. In Present-day English, however, they do not seem to be occurring as much as in Late Modern English. A search into the COHA shows that the occurrence rate of these agentive nouns during the latter half of the Late ModE period (1810–1900) was fifteen percent, while that of the PE period (1970–2000) is 0.6 percent.[6] A search into the MEC and the BNC shows similar rates: fifteen percent in Late ModE and one percent in PE. There has been an obvious decrease of these agentive nouns and the intermediate usage may also have been falling into disuse.

2.3 The acquisition of psychological meanings

The first illustrative quotation of *surprise* in a psychological sense in the

---

6) These nouns occur 50 times out of a total of 325 occurrences of *surprised by*, while in PE they occur twice out of 355 occurrences.

OED is the one of 1655.[7] In *A Shakespeare Glossary* compiled by Onions, however, there is a description of psychological use of *surprise* as follows:

> surprise: to perplex, bewilder, dumbfound Wint. III.i.10 the ear-deafening voice ... so surpris'd my sense, Tit. II.iii.211 surprised with an uncouth fear, Tim. V.i.161 You ... Surprise me to the very brink of tears,

It can be assumed that the first psychological use may have occurred around the time when Shakespeare was writing his plays. It may antedate the first *OED* quotation of 1655 by about fifty years.

Our examination of these illustrative quotations, however, shows that Onions' definition of 'to perplex, bewilder, dumbfound' may not really convey the precise meanings of them. The quotation in *Winter's Tale* may be said to be a forerunner of the intermediate usage in that 'the ear-deafening voice' as an agentive noun is perceived to affect the mind as well as sensory organs, that is, the ears being deafened. This sentence is adopted to illustrate the sense 1b,[8] not sense 5, of *surprise* in the *OED*.

The quotation in *Titus Andronicus* reminds us of the definition of sense 1 of *surprise*, which is 'to be seized with (or of) a desire, emotion, etc.' This use is obsolete now and is different from a typical psychological use.

The verb *surprise* in the quotation of *Timon of Athens* is given the gloss of 'overcome' in *The Riverside Shakespeare* (1974). The meanings implied in these three illustrative quotations may not necessarily match Onions' definitions. Why is this?

The publication of Onions' *A Shakespeare Glossary* was in 1911 and the compilation of lexical items of *su–sz* in the *OED*, which include *surprise*, began in 1914 and finished in 1919.[9] The definitions Onions gave to Shakespeare's use of *surprise* in 1911 may have been more or less too broad and sketchy to impart the exact meanings. After a few years of the editing

---

7) The first illustrative quotation of *surprise* being used in a psychological sense is that of 1655 Theophania 103, which goes, "Alexandro acquainted him with the occasion of their coming thither, with which he was exceedingly surprised at first."

8) The sense 1b of *surprise*, now obsolete, is as follows: "To overcome, overpower (the mind, will, heart); to captivate. *Obs.*"

9) *OED*, 1933: Vol.1: xxxv–xxvi.

process of *surprise*, the lexicographer may have reached such subtle and elaborate definitions as are provided in the *OED*. Shakespeare's use of *surprise* seems to show that the verb was acquiring the rudimentary stage of psychological meanings.

2.4 The illustrative quotations in the *OED*

Although the definitions of sense 5 of *surprise* in the *OED* does not include any description of *by* nor are there any illustrative quotations containing it, a text-search of its CD-ROM reveals that there are as many as fifteen illustrative quotations containing *surprised + by*. Let us show some of them in (6). Each quotation illustrates the word in parentheses.

(6) 1786 F. Burney At the desert I was very agreeably **surprised by** the entrance of Sir Richard Jebb, who stayed coffee. (*stay* v. 17); 1845 Darwin *Voy. Nat.* I was a good deal **surprised by** finding two species of coral . . . possessed of the power of stinging. (*sting* v. 3); 1855 Macaulay *Hist. Eng.* In the spring of 1691, the Shepherds . . . were **surprised by** glad tidings. (*spring* n. 5e); etc.

The earliest quotation is the one of 1786, but a search into the Late ModE corpora retrieves instances earlier than this one, as in (7).

(7) We were suddenly **surprised by** the unexpected return of her husband . . . (Fielding, *A Journey from This World to the Next*, 1749); He **is surprised by** sudden alterations of the state of things. (S. Johnson, *The Rambler*, No.14, 1750); I was never more **surprised** than **by** his behaviour to us . . . (Austen, *Pride and Prejudice*, 1813); He was disagreeably **surprised by** a *visit* from the professor, whom he had scarcely thought of for whole weeks. (Hawthorne, *Rappaccini's Daughter*, 1846); etc.

The first writer who is assumed to have used this construction was Henry Fielding and the first citation is that of 1749, followed by such eminent writers as Samuel Johnson, Jane Austen in Britain and Nathaniel Hawthorne in America.

The psychological use of the passive of *surprise* began to appear in the

17th century, occurring with the agentive prepositions *with* or *at*, later joined by the agentive *by*. The use of *by* gradually established itself throughout the centuries up to the present time when it has become the most dominant preposition.

III. The principle of the semantic shift

3.1 The process of the semantic shift of the passive of *surprise* + *by*

The sematic shift of the passive of *surprise* occurring with *by* from the physical to psychological may be shown in the simplified continuum from (8a) to (8e) below, first proposed in my 1999(c) article.

(8)
  a. The soldiers **were surprised by** the enemy and many were killed. [phy]
  b. The soldiers **were surprised by** a bomber and took shelter. [semi-phy]
  c. The soldiers **were surprised by** the air-raid sirens. [phy+psy]
  d. The soldiers **were surprised by** the appearance of the MP. [semi-psy]
  e. The soldiers **were surprised by** the spaciousness of the barrack. [psy]
  [phy=physical, psy=psychological]

The reality, of course, is not as simplistic as this. The sentences in this spectrum may have coexisted or intermingled with each other for a certain span of time. There may have been a cohabitation or rivalry with the *surprised* + *at* construction. From such an entwined or entangled situation, the type of the meaning in each developmental stage was extracted and arranged in such a simplified order as to form the continuum shown above. The sentence (8a) is the most typical of the physical use and its opposite end is (8e), the most typical psychological use. The sentence (8b) possesses a physical meaning but it is not as strong as (8a) since the direct corporal effect is not involved. The sentence (8c) lies on the borderline with a shade of psychological meaning also contained. The sentence (8d) has mainly a psychological meaning with a shred of a physical or physiological meaning. The sentences (8c) and (8d) can be interpreted to be at the intermediate stage.

The following sentence (9) retrieved from the COHA looks like a combination of the two stages of (8c) and (8d).

(9) The soldiers, **surprised by** the sudden shots and even more the sudden entry of the officers, were galvanized into action.
(COHA, Fiction, 1972)

This sentence may be able to confirm the spectrum presented above: it is not an imaginary concoction but it is something that could be happening as a linguistic reality. This will be further reinforced in the next section by the examples found in novels.

3.2 The semantic shift observed in novels

The process of the semantic shift proposed above is partly but conveniently exemplified in Washington Irving's novels. Irving used the *surprised + by* sentences of the three different stages: physical, intermediate and psychological, as in (10).

(10) a. Exhausted by fatigue and watching, they fell into a sound sleep, and in that state were **surprised by** the savages. (*Astoria*) [physical]
 b. While in this moody state, he was **surprised** . . . **by** the sudden appearance of M'Kenzie . . . (*Astoria*); In the evening the travellers were **surprised by** an unwelcome visit from several Crows belonging to a different band . . . (*Astoria*) [intermediate]
 c. He began to kiss and caress the animal, who . . . seemed by no means **surprised** or displeased with his salutation. (*Astoria*); I could not but feel both **surprised** and gratified **by** such unexpected attentions on the part of this benevolent cut-throat: (*Tales of a Traveller*) [psychological]

Irving's use of sentences of the three stages in one novel (*Astoria*, 1836) plus another one seems to suggest that the intermediate and psychological stages were derived from the physical use. The theoretical semantic continuum in (8) could be substantiated to be a real shift, not something imaginary or fictitious, as it is actually seen to occur in novels. It seems certain that the actual semantic process was taking place in a novelist's head and it was represented in the sentences of his writing.

IV. The semantic shift of synonymous verbs

Not only *surprise* but other synonymous verbs such as *startle* and *stun* also underwent a similar semantic shift from physical to psychological, with the intermediate stage taking place in between. Let us see how these verbs went through their semantic developments.

4.1 *Startle*
Etymologically, the verb *startle* possessed such a physical meaning as 'to awake with a start, to move as if surprised or frightened.' Then the verb underwent an intermediate stage, as in (11).

> (11) Marianne, whose nerves could not then bear any sudden noise, was **startled by** *a rap* at the door. (Austen, *Sense and Sensibility*, 1811); "O dear!" said Anne, with a sudden start away. "How nervous you are, child, to be **startled by** *fireworks* so far off," said Mrs. Loveday. (Hardy, *The Trumpet-Major*, 1880); the fishermen of West Colebrook had been disturbed and **startled by** *heavy knocks* against the walls of weatherboard cottages, and **by** *a voice* crying piercingly strange words in the night. (Conrad, *Amy Foster*, 1901); etc.[10]

Its passive predicates occur with the agentive nouns that affect minds or nerves, apparently giving some effects to sensory organs and maybe causing some physical motions or physiological reactions. A large number of occurrences of *by* may have to do with the frequent use of these agentive nouns.

---

10) The agentive noun phrases include such phrases as: *a smart rap at the door, a loud ringing at the front door bell, a scream from the same quarter, the sound of a horse's feet, a hasty knock at the door, a voice of command, the sound of the great bell pealing, a sudden cry from within the house*, etc.

Chapter 5

The passive of *startle* also occurs with nouns of 'appearance/entrance', as in (12).

(12) "What is the matter?" cried Amabel, **startled by** her agitated *appearance*. (Ainsworth, *Old Saint Paul's*, 1841); Patty had been very much **startled by** the sudden *entrance* of the landlady's rough lodger. (Collins, *Hide and Seek*, 1854); "Yes," replied Arthur, who had been **startled by** Helen's *entrance*, his pulses throbbing with delight at the sound of her voice. (Gissing, *Workers in the Dawn*, 1880); He is **startled by** the *entry* of a wounded Roman soldier, (Shaw, *Caesar and Cleopatra*, 1901); etc.

It is interesting to note that Gissing's 1880 example shows that it causes a physiological reaction of 'his pulses throbbing' and my assumption that physiological reactions can be involved in the intermediate stage seems to be substantiated by this example.

At the final stage of the shift, we find abundant examples of the verb used in a psychological sense, as in (13).

(13) She was **startled by** the bloodlessness of the face, (Yonge, *Heasrtsease*, 1854); The major was **startled by** her eloquence, and **by** the indignant tone of voice . . . (Trollope, *The Last Chronicle of Barset*, 1867); he might well have been **startled by** the vividness of her eyes . . . (Eliot, *Romola*, 1862–63); etc.

The verb *startle* is very much similar to *surprise* in the way that the semantic shift took place. What may be different is that this verb has a strong affinity with *by*. In fact, the investigation in Chapter 3 shows that the ratio of *at* and *by* was approximately 1 : 4 in Late Modern English, while that of Present-day English is 1 : 7.[11]

---

11) *By* occurs 425 times and *at* 108 times with *startled* in Late Modern English, while in Present-day English, *by* occurs 238 times and *at* 32 times (see Tables 2 and 3 in Chapter 3). The calculation of these figures leads to the ratios mentioned above.

4.2 *Stun*

The verb *stun* had originally such a physical meaning as 'to faint (with a blow)' and it is still used in this sense. The word *stun gun* may be a good illustration of the physical use. Then the verb went through the intermediate stage and eventually developed a psychological meaning of 'to be shocked or astounded'. The following sentences in (14) will show the intermediate stage.

(14) **Stunned by** *that loud and dreadful sound*, which sky and ocean smote... (Coleridge, *The Rime of the Ancient Mariner*, 1798); Fanny and I... utterly **stunned by** *the uproar of the wind* among the trees... (Stevenson, *The Silverado Squatter*, 1883); a woman of seventy-eight... was **stunned by** *an extremely vivid flash of lightning* and fell back unconscious into a chair. (Gould, *Anomalies and Curiosities of Medicine*, 1896); etc.

Basically giving a mental astonishment, an agentive noun of a sound (the 'uproar') or a light ('flash of lightning') gives a stimulus to or exerts an influence on sensory organs (that is, eyes or ears), causing possibly a physical or physiological reaction. Gould's 1896 example exhibits such an influence of "fell back unconscious into a chair." In this sense, the effect may be said to be physiological, and naturally, *by* should be employed as the agentive preposition.

The following sentences show the final stage of the development, or the psychological stage.

(15) Ravenswood was at first **stunned by** this new and unexpected calamity; (Scott, *The Bride of Lammermoor*, 1819); She went away, leaving Sylvia almost **stunned by** the new ideas presented to her. (Gaskell, *Sylvia's Lovers*, 1860); She was **stunned by** his cruelty, and did not hear. He had not the faintest notion of what he was saying. (Lawrence, *Sons and Lovers*, 1913)

The agentive nouns include static nouns and many of them are abstract nouns. They occur with *by* presumably because of the continuation from the previous stage where *by* was chosen on the analogy of physical use. Like *startle*, the passive of *stun* seems to possess a closer affiliation with *by*. The search of the BNC shows that the predicate occurs with *by* much more frequently than with other prepositions: it occurs with *by* 110 times, *at* 16 times and *with* 6 times.

We have seen the verbs *startle* and *stun*, just like *surprise*, have gone through a similar semantic process. Other synonymous verbs did not seem to have gone through the three semantic stages, but all of them at least experienced the shift from physical to psychological.[12]

4.3 Theorems of the semantic shift

The shift of meaning from physical to psychological is not only confined to the psych-verbs but it seems to involve an issue of general semantics. Bradley, one of the most distinguished scholars of the English language more than a century before, states in his renowned book, *The Making of English* (1904: 173), as follows:

> It is hardly necessary to dwell on the well-known fact that most of the words that are now used to describe mental states or qualities have obtained these meanings through metaphorical use, their earlier sense having been purely physical. This is indeed, the ordinary course of development in all languages.

It follows that the semantic shift from physical to psychological, which occurred to verbs like *surprise*, *stun*, *startle* and so forth, was not uncommon. Rather, it is a natural phenomenon that could normally happen to any language change.

Ikegami (1975: 287) cites an example of an adjective, *profound*. He says that the adjective *profound* ('deep'), which had been borrowed from Old French, went into a rivalry with the word *deep* of the OE origin and presumably to avoid competition and to survive, it began to take the psychological meaning that it possesses now.

---

12) The original meanings of some of these verbs are as follows: *appall* 'to make or become pale', *astound* 'make faint', *astonish* 'to deprive of sensation, as by a blow', *bewilder* 'to lose in pathless places, to confound for want of a plain road', *shock* 'to collide with, to assail with a sudden and violent attack', etc.

Furthermore, Ikegami (1978: 139-40) claims that the change of meaning from 'concrete' to 'abstract' is assumed to take place due to the way of our mental activities. The change in our way of recognition through the physical or sensory organs to mental or psychological recognition may be linguistically represented as the change from 'concrete' (i.e. physical) to 'abstract' (i.e. psychological) meaning. Ikegami's claim seems to confirm the semantic shift we have presented so far.

V. Summary

This chapter attempts to clarify the process of the semantic shift of the passive of *surprise* and its synonymous verbs *startle* and *stun*. This is also an attempt to discover why their passives are more likely to occur with *by* rather than *at* as the preposition of an agent.

The verb *surprise* had originally such a physical meaning as "to attack suddenly or unexpectedly" and its passive sentences naturally occurred with *by* as an agentive preposition. Gradually it acquired a psychological meaning of "to cause someone to be astonished or shocked" and during this process of the semantic shift, what I call the 'intermediate' stage presumably took place. The passive of *surprise* at this stage, with the sensory organs like eyes and/or ears being affected and possibly with a physiological response, chose *by* on the analogy of the physical use.

Another intermediate stage is also observed to have taken place. At this stage one gets mentally confused or panicky because of a sudden and unexpected 'appearance', 'entrance', 'arrival' and so forth of an entity as an agentive noun, as in such a sentence as *we were surprised by the sudden appearance of the enemy*. I refer to these nouns as nouns of 'appearance/ entrance'. The passive of *surprise* at this stage, showing some vestiges of the physical use, may have chosen to occur with *by*. This use of *by* may have been extended to a psychological use as well, thus the perceived increasing use of *by* with the passive of *surprise*.

The synonymous verbs *startle* and *stun* also underwent a similar semantic shift to that of *surprise*. In developing a psychological meaning, they went through the intermediate stage. Their passives occurred with such dynamic agentive nouns as *a loud ringing at the front door bell, a scream from the same quarter, a flash of lightning*, etc. or nouns of 'appearance/entrance'. Their passives are most likely to occur with *by* and the use of *by* at this stage may have been applied to the psychological use.

I have proposed a spectrum of the semantic shift from physical to psychological and this hypothetical spectrum has proven to be confirmed by the sentences actually occurring in the corpus or novels. The semantic shift from physical to psychological, which we saw happen to psych-verbs, is not an uncommon phenomenon but it is a natural and normal process in general semantics, as claimed by Bradley or Ikegami.

Chapter 6
The decline of gerunds with psych-passives

The Tale of Heike, an epic chronicle of medieval Japan depicting the rise and fall of the Taira clan (Heike), begins something like, "The pealing of the bells of the temple ring with the sound of the impermanence . . . The color of the trees gives witness to the truth that all who flourish must necessarily perish." The gist of it is that what has flourished will eventually and inevitably perish. This axiom may be true of a language and there may be flourishing and perishing happening in the usages of English grammar. Are English gerunds occurring with psych-passives perishing like the ringing of the bell after they flourished in the earlier period?

I. Introduction

1.1 Gerunds in Late ModE

In examining the shift of the agentive prepositions from *at* to *by* with the passive of *surprise*, I noticed that considerable changes have been taking place in prepositional complements. The changes are particularly characterized by the decrease of gerunds and by the increase of *how*-clauses. Are the gerunds now perishing after having flourished in the earlier period? We will treat the decrease of gerunds in this chapter and the increase of *how*-clauses in the next.

In the data obtained from the Late ModE corpora, gerunds as in (1) are observed to occur quite frequently.

(1) I own I was a little **surprised at** *seeing* Cromwell here; (Fielding, *A Journey from This World to the Next*, 1749); "I am no longer **surprised at** *your knowing* only six accomplished women." (Austen, *Pride and Prejudice*, 1813); I was **surprised at** *this door being shut*, for all summer

long it was open from morning to night; (Gaskell, *Cousin Phillis*, 1864); etc.

In the PE corpora, however, gerunds seem to occur only so occasionally as to give us the impression that their use has considerably declined. I will show the decline statistically in what follows, but let us first examine how dictionaries have treated the construction.

1.2 The treatment in dictionaries

The sentences containing a gerund occurring with the passive of *surprise* seem to have been prevalent from Late Modern English, as is evident from the fact that they are adopted in dictionaries as illustrative quotations, as in (2).

(2) I'm *surprised at* you wanting a man like that. (*Progressive*); We were *surprised at* finding the house empty. (*New College*); He was *surprised at* receiving a telegram from his parents. (*Royal*); etc.

These quotations in dictionaries suggest that the construction has been accepted as an established and standard usage. However, considering the decrease of gerunds we have observed in the PE corpora, a question arises as to whether it is still a prevalent construction or it may be an outdated one. Newer dictionaries or new editions of dictionaries do not seem to adopt sentences with a gerund as an illustrative quotation and it may be a reflection of the real usage.[1]

Strang (1970: 100) claims that gerunds have been "gaining ground" over *to*-infinitives as the object of verbs and so does Blake (1996: 330). Gerunds may be increasing in some contexts, while our investigation shows otherwise in different environments. It would be worthy, therefore, to try to find out the true linguistic situations of the use of gerunds by showing the statistical evidence. After examining the statistics, I will discuss how and why these

---

1) Some dictionaries such as *Readers* (2nd, 2012), *Wisdom* (3rd, 2012), *O-lex* (2013), *Genius* (5th, 2015), etc. do not carry quotations containing a gerund with *surprised*. The treatment in these dictionaries may be more appropriate. [For the full names of the dictionaries, see the Bibliography.]

changes have been taking place and propose some hypotheses of the reasons for the decrease.

II. Gerunds with the passive of *surprise*

To collect the samples of gerunds occurring with the passive of *surprise*, we used the MEC and the VLSA for Late Modern English, and the BNC and the COCA for Present-day English. The COHA was also used to confirm the results obtained from the other corpora. The decrease of gerunds will be shown statistically in the following sections.

2.1 Late Modern English

The following are examples used by such writers as Jane Austen, Wilkie Collins, George Eliot and Henry James, who particularly seem to have preferred to use gerunds with the predicate.

(3) "A fortnight!" she repeated, **surprised at** *his being* so long in the same county with Elinor without seeing her before. (Austen, *Sense and Sensibility*, 1811); "If you are **surprised at** *not having heard* from me the moment you got back . . . " (Collins, *No Name*, 1862); Certainly all Tipton and its neighborhood . . . would have been **surprised at** *her beauty being made so much of.* (Eliot, *Middlemarch*, 1871); Miss Chancellor went on, "I am **surprised at** *your not perceiving* how little it is in my interest to deliver my—my victim up to you." (Henry James, *The Bostonians*, 1886); etc.

Let us show the frequencies of occurrence of gerunds. From the MEC, we found 79 examples of gerunds with *at* and 14 examples *with* by and from the VLSA, 109 examples with *at* and 17 examples with *by*. Figure 1 shows the statistics.[2] 'All' means all the prepositional complements. The ratios between the gerunds and all the complements between Late ModE and PE will be compared later to show the decline.

---

2) The data from the MEC was obtained in writing my 2001 article and the data from the VLSA was collected in writing my 2015 articles.

Chapter 6

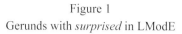

Figure 1
Gerunds with *surprised* in LModE

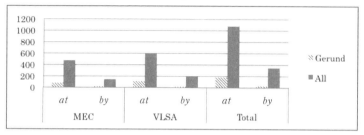

From the total statistics, we find that gerunds occurring with *at* account for 17.4 percent and those with *by* 8.7 percent. The impression we get that gerunds were occurring fairly frequently in Late Modern English seems to be confirmed by the statistics.

2.2 Present-day English

We used the BNC and the two sub-corpora of the COCA: the COCA (1), which covers the period from 1991 to 1995 and the COCA (2) from 2011 to 2015. The data from the two different periods may be expected to yield different results as in Chapter 1. Some of the samples retrieved by the search into the PE corpora are shown in (4).

(4) The major looked **surprised at** *being introduced* to a prisoner, but he played along with it. (BNC, Fiction, 1991); It's the Archduke, very **surprised at** *being treated* this way. (COCA (1), Fiction, 1994); I'm **surprised at** *you saying* that, Donald. (COCA (2), Spoken, 2014); on more than one occasion I was indeed left **surprised by** *not knowing* the detail. (COCA (1), Spoken, 1991); etc.

We obtained the following results: from the BNC, 16 examples of gerunds with *at* and none with *by*, from the COCA (1), 12 examples with *at* and 6 examples with *by*, and from the COCA (2), 6 examples with *at* and 3 examples with *by*.

I use the logarithmic scale in Figure 2 below as the quantity gap between the gerunds and all the prepositional complements is so large that the statistics of the gerunds are nearly invisible in an ordinary chart.

Figure 2
Gerunds with *surprised* in PE

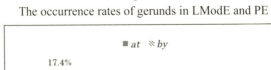

[logarithmic scale]

Gerunds occurring with *at* account for 2.4 percent and those with *by* 0.5 percent. There seems to be a considerable decrease, compared to the results of Late Modern English.

Furthermore, the decrease can be seen, if only slightly, even during the period of current English. We can see the occurrence of gerunds going down from the COCA (1) to the COCA (2) and this is probably due to a gap of two decades between the two sub-corpora. Gerunds may be going more and more out of fashion in this particular linguistic context with each decade at this present time.

The comparison of the percentages of gerund occurrence between Late ModE and PE is shown in Figure 3 below.

Figure 3
The occurrence rates of gerunds in LModE and PE

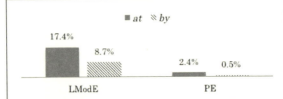

The quantitative decrease is quite visible and it is a drastic decline. It confirms our empirical observation that gerunds occurring with the passive of *surprise* might be decreasing from Late Modern English to Present-day English.

The results obtained so far can be confirmed by the examination of the data from the COHA. Rather than repeating similar statistics, they are presented in Appendix I.

III. Gerunds with psych-passives

The decrease of gerunds seems to be true of other synonymous psych-verbs as well. The quantitative decline of gerunds with psych-passives from Late ModE to PE will be shown in what follows.

3.1 Late Modern English

Using the VLSA, the use of gerunds with psych-passives in the Late ModE period was examined. Many samples were retrieved from the corpus, some of which are presented in (5).

(5) a. His attention was instantly diverted to the keys; he was **astonished at** *having forgotten* them. (Collins, *Jezebel's Daughter*, 1880); We were rather **dismayed at** *their bringing* two servants with them. (Gaskell, *Cranford*, 1853); and then she felt **shocked at** *having obtruded* the subject on him at all, (Yonge, *The Clever Woman of the Family*, 1865); etc.

b. the servants at Porthgenna were **amazed by** *receiving* directions to pack the trunks for travelling, (Collins, *The Dead Secret*, 1857); Charles was actually **startled by** *her entering* the dressing-room, (Yonge, *The Heir of Redclyffe*, 1853); etc.

The corpus yields 105 examples of gerunds with *at* (Britain 74, America 31) and 83 examples with *by* (Britain 55, America 28). Figure 4 shows the statistics.

Figure 4
Gerunds with psych-passives in LModE

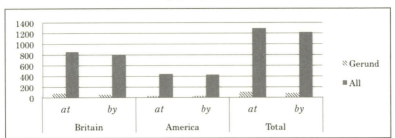

Gerunds occurring with *at* account for 8.1 percent and those with *by* 6.8 percent. We can see there were quite frequent occurrences of gerunds with psych-passives in Late Modern English.

3.2 Present-day English

Now let us see how gerunds with psych-passives are occurring in Present-day English, using the BNC and the COCA. Some of the samples retrieved from the corpora are presented below.

(6) I was quite **amazed at** *her being* able to use the terminology . . . (BNC, Biography, 1988); She was **appalled at** *being forced* to accept this. (BNC, Fiction, 1988); I was very **shocked at** *looking* at her eyes. (COCA, Spoken, 2013); I was just so **startled by** *O.J. being* there. (COCA, Spoken, 2007); etc.

The PE corpora yield the following results: 15 examples of gerunds with *at* and 11 examples with *by* from the BNC and 11 examples with *at* and 6 examples with *by* from the COCA. (Note that the raw data from the COCA was divided by five in order to make easier comparison with the data of the BNC.) Figure 5, using logarithmic scale, shows the statistics.

Figure 5
Gerunds with psych-passives in PE

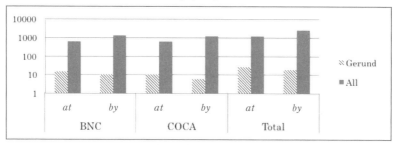

[logarithmic scale]

Gerunds occurring with *at* account for two percent and those with *by* 0.7 percent.

Figure 6 shows the rates of occurrence in Late Modern English and Present-day English.

Figure 6
The occurrence rates of gerunds in LModE and PE

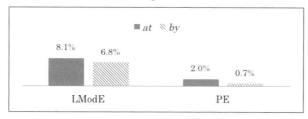

Statistically, the decrease of gerunds is clearly seen from the chart. A comparison of the occurrence rates between LModE and PE may lead to the conclusion that there has been a drastic decline in the use of gerunds with psych-passives.

This conclusion can be confirmed by the examination of the data from the COHA and the results are shown in Appendix II to avoid repeating the statistics similar to those of Figures 5 and 6.

IV. Types of gerunds

The gerundial constructions of Late Modern English shown in (3) are so complex as to involve the gerundial subject (*his being so long*), perfect aspect (*having heard from me*), passive (*her beauty being made so much of*) and/or negative (*your not perceiving*). Gerunds during this period seem to have developed complex forms to perform quite complicated functions.

First, there are gerunds characterized by the frequent use of a nominal subject in the genitive case. Jane Austen and Charles Dickens are the writers who seem to have favored this type of construction, as in (7) below, which, however, rarely occur in the PE corpora.

(7) a. It is impossible to be **surprised at** *Miss Palmer's being* ill. (Austen, *Jane Austen's Letters*, 1817)
　　b. He was not so much **surprised at** *the man's being* there. (Dickens, *Martin Chuzzlewit*, 1843–44)

Some types of gerunds are seen to occur quite frequently in Late Modern English but hardly appear in Present-day English. The sentences in (8) will be a good illustration.

(8) a. I am **surprised at** *his not having done* so sooner. (Andrew Lang, *Red Fairy Book*, 1890)
　　b. I was **surprised at** *there remaining* so many mechanical specimens as are seen in the museums. (Samuel Butler, *Erewhon*, 1872)

The gerund in (8a) takes a complex form involving a gerundial subject, a negative adverb and the perfect aspect. (8b) is a construction with existential *there* serving as a gerundial subject in the accusative case.

It may be summarized that in Present-day English, gerunds with *surprised* + *at*/*by* have not only declined in terms of quantity but have changed their quality, or their characteristics as well. We will explore why these changes have occurred and provide some hypotheses as to the causes of these changes in the next section.

Chapter 6

V. Some hypotheses on the causes of the changes

In considering a language change, it may be possible to describe how a certain change has occurred, but it might be difficult or even impossible to explain why. Nevertheless, it is interesting and worthwhile to attempt to look into why the kind of changes mentioned above have actually taken place.

5.1 The replacement of gerunds by *to*-infinitives

The decreasing use of gerunds may be attributed to the coexistence and competition between gerunds and *to*-infinitives,[3] as in (9), and to the possible replacement of gerunds by *to*-infinitives.

(9) a. I was a little **surprised at** *seeing* Cromwell here. (= (1a))
　　b. I was a little **surprised** *to see* Cromwell here. (a paraphrase of (9a))

The two constructions are assumed to possess practically the same meaning, as Kruisinga (1931: §390) says as follows:

> When nouns or adjectives take both a stem and a prepositional ing (*surprised to hear it, surprised at hearing it*) the difference in meaning between the two constructions is that between an adverb adjunct and a prepositional object. It may be compared with the difference between clauses with *that* and those with a conjunctive adverb, e.g. *I am surprised that he is not coming, I am surprised because he is not coming*.

There is a description in dictionaries that the two constructions have the same meaning:

> I was much *surprised at* (receiv*ing*) a telegram. = . . . *to* receive a telegram. (*Genius*, 1988)[4]

---

3) Curme (1931: 491) says, "It [gerund] often competes with the infinitive in many categories."
4) This description in the first edition (1988) has been deleted in the 5th edition (2015), for instance.

We were *surprised at* find*ing* the house empty. = We were *surprised to* find the house empty. (*New College*, 7th ed., 2010)

As *to*-infinitives possess the same meaning as gerunds and the former are the more predominant construction of the two in a competitive environment, gerunds may have been felt to be a redundant construction and they may have been being ousted by *to*-infinitives.

Let us now present the occurrence ratios between *surprised at* + gerunds and *surprised* + *to*-infinitives, using the MEC and the BNC. The results are approximately 1 : 16 in Late Modern English and 1 : 90 in Present-day English.[5] Evidently, gerunds have decreased relatively from Late ModE to PE, compared to *to*-infinitives, which have shown a great deal of increase.

A similar phenomenon is observed in the alternation of 'aim to do' and 'aim at doing' constructions as Tajima et al. (1995: 31–42) claim, as in (10).

(10) a. We must *aim at increasing* exports.
 b. We must *aim to increase* exports. (Tajima et al., 1995: 31)

It has been described in grammar or usage books that 'aim at doing' is a British usage while 'aim to do' is a dialectal or American idiom. Tajima et al. (1997: 38), however, draw a conclusion that "without doubt the infinitives have become practically a standard usage today, not only in American English but also in British English."

From what has been discussed so far, the replacement of gerunds by *to*-infinitives may be considered to be a possible reason for the decreasing use of gerunds with the passive of *surprise*.

5.2 The replacement of gerunds by clauses
5.2.1 *that*-clause

Difficulties in having to choose the subject of a gerund in the proper case may be another reason for the decrease in the use of gerunds. The choice of

---

5) In the MEC, gerunds with no subject occur 44 times and infinitives over 700 times. In the BNC, the occurrence of subjectless gerunds counts merely 9 times while that of infinitives more than 800 times. These figures lead to the ratios presented above. These data were obtained when I was writing my 2001 article.

the case for the subject, either the genitive or the accusative,[6] has been discussed by a number of scholars (e.g. Curme 1931: 485–91; Quirk et al. 1985: §15.12–13; Blake 1996: 330). Quirk et al., for example, argue that "some are troubled by the choice of case," as in (11a), and that "in some instances, an acceptable alternative is a *that*-clause, which is normally extraposed," as in (11b).

(11) a. *My forgetting her name* was embarrassing.
b. *It* was embarrassing *that I forgot her name*.
(Quirk et al., 1985: §15.12)

Although the subject in the genitive case is more common, as can be seen in the instances presented in (3) and (12a) below, the accusative case, rare though it may be in our data of Late Modern English, is also used, as in (12b).

(12) a. "I am only **surprised at** *Sir Patrick's delivering* it." (Collins, *Man and Wife*, 1870)
b. "I suppose you are **surprised at** *Hetty coming* with us." (Doyle, *The Stark Munro Letters*, 1895)

These will be a good illustration of the difficulty involved in the choice of the proper case for the subject of gerunds. In order to avoid the extra cognitive burden in making an appropriate choice, writers and speakers may have begun to use a clause, as in (13b), in which the choice of the case is not forced upon them, instead of the controversial gerund, as in (13a).

(13) a. I am **surprised at** *John's/John talking* so rudely.
b. I am **surprised** *that/because John talks/talked* so rudely.

The following statement made by Curme (1931: 486) may also support the assumption that the decreasing use of gerunds occurred because of the case:

---

[6] Different terms for the accusative case are used by different scholars. Quirk et al. refer to it as the "objective" and "common" case. Blake uses the term "oblique". For the sake of convenience, following Curme, "accusative" is used throughout.

The development of the gerundial construction is hampered at the present time by the lack of *s*-genitive forms in current English and by the lack of a clear form for the possessive referring to a female.

Decreasing use of gerunds may also be explained by the ambiguous nature inherent in gerunds. Concerning no-referentiality of the tense in gerunds, which may lead to ambiguity, Jespersen (*MEG* IV, 1935: 7.8 (1)) says as follows:

> the ing (the verbal substantive in ing) had originally, and to a great extent still has, no reference to time: *on account of his coming* may be equal to 'because he comes' or 'because he came' or 'he will come', according to the connection in which it occurs.

The sentence of (14a) below could be an ambiguous example in terms of tense if it were taken out of context. The sentence of (14b), a paraphrase of (14a), would be clearer and more explicit with the self-evident tense or aspect.

(14) a. My uncle is quite **surprised at** *my hearing* from you so often; (Austen, *Jane Austen's Letters*, 1799)
 b. My uncle is quite **surprised** *that/because I hear/have heard/heard* from you so often.

5.2.2 Concealed exclamation

Some of the gerunds used in an emphatic context could be interpreted to be what theoretical linguists call 'concealed exclamations'[7] and paraphrased with a *how*-clause, as in (15), which occurs abundantly in Present-day English.

(15) a. I am quite **surprised at** *your being so very thoughtless*. (Dickens, *Nicholas Nickleby*, 1838–39)

---

[7] 'Concealed exclamations' (e.g. Fukuchi 1995: Ch.3) are sentences in which a noun phrase can be paraphrased with such exclamatory words as *how* or *what*. Fukuchi (p.62) paraphrases the sentence *You'd be surprised at the big cars he buys* into *You'd be surprised at what big cars he buys*.

b. I am quite **surprised at** *how thoughtless you are/were.*

Not only would (15b) remove the obscurity of the tense of (15a) but it also seems to sound more colloquial, vivid and emphatic by using a *how*-clause than a gerundial construction in terms of style.

In connection with style, such gerunds as already shown in (8) may be rewritten with a clause, as in (16) and (17).

(16) a. I am **surprised at** *his not having done* so sooner. (= 8a)
b. I am **surprised** *that/because he did not do/has not done* so sooner.

(17) a. I was **surprised at** *there remaining* so many mechanical specimens as are seen in the museums. (= 8b)
b. I was **surprised** *that/because there remained* so many mechanical specimens as are seen in the museums.

By rewriting with a clause, a writer may be able to remove a bookish and literary tone and a shred of affectedness or awkwardness and to achieve a more colloquial and plain style. This may have to do with the trend of writing in "plain English,"[8] towards which society seems to have been headed.

In general, gerunds are said to be a concise and useful means of expressing simply and tersely what is conveyed by clauses (e.g. Curme, 1931: 485; Jespersen, 1938: 186), but they are seemingly being replaced by infinitives or clauses in certain contexts. Our investigation shows that gerunds are declining in such an environment as after psych-passives, where gerunds and infinitives are in competition, or where gerunds involve such ambiguity or unnaturalness as to be removed by the employment of clauses.[9] The same phenomena may have been occurring in similar contexts and would be worth investigating.

---

8) Refer, for example, to David Crystal (1995: 376–77).
9) Needless to say, this is not to imply that gerunds in general are declining. On the contrary, some gerunds are supposed to be still prevalent in other environments in Present-day English, as mentioned in §1.2.

VI. Summary

Utilizing computer corpora, a historical shift of gerunds with psych-passives was examined. The decrease of gerunds is observed to have occurred from Late Modern English to Present-day English. Not only the quantitative decrease but qualitative changes from complex constructions to simpler forms are also observed to have taken place.

Some hypotheses have been presented to explain the causes for these changes. First, the decrease of gerunds may be explained as a result of their possible replacement by *to*-infinitives. *To*-infinitives, which convey the same meaning, have become the more predominant of the two constructions and seem to have been replacing gerunds.

Secondly, gerunds seem to have been replaced by clauses for various reasons. Difficulty in choosing the grammatical case of gerundial subject, either in the genitive or in the accusative, may be leading to the employment of clauses. Ambiguity in gerunds in terms of tense or aspect may be another reason for the replacement by synonymous clauses.

Some gerunds, being 'concealed exclamations', may be replaced with *how*-clauses. Some others, which sound stylistically too bookish, literary or unnatural in an informal context, may be rewritten with a more colloquial and plain clause.

In this chapter, we have shown the decrease of gerunds with psych-passives from Late Modern English to Present-day English. The reasons for the decrease have been discussed and some hypotheses are presented. It may be interesting to examine why the decrease of gerunds has been happening when they are supposed to be gaining ground in other contexts.

Chapter 6

Appendix I

Gerunds with *surprised* in the COHA

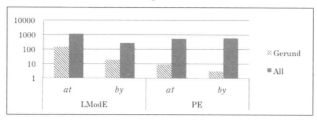

[logarithmic scale]

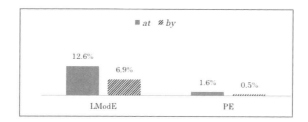

Appendix II

Gerunds with psych-passives in the COHA

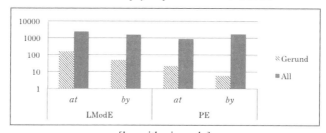

[logarithmic scale]

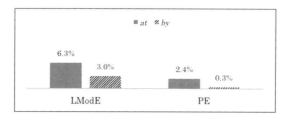

Chapter 7

The rise and growth of *how*-clauses with psych-passives

As happened in *The Tale of Heike*, when there are things that are perishing, there are other things that might be flourishing. The rise and fall is the way of the world and languages cannot escape from this law. In the world of English grammar, gerunds with psych-passives may be perishing, while *how*-clauses seem to be blossoming in full bloom. It is surprising that what hardly existed a century before is now as flourishing as the bamboo shoots sprouting after the spring rain.

1. Introduction

Language has been constantly changing and quite big changes—grammatical or stylistic—can take place in a fairly short time span, say, over several decades. We will deal with such a change as has been taking place in the usage of English grammar.

The statement in (1) was made by Kazuo Ishiguro, the Nobel laureate, when he received the message from Sweden in the autumn of 2017.

(1) "Eventually a very nice lady called from Sweden and asked me first of all if I would accept it . . . **I was surprised at** *how* low-key they were, it was like they were inviting me to some kind of party."

(Reuters, Oct. 5, 2017)

In expressing his surprise, the novelist used the agentive *at* + *how*-clause with the predicate in his utterance. Sentences of this construction hardly existed a century before but they are now prolific enough to be occurring abundantly in current English, as in (2).

(2) She was **amazed at** *how* little he wore and *how* impervious he was to the cold. (BNC, Fiction, 1989); Neil was **astonished at** *how* pleasant the evening had been. (BNC, Fiction, 1993); I was really **surprised at** *how* down to earth she was. (BNC, Popular Lore, 1991); etc.

This construction seems to be a fairly new development, while the construction without the preposition, as in (3), is observed to have occurred in earlier English.

(3) I **was amazed** *how* the creature go thither. (Defoe, *Robinson Crusoe*, 1719); some wondered how it could be got out, but still more were **amazed** *how* it ever got in. (Goldsmith, *The Vicar of Wakefield*, 1766); You'll be **surprised** *how* those girls are stowed away. (Dickens, *David Copperfield*, 1850).

What we are chiefly concerned with in this chapter is the rise and growth of the 'psych-passive with *at* + *how*-clause' construction,[1] which was rarely seen in Late Modern English and yet has become quite popular in Present-day English. It would be worthwhile to make an investigation into the extent to which the construction has been on the increase and into how and why this usage came into existence when there had been an alternative construction (i.e. the psych-passive + *how*-clause).

First, the treatment of the construction in dictionaries and English usage books will be examined to look into its linguistic legitimacy. Secondly, the increase of the construction will be shown statistically. Finally, hypotheses will be presented to show how and why it came into being despite the existence of the synonymous construction without a preposition.

---

1) We will deal with the construction with the agentive *by* in §6. It began to appear around the middle of the 20th century, much later than the construction with the *at* + *how*-clause. The number of its occurrence is much smaller than that of the latter. Possibly for that reason, dictionaries have yet to cite the construction as illustrative quotations. So, the formula '*at* + *how*-clause' is used here for the sake of simplicity.

II. The treatment in dictionaries and usage books

How have grammarians and lexicographers treated these two types of constructions? We will focus on the verb *surprise* and examine its passive occurring with the *(at) how*-clause. The examination will reveal how the scholars judge the appropriateness or legitimacy of the usage.

2.1 Dictionaries

A number of English-Japanese dictionaries adopt the construction with a *how*-clause as an illustrative quotation, as in (4).

(4) You'll be *surprised how* beautiful she is. (*New College)*; You'll be *surprised how* ignorant they are of that matter. (*New Crown*); You'll be *surprised how* kind he is. (*Genius*); You'd be *surprised how* many people aren't interested in sex. (*Royal*); You'd be *surprised how* well thought of you are amongst our leaders. (*Royal*): etc.

The adoption of these sentences as illustrative quotations suggests that the construction has been widely-used and accepted as a standard usage. Especially, *Royal* gives two quotations, an indication that this is a fairly frequent usage. As it is also used with the archaic word *amongst*, it may suggest that it is a slightly older usage.

These dictionaries, however, do not quote the construction with the preposition. Considering their frequent occurrence in Present-day English, the lexicographers may not do justice to this usage.

There is a dictionary, however, which adopts the following sentence as an illustrative quotation.

(5) Helen was surprised at how small the room really was.
(*Longman Language Activator*, 1993)

The dictionary was published in Britain in 1993. The year of publication suggests that the construction has become popular and prevalent in relatively recent decades.

Sanseido's *Wisdom* gives a description in which the use of the prepositions is indicated, as in (6).

(6) I was pleasantly surprised (*by* [*at*]) how easy it was. [Before a *wh*-clause, *at* or *by* often accompanies]

It may be a better description since it shows the use of the prepositions but it is not without shortcomings. When a preposition is absent, *how*-clauses are very likely to be introduced by *you'd* (*you'll*) *be surprised*, as may be known by the quotations in (4). Moreover, *at* occurs much more frequently than *by*, so *at* should be placed before *by* in parentheses. Basically, this is a good description in a limited space of a dictionary but it may need a slight emending.

2.2 English usage books

Peters (1995: 730) gives the following quotations in differentiating the usage of *surprised at* and *surprised by*.

(7) a. They were surprised by a night watchman.
    b. She was surprised at how quickly it had grown.
            (*Australian English Style Guide*, 1995: 730)

(7a) is an example of physical use, not psychological, so Peters' contrast of the two constructions seems to be somewhat irrelevant. The adoption of (7b) as an illustrative quotation, however, shows that *how*-clauses have become popular and that they are very much compatible with the current usage of the predicate.

There is an awkward explanation in Konishi (1985: 1551), however. Konishi, providing a quotation in (8), describes the usage as the one which "drops *at* when it is followed by a clause."

(8) You'd be surprised how many times a girl has to lie in this world.

This description seems to be a little odd as we now know that the construction with the preposition has been a fairly recent development, while the construction without it had existed for several centuries. The latter could not have been derived from the former, which had not been in existence.

Accessible data may have been too scarce for Konishi to have made an appropriate judgment. Konishi is not to blame, however, because when he was engaged in editing the book, computer corpora barely existed and he would not have been able to gather even a fraction of the data we are collecting now.

In what follows, we will look into how psych-passives with the *at* + *how*-clause did rise and grow, when there had been the alternative construction (without the preposition) available.

III. Early Modern English

In order to identify when the constructions first began to appear, I used the *OED* on CD-ROM and the EEBO, the corpus of Early Modern English, for data collection.

3.1 The *OED* on CD-ROM

The sentences in (9) are the samples retrieved through the text-search of the *OED* on CD-ROM.

(9) He stands **amazed** *how* he thence should fade. (Spenser, *Faerie Queene*, 1599); Many parents are solicitously **perplexed**, *how* their children doe when they are dead. (T. Adams, *Semper Idem* Wks., 1614); If I were not misted, and confounded, and **astonished** *how* to be thankful. (Rutherford, Lett. 1637); He was **amazed**, *how* so impotent and groveling an Insect as I, could entertain such Inhuman Ideas, (Swift, *Gulliver's*, 1726); You'd be **amazed** *how* fast I can write when my pencil can actually form legible letters. (*New Yorker*, 28 Jan, 1975).

The earliest quotation is the one of Spenser's *The Faerie Queene* in 1599. The construction seems to have begun to appear as early as in the late 16th century and continued to occur through the 17th and 18th centuries till the present day. Samples of the construction with the preposition cannot be found from this corpus.

3.2 EEBO (Early English Book Online)

This corpus covers the period from the 1470s to the 1690s. The search retrieves slightly earlier instances than the data obtained from the *OED*, as in (10).

(10) and afterwardes stand in a dumpe **amazed** *how* you may colorably pray pardon of so great a crime so maliciously conceaued. (1581); Giue such a one fourty or fifty Crownes, 100: or 10: pounds: so as the treasurer rested euermore **perplexed** *how* to perform the dukes pleasure. (1595); who puffed vp with vaine glorie, was **astonished** *how* any durst denounce warre against him. (1597); this admirable Semstress . . . thus **surprised** *how* any body should come into her garden, (1673); etc.

The construction occurred for the first time with the verb *amaze* in 1581, followed by *astonish* and *perplex*. *Surprise* appeared a century later. *Perplex* occurs with *how* + *to*-infinitives and this characteristic seems to be continuing to the present day. The construction with the preposition cannot be found from this corpus, either. Figure 1 shows the statistics from the two corpora.

Figure 1
Psych-passives + (*at*) *how*-clause in EModE

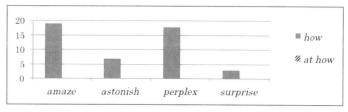

[no instances of the *at how*-clause retrieved]

Amaze and *perplex* are the main verbs that occur with the construction, with *astonish* and *surprise* following them. The psych-passive + *at how*-clause does not seem to have appeared yet in the Early Modern English period.

IV. Late Modern English

We used the MEC, the VLSA and the COHA to collect data from Late Modern English. From the COHA we obtained the data from 1810 to 1900, which covers the latter part of Late Modern English. The COHA will be treated separately because its data may show different results as the genres of its texts are different from those of the MEC and the VLSA.[2]

4.1 The MEC and the VLSA

Let us present some examples retrieved from the corpora.[3] The sentences of (11a) are the construction without the preposition and (11b) are the sentences with it.

(11) a. First, I was **amazed** *how* the creature got thither; and then, *how* he should just keep about the place, (Defoe, *Robinson Crusoe*, 1719); Indeed I am **astonished** *how* you have filled up, or rather killed, so much of your time. (Fielding, *Tom Jones*, 1749); Bathsheba had been **perplexed** *how* to *act*, for she was not much more than a slim young maid herself, (Hardy, *Far From the Madding Crowd*, 1874); I am **surprised** *how* anybody can like to look at them. (Thackeray, *Roundabout Paper*, 1863); etc.

b. The King was beside himself with joy, and was **astonished at** *how* clever a man Ring was in all kinds of feats, (Lang, *The Yellow Fairy Book*, 1894); I've told you how I first saw Captain Trent in the saloon in 'Frisco? . . . and how I saw him afterwards at the auction, frightened to death, and as much **surprised at** *how* the figures skipped up as anybody there? (Stevenson, *The Wrecker*, 1892); etc.

---

2) While the former includes fiction, non-fiction, newspapers and magazines, the latter are mostly literary works, as already mentioned in Chapter 3.

3) The data from the MEC and the VLSA were collected in writing my 2015(c) article when the MEC was still available.

Chapter 7

After the first appearance in the late 16th century, a number of sentences of the construction with the *how*-clause can be observed during the Late ModE period and are still in wide use in today's English. The construction with the preposition, on the other hand, made its first appearance in the late 19th century and only three samples are retrieved from the corpora. The statistics are shown in Figure 2 below, together with the statistics from the COHA.

4.2 The COHA

The construction with the *how*-clause occurs with similar verbs but the instances of *amaze* and *bewilder* are not found in this corpus. *Perplex* shows higher frequency in this corpus. The difference may come from the different genres of the texts. There is only one instance taking the preposition.

4.3 The results

The results of the search into the three corpora are shown in Figure 2.

Figure 2
Psych-passives + (*at*) *how*-clause in LModE

Several dozen instances of the psych-passive + *how*-clause are found in the corpora. *Amaze*, *perplex* and *surprise* are the main verbs that occur with this construction. Only a few instances with the *at* + *how*-clause are found to occur with *astonish* and *surprise*. The statistics confirm our observation that the construction without the preposition occurred occasionally in Late Modern English, while its future rival rarely appeared during the same period.

V. Present-day English

We used the BNC, the Wordbanks, the COCA and the COHA to collect data. As for the COHA, the data from 1970 to 2010 was used. The size of this sub-corpus is approximately 104 million words (Davies, 2012: 123), very similar to that of the BNC or the Wordbanks, so we can make a fair comparison between the corpora. The COCA is a corpus of 500 million words, roughly five times larger than the other corpora. To make a fair comparison, the raw data from the COCA was divided by five.[4]

5.1 Psych-passives + *how*-clause

Some of the samples collected from the corpora are shown in (12).

(12) You'd be **amazed** *how* little we know about the polar regions, (BNC, News, 1989); I am **astonished** *how* little money there is in politics. (COCA, News, 2012); You would be **surprised** *how* many people quit when faced with obstacles, (COHA, Magazine, 1992); You'd be **surprised** *how* small this world is when you get right down to it. (COCA, Spoken, 2014); etc.

The statistics are presented in Figure 3. Verbs with no occurrence are excluded.

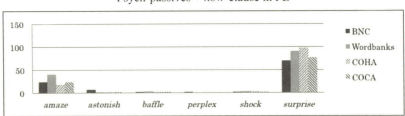

Figure 3
Psych-passives + *how*-clause in PE

---

4) In Chapter 3, the raw data from the COCA was divided by 4.5. This is because this corpus has constantly been updated with 20 million words being added each year. There is an increase of total words from the previous research, thus the division by five.

It is to be noted that the construction occurs almost exclusively with *surprise* and *amaze*. Other verbs occur only to a negligible degree. It looks as if the usage was confined to these two verbs, especially to *surprise*.

5.2 Psych-passives + *at how*-clause

A very large number of samples were retrieved, only a fraction of which are presented in (13).

(13) I was **amazed at** *how* well we were welcomed—after their initial shock. (BNC, Popular Lore, 1992); I've been **amazed at** *how* many plagiarized papers I've gotten from students. (COCA, News, 2010); I'm **shocked at** *how* foolish people can be. (COCA, Magazine, 2011); You'd be **surprised at** *how* many people give money to the cause. (BNC, Fiction, 1992); You'll be **surprised at** *how* greatly your writing will improve over time. (COCA, Fiction, 2008); etc.

Figure 4 shows the statistics. Verbs with no occurrence are excluded.

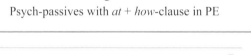

Figure 4
Psych-passives with *at* + *how*-clause in PE

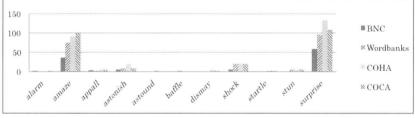

The construction occurs chiefly with *surprise* and *amaze*. *Shock* and *astonish* come in a distant third and fourth place. Other verbs make such a sporadic occurrence that they are hardly visible in the chart. The overall pattern is similar to that of the construction with the *how*-clause except that this construction occurs nearly three times more frequently with *amaze* and slightly more frequently with *surprise*.

Psychological Passives and the Agentive Prepositions in English

5.3 A large increase from Late ModE to PE

The total numbers of the occurrences of psych-passives + (*at*) *how*-clause in each period are shown in Figure 5.

Figure 5
Psych-passives + (*at*) *how*-clause in each period

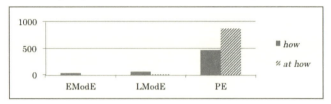

Evidently, the two constructions show a drastic increase in Present-day English, allowing for the different sizes of the corpora.[5] The construction with the preposition occurs nearly twice as much as its rival in Present-day English.

5.4 A historical shift of *surprised* + (*at*) *how*-clause

Using the data obtained from the COHA, we will be able to show the increase of the two constructions with *surprise*. Figure 6 shows the shift from the 1830s to the 2000s.[6]

Figure 6
Surprised + (*at*) *how*-clause from the 1830s to the 2000s (COHA)

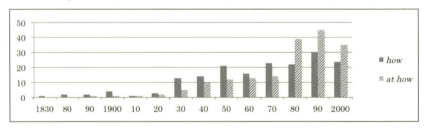

---

5) The sizes are: EModE about 780 million, LModE probably around 200 million and PE a little over 400 million. Despite the different sizes, the increase is evident.
6) No samples are found between the 1840s and the 1870s.

The gradual increase of the two constructions from the early 20th century to the present time can be clearly seen. As if abruptly, the constructions began to increase from around the 1930s. The 1980s saw a drastic rise in the construction with the preposition, which surpassed the occurrence rate of the other during this decade. Why the two constructions have existed side by side for several decades to the present time may be an interesting issue and we will discuss it later in terms of stylistic variation.

VI. Psych-passives with *by* + *how*-clause

Let us now examine the behaviors of the 'psych-passive with *by* + *how*-clause' construction, especially, the construction with *surprise*. This structure seems to have appeared for the first time in the last part of the 20th century. I happened to encounter the exclusive occurrence of this construction in the work of this particular author, as in (14).

(14) I am **surprised by** *how* human, even likable, he is. (Helen Prejean, *Dead Man Walking*, 1993, p.40); I am **surprised by** *how* thick his accent is. (ibid. p.55)

One swallow does not make a summer, but it signals the approaching summer. Likewise, the instances like this may presage the surge of the construction taking place. The verb *surprise* seems to be occurring quite often with this construction in Present-day English. How about other synonymous verbs? The search of the PE corpora yields the results in Figure 7 below.

As expected, the verb which occurs most frequently is *surprise*, followed by *amaze* and *shock*, with *startle* and *stun* trailing after them. It is puzzling that the construction with *surprise* shows much higher frequency in the American corpora than in the British corpora. We are not certain if there is a regional difference involved in this peculiar phenomenon.

Startle and *stun* show a relatively higher profile than in the previous statistics (Figure 4). This may reflect the fact that these verbs have a strong affinity with *by*, which leads to more occurrences with this construction.

Figure 7
Psych-passives + *by how*-clause in PE

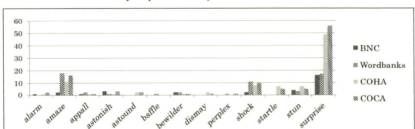

Comparatively small figures of *amaze* and *shock* in the BNC are puzzling. This deviation may have to do with the regional difference or the periods that the texts cover. Other verbs occur in such a way that they are scarcely visible in the chart.

To find out how this construction behaves in spoken English, we searched for samples of this construction in the CASO (the Corpus of American Soap Opera). Only nine instances are found from the search: four instances with *amaze*, three with *surprise* and one each with *shock* and *stun*. The result seems to suggest that the construction is not very likely to be used in spoken English. This finding may confirm our observation made already to the effect that *at* tends to occur in colloquial English in expressing one's emotion and *by* is likely to be used in writing to mention a fact.

I will show the developmental history of this construction with *surprise*, using the COHA. Figure 8 shows the frequency of occurrence of the construction in each decade from the 1930s to the 2000s.

Figure 8
A historical shift of *surprised by* + *how*-clause in PE (COHA)

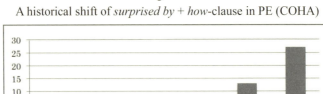

The construction seems to have begun to appear practically in the 1960s and it has been gradually on the increase. Especially, it shows a rapid growth over a couple of decades from the 1980s to the 2000s. This may be a reflection of a synchronization with the increasing use of *by* with psych-passives. The frequencies of occurrence of the two constructions (i.e. the *how*-clause with *at* or *by*) are shown in Figure 9. The raw data from the COCA was divided by five to make an easier comparison.

Figure 9
Surprised at or *by* + *how*-clause in PE

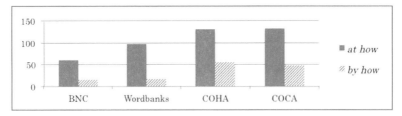

The chart shows that the construction with *at* occurs a couple of times more frequently than the construction with *by*. The latter, however, may be making a rapid chase after its rival construction, just as the agentive *by* has overtaken *at* and surpassed it in the occurrence rate with the passives of *surprise* and its synonymous verbs in the recent decades.

VII. Stylistic variation

Analyzing the data, it was brought to my attention that stylistic variation might be involved in the choice of the construction. *How*-clauses have a tendency to be introduced by *you'd be surprised*, while the construction with *by* + *how*-clause seems more likely to be used in the past tense or perfect aspect.

7.1 *You'd be surprised* + *how*-clause

We observe an unusually frequent occurrence of the *how*-clause introduced by *you'd be surprised*, as in (15).

(15) **You'd be surprised** *how* much things haven't changed. A lot has, we still have a way to go. (COCA, *New York Post*, 2017); Oh, **you'd be surprised** *how* many cars make you squeeze through a needlessly narrow opening. (COHA, *USA Today*, 2002); **You'd be surprised** *how* humbling yourself like that can accomplish something. (CASO, *All My Children*, 2002); etc.

The sentences of this type occur so frequently that they look as if they were used as a near-idiomatic expression. Especially in the CASO, their occurrence rate is nearly 70 percent. It may be said that the construction goes along well with spoken English.

We also see a fairly frequent occurrence of *you'll be surprised* with the *how*-clause, especially in the British corpora. The two constructions combined, the occurrence rates are very high; in fact, roughly 50 to 70 percent of *how*-clauses are occurring with *you'd* (*you'll*) *be surprised*,[7] as is shown in Figure 10.

Figure 10
You'd (you'll) be surprised + *how*-clause in PE

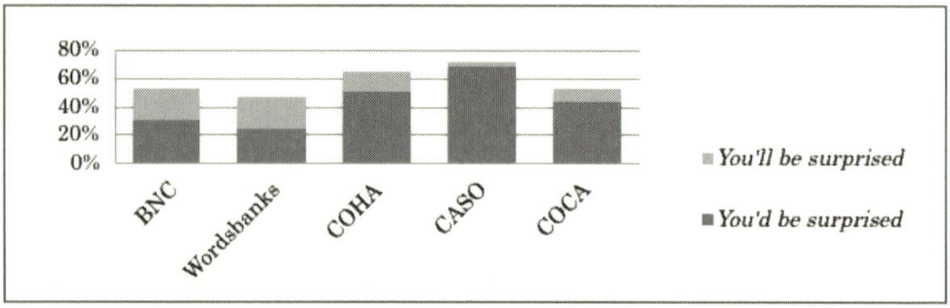

[Bar chart showing percentages for BNC, Wordsbanks, COHA, CASO, COCA with two series: "You'll be surprised" and "You'd be surprised"]

7.2 *Surprised by* + *how*-clause in the past tense or perfect aspect

As opposed to the future tense as in *you'd* (*you'll*) *be surprised*, the construction with *by* + *how*-clause seems to have a tendency to occur in the past tense or perfect aspect, as in (16).

---

[7] This is more true of *what*-clauses introduced by *you'd* (*you'll*) *be surprised*. In the data from the COHA, 90 percent of *what*-clauses occur with *you'd* (*you'll*) *be surprised*.

(16) Yes, I was actually somewhat **surprised by** *how* critical he was about Hillary Clinton. (COCA, Spoken, 2016); I used to be **surprised by** *how* readily older people downsized their lives. (COCA, Magazine, 2010); I have been pleasantly **surprised by** *how* much they have taught me about perseverance and grit. (COCA, Magazine, 2014); etc.

Figure 11 shows the percentages of the construction occurring in the past tense or perfect aspect in each PE corpus.

Figure 11
Surprised by + *how*-clause in the past tense or perfect aspect in PE

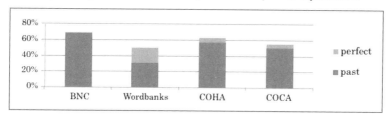

It shows that a fairly large number of instances are likely to occur in the past tense or perfect aspect. In other words, this construction tends to be used to describe what happened in the past or has been happening from the past. It looks as if the two constructions were making what is called a complementary distribution in terms of tense or aspect, partial though it may be. Stylistically, on the other hand, the predicate with *at* + *how*-clause seems to be an all-round player, which does not seem to choose any particular tense or aspect.

VIII. Hypotheses for the rise of *how*-clauses with *at*

I will present some hypotheses how and why the construction with the preposition came into being when there had been the alternative construction without it. First, we assume that *at* came to be inserted on the analogy of *what*-clauses, which occurred with a preposition quite frequently in the earlier period. Secondly, *the way*-clauses and *the N with which*-clauses may have been replaced with the syntactically equivalent *how*-clauses to make the structure simpler and plainer and to emphasize the exclamatory effect.

8.1 Insertion of *at* on the analogy of *what*-clauses

We assume that the agentive *at* came to be inserted before *how*-clauses on the analogy of *what*-clauses that occurred quite frequently with a preposition in the Late ModE period, as in (17).

> (17) I am often **astonished at** *what* I hear. (Austen, *Emma*, 1815); He was **dismayed** . . . **at** her face and *what* it portended. (H. James, *The Bostonians*, 1886); You pretend to be **shocked by** *what* I have said. (Ch. Brontë, *Jane Ayre*, 1847); etc.

In the data from the sub-corpus of the COHA (1810–1900), *what*-clauses are found to occur with the preposition 112 times (*at* 77 times, *by* 35 times), while there are only some twenty *how*-clauses (without a preposition). It would be little wonder if psych-passives had begun to take a preposition with *how*-clauses by analogy with *what*-clauses due to their syntactic similarity as an interrogative pronoun or an exclamatory word.

8.2 The replacement of *the way*-clauses by *how*-clauses

The way-clauses, which had existed from the earlier period as in (18), may have been replaced by *how*-clauses.

> (18) Amabel . . . had been very much **alarmed at** *the way* in which Guy clambered about, (Yonge, *The Heir of Redclyffe*, 1853); He's **shocked at** *the way* your father goes on in. (Dickens, *Pickwick Papers*, 1837); before it probably had time to **be surprised at** *the way* the thing was done. (Mark Twain, *Political Economy*, 1870); etc.

Since *the way*-clauses are syntactically equivalent to *how*-clauses (e.g. Quirk et al., 1985: §17.18),[8] the former may well have been replaced by the latter. The sentences in (18) would be rewritten as in (19) with the *how*-clause.

---

8) Quirk et al. cite the following two sentences as synonymous: *That's the way she spoke* = *That's how she spoke.*

(19) Amabel ... had been very much **alarmed at** *how* Guy clambered about; He's **shocked at** *how* your father goes on in; before it probably had time to be **surprised at** *how* the thing was done.

8.3 The replacement of *the N with which*-clauses by *how*-clauses

Another hypothetical replacement is that *how*-clauses may have taken the place of *the N with which*-clauses. The latter could be what theoretical linguists call 'concealed exclamations' and if so, they can be replaced by the exclamatory *how*-clause.

Fukuchi (1995: 62) says that (20a) is a 'concealed exclamation' as it can be paraphrased into (20b) with the *what*-clause, which conveys an exclamation.

(20) a. You'd be surprised at *the big car* he buys.
    b. You'd be surprised at *what big car* he buys. (Fukuchi, 1995: 62)

In the same vein, the sentences containing *the N with which*-clause as in (21),[9] apparently concealed exclamations, can be paraphrased with the exclamatory *how*-clause.

(21) The reader may have been **surprised at** *the ease with which* Mr. Frost expressed himself in his speech. (COHA, Fiction, 1864); Andy was **surprised at** *the kindness with which* he was treated. (COHA, Fiction, 1895); You would be **surprised at** *the rapidity with which* she acquires knowledge. (COHA, Fiction, 1896).

Such phrases as *with ease, with kindness* and *with rapidity* in (21) can be rewritten with the cognate *-ly* adverb into *easily*, *kindly* and *rapidly*, respectively (e.g. Leech and Svartvik, 1975: §192). It is, then, possible to paraphrase the sentences in (21) with the *how*-clause and an *-ly* adverb, as in (22).

---

[9] This formula subsumes such a usage with a different preposition as *the length to which* my story has run (COHA, Fiction 1827) or as *the cool manner in which* his absence was treated. (COHA, Fiction 1857).

(22) The reader may have been **surprised at** *how easily* Mr. Frost expressed himself in his speech; Andy was **surprised at** *how* kindly he was treated; You would be **surprised at** *how* rapidly she acquires knowledge.

As many as forty instances of *the N with which*-clauses are found in the Late ModE sub-corpus of the COHA (1810–1900), while there are only three instances of them in the PE sub-corpus (1970–2010). The small occurrence in the PE sub-corpus suggests that this usage is now out of favor in Present-day English. Although this decrease may not necessarily confirm the validity of my hypothesis, it may not be far wide of the mark to assume that it could be substantiated, if indirectly, by the statistics as Bradley (1904: 17) is insightful enough to say as follows:

> the dying out of the ancient forms created a need which had to be supplied by the invention of new modes of expression (Bradley, 1904: 17).

Why did the replacement take place at all? English speakers may have found the one-morpheme *how*-clause simpler and plainer, more convenient and expressible than the four-word alternative to express the same conceptual meaning. It may be a natural course to take in order to avoid using *the N with which*-clauses, which may sound pompous and superfluous, and may even be cumbersome to deal with because of their complex structure and abstract nature.

Furthermore, the colloquial characteristics of *how*-clauses may have been responsible for the replacement. Exclamatory *how*-clauses are often used in a colloquial style, or in spoken English by nature as exclamations usually take place in speech or colloquial contexts. The replacement may be a natural linguistic sign in society in which the plain and simple writing has been advocated (Gowers, 1973; Crystal, 1995).[10]

---

10) Gowers, for instance, advocates in his *The Complete Plain Words* (1973: 81–103) that writers should avoid superfluous words and choose familiar words. In his *Encyclopedia* (1995: 376–77), Crystal explains 'the Plain English Campaign', which was launched in 1974.

IX. Summary

We have attemted to clarify the behaviors of psych-passives with the *how*-clause with or without a preposition. The 'psych-passive + *how*-clause' construction has existed for several centuries since the late 16th century and is still popular in Present-day English. The construction with the agentive *at* made its first appearance in the late 19th century and occurred only occasionally until the present day when it has shown a drastic increase, especially during the past few decades. The construction with the agentive *by* has also shown a rapid increase during the recent couple of decades after it made what was virtually the first entrance in the 1960s.

Surprise and *amaze* are the main verbs used with these constructions, showing a near exclusive occurrence. The runner-up verbs *astonish* and *shock* occur with the (*at*) *how*-clause and the third string *startle* and *stun* with the *by* + *how*-clause, exhibiting their penchant for a particular preposition. Other verbs only occur to a negligible degree.

Why are the three constructions existing side by side? There seem to be stylistic reasons involved in the choice of the construction: *how*-clauses are likely to be introduced by *you'd* (*you'll*) *be surprised* in the future tense (or hypothetical future), while the construction with *by* + *how*-clause tends to occur in the past tense or perfect aspect, seemingly making a partial complementary distribution. Psych-passives + *at how*-clause do not seem to adhere to any particular tense or aspect.

To explain how and why the increase of the *at* + *how*-clause with psych-passives has taken place, some hypotheses are presented. First, the insertion of *at* may have occurred before *how*-clauses on the analogy of *what*-clauses (*I am often astonished at what I hear*), which have been fairly frequently used with the preposition since the Late ModE period and have shared similar functions.

Secondly, the *way*-clauses (*I was surprised at the way she spoke*) may have been replaced by the equivalent *how*-clauses (*I was surprised at how she spoke*).

Thirdly, the *N with which*-clauses (*We were amazed at the ease with which he did the job*), so-called 'concealed exclamations', may have been taken over by *how*-clauses with an exclamatory tone (*We were amazed at how easily he did the job*).

    How-clauses, because of their plainness and lucidity plus an exclamatory effect, may have been preferred and increasingly used, as compared to *the way*-clauses or *the N with which*-clauses, which convey only conceptual meanings with little emotion. Particularly, the latter may sound superfluous and are even cumbersome to handle. The employment of *how*-clauses, being colloquial and simple, may be instigated by the trend in society which has been headed toward simple and plain writing.

Chapter 8

How Onions treated the 'passive of *surprise* + *by*' construction in the *OED*

"A harmless drudge, that busies himself in tracing the original, and detailing the signification of words." Any dictionary lover should be familiar with this famous definition of a 'lexicographer' by Dr. Johnson. How would Murray or Bradley, chief editors of the *OED*, have read this definition of Johnson's? Would they have smiled at it, appreciating Johnson's humor or irony? Would they have taken offence, if slightly, at this somewhat derogatory comment if they had believed dictionary editing as something serious and even solemn? No matter what they think of it, the fact remains that they made the most significant contribution to the completion of this lexicographical monument and we cannot thank them enough for their dedicating their life and soul to it.

I. Introduction

The passive forms of such psych-verbs as *amaze*, *astonish*, *surprise*, etc. have been said to occur with the agentive prepositions other than *by* but actually they are observed to be occurring with *by* in increasing numbers in Present-day English. The increasing use of the agentive *by* with psych-passives may be reflected in the treatment of dictionaries and usage books today. Psych-passives with the agentive *by* are shown to be an acceptable and legitimate usage in many of them. Kenkyusha's *Luminous* (2005, 2nd ed.), for instance, gives the following illustrative quotations and usage description for the verb *surprise*.

(1) We were very [pleasantly] *surprised by* [*at*] the news; We were *surprised at* [*by*] his behavior.

The active-voice sentence of *We were very* (*much*) *surprised by the news* is *The news surprised us very much*; *By* is a colorless preposition used to mention a fact, whereas when *at* is used, a strong shock or an emotional response or reaction can be felt. (*Luminous*, s.v. *surprise*)

Taishukan's *Genius* (2015, 5th ed.) gives a similar treatment to other psych-verbs such as *please, scare* and *worry*, for instance, and provide them with quotations in which the agentive *by* as well as the conventional prepositions are used, as in (2).

(2) a. I'm very *pleased* with [about] my new job; I was *pleased* by her admiration.
    b. I'm *scared* of spiders; I was *scared* by the strange noise.
    c. I was *worried* about [over] nothing; I'm not so much *worried* by the result.   (*Genius*, s.v. *please, scare, worry*)

These quotations with the agentive *by*, indicated explicitly as acceptable, are not confined to these dictionaries alone. They are also seen in other dictionaries. Judging from the proper quotations and apt descriptions employed in many dictionaries, it can be safely said that the 'psych-passive + *by*' construction has been gaining recognition as a standard and acceptable usage in Present-day English.

The linguistic situations in the late 19th and early 20th centuries, however, were different from those of today. Psych-passives occurring with the agentive *by* do not seem to have been considered to be an acceptable and legitimate usage during the period, when the *OED* was compiled. What, then, were the attitudes of the editors of the *OED* toward the sentences of the 'psych-passive + *by*' construction, which was not necessarily the standard usage? Did they treat them as non-standard or unacceptable? Did the four editors treat them in the same way or differently?

The theme of this chapter and the next will be how the editors of the *OED* treated the agentive prepositions that occurred with psych-passives. The editors that we will deal with are Charles Talbut Onions and Henry Bradley but we will also refer to James Murray and William Craigie. Onions' treatment of the 'passive of *surprise* + *by*' construction will be examined in this chapter and how Bradley treated the 'psych-passive + *by*' construction will be in the next chapter.

II. Quotations with *surprised* + *by* in the *OED*

As already noted, a number of great and popular writers of the Late ModE period such as Austen, Dickens, Trollope, Collins, Conrad and so forth had already made rather frequent use of the '*surprised* + *by*' construction, supposedly a non- or sub-standard usage at that time. They seem to have given the usage such currency that the construction may have been gaining popularity and legitimacy during the period.

However, the definition of *surprise* in a psychological sense in the *OED* has no reference to *by*, nor are there any illustrative quotations provided under the entry. We will delve into why Onions did not include any reference to *by* in the definition despite the apparent spread and dispersion of the construction to such an extent in society.

The *OED* may have exerted a tremendous influence on later lexicographers,[1] who may have refrained from referring to *by* because of its absence in the definition in the *OED* even if the construction was in fairly wide use. Considering this, this investigation would be necessary and worth conducting.

2.1 A text-search of *surprised* + *by*

A text-search of the phrase *surprised* + *by* and its variant forms in the *OED* yields twenty-two quotations with the predicate used psychologically. After excluding the seven quotations obtained from Burchfield's supplementary volumes,[2] we will have the fifteen quotations,[3] shown in (3). Each

---

[1] Landau (1989: 69–70), for instance, says, "Every dictionary thereafter is indebted to it [*OED*]. It is ... unthinkable that any contemporary lexicographers be without *OED* ... "
[2] Burchfield was Chief Editor of *Supplement to the OED* (1972–86).
[3] The search of the *OED Online* (The Third Edition) shows that some dates in the illustrative quotations turn out to be different from those of the First Edition and that some quotations are slightly changed. In the 1845 quotation, for instance, the date is changed

quotation is used to illustrate the word in parentheses. The 1794 quotation is used to illustrate two entries, i.e. *lobster* and *unmercifully*.

(3)

1786 F. Burney *Diary* 27 July (1842-6) III. 37 At the desert I was very agreeably **surprised by** the entrance of Sir Richard Jebb, who stayed coffee. (*stay* v.17)

1794 C. Pigott *Female Jockey Club* 139 She faints at the approach of a mouse; is **surprised by** the sight of a black lobster, she screams unmercifully. (*lobster* n. 1; *unmercifully* adv.)

1816 *Sporting Mag.* XI. VII. 43 The other horse . . . determined not to be again **surprised by** a go-by. (*go-by* n. 1)

1823 Rutter Fonthill 7 **Surprised by** the modest pretensions of the entrance. (*modest* a. 5)

1830 W. Taylor *Hist. Surv. Germ. Poetry* II. 320 He is **surprised by** a nymph. who is at length seized by the supervening Itifal, a Sacripant of knighthood. (*Sacripant* n.)

1838 Lytton *Alice* 21 Miss Merton was . . . **surprised by** the beauty . . . of the young fairy before her. (*fairy* n. 5b)

1840 *Moore Mem.* (1856) VII. 275 Russell's berth was . . . the chief object of our attention, and I was most agreeably **surprised by** its roominess. (*roominess* n.)

1844 C. E. A. Yng, *Communicants* (1848) 21 The party of visitors . . . were much **surprised** and disedified **by** this scene in a convent school. (*disedify* v.)

1844 J. H. Newman *Lett.* (1891) II. 442 He was **surprised** and thrown out **by** finding I did not seem to be what he had fancied. (*throw* v. 44.1)

1845 Darwin *Voy. Nat.* xx. (1879) 464 I was a good deal **surprised by** finding two species of coral . . . possessed of the power of stinging. (*sting* v. 3)

1855 Macaulay *Hist. Eng.* xvii. IV. 12 In the spring of 1691, the Waldensian Shepherds . . . were **surprised by** glad tidings. (*spring* n. 5e)

1865 Dickens *Mut. Fr.* II. i. 'I don't like that', said Bradley Headstone. His pupil was a little **surprised by** this striking-in with so sudden . . . an

---

to 1839 and the word "power" is altered to "property". These apparent corrections, however, do not seem to have any effect on the analysis of the construction we are concerned with.

objection. (*striking* n. 1b)

1878 Black *Green Past.* v. 37 **Surprised** and chagrined **by** the coldness of her manner. (*chagrin* v. 2)

1879 G. C. Harlan *Eyesight* vi. 69 Old people who have been using glasses . . . are sometimes **surprised by** a return of the ability to read without them. (*return* n. 3)

1889 Jessop *Coming of Friars* vii. 325 Prophets are never at a nonplus, and never **surprised by** a question. (*nonplus* n. 1)

These quotations must have been judged to be better sentences among many other candidates for illustrating the entry words. In this sense, they may be considered to be examples of 'random sampling' and are therefore supposed to represent the linguistic situations of the period we are concerned with.

As we have already shown in Chapter 1, the 'passive of *surprise* + *by*' construction began to appear in the late 18th century and seems to have become quite popular during the 19th century. In fact, it was so popular as to be used by such eminent figures as Dickens, Darwin and Macaulay in the quotations of (3).

We have also shown that the agentive *at* has been the most predominant preposition with the 'passive of *surprise*' construction throughout the ModE period since its first appearance in the 17th century. A text-search of *surprised* + *at* and its variant forms yields 59 quotations (with the quotations from Burchfield's *Supplement* excluded). As compared to 59 quotations of *surprised at*, 15 quotations of *surprised by* do not seem to be too small a figure to be disregarded. Besides, the occurrence rate of *by* during the Late ModE period, when the editing of the *OED* was taking place, is assumed to have been more than 20 percent. An occurrence rate of more than 20 percent does not seem to be too small a figure to overlook, either.

2.2 Potential illustrative quotations from Late ModE writers

We have found a couple of hundred samples containing *surprised by* which were used by some of the greatest and most popular writers of Late Modern English. These include Samuel Johnson, Jane Austen, Charles Dickens,

Anthony Trollope, Wilkie Collins, George Gissing, Joseph Conrad from Britain and Washington Irving, Ralf Waldo Emerson, Nathaniel Hawthorne, Jack London and Edith Wharton from America (see Appendix in Chapter 1).

The publication of the fascicle containing the entry *surprise* took place in 1918. Almost all the retrieved samples, therefore, must have been from the works published before the date of compiling. As it is, they may have stood a chance of coming into the hands of, or at least may have caught the eye of, the editor or sub-editors (see §3.2).

This is significant for two reasons. First, as these writers were all such popular and renowned writers, the construction may have come to be recognized as legitimate and acceptable simply because they used it. Secondly, a number of sentences containing the construction in these great writers' works must have been submitted in citation slips to the editors by voluntary readers. Why, then, is any reference to *by* not made in the definition of *surprise* nor are there any illustrative quotations adopted under the entry? My speculation is that this seemingly insufficient treatment may have to do with the editorial attitude of Onions, the fourth editor of the *OED*, who compiled the entry *surprise*.

III. Onions, the fourth editor of the *OED*

3.1 Four editors

There were four editors, who dedicated themselves to the compilation of the *OED*, probably the most important and valuable dictionary in history. It was James Murray (1837–1915) who virtually set sail for the uncharted waters of this lexicographical enterprise,[4] followed by Henry Bradley (1845–1923)

---

[4] Herbert Coleridge was appointed the first editor of the dictionary undertaken by the Philological Society. After his sudden death at the age of thirty-five, F. J. Furnival succeeded Coleridge. Both Coleridge and Furnival did preliminary work for the dictionary, which, however, had been at a standstill and could have been abandoned. Then James Murray was persuaded to take up this great enterprise. It was Murray who actually began the work of editing the dictionary, compiled almost half of it and set the stage for its completion with the cooperation of three other editors (*OED*, Vol. I, Historical Introduction; Baugh, 1935: §234; Landau, 1989: 68–69).

as a joint editor and later joined by William Craigie (1867–1957) and finally by Charles Talbut Onions (1873–1965).

Murray edited more than half of the pages of the *OED* as Editor-in-Chief[5] and he is referred to as the greatest lexicographer by Burchfield.[6] Without Murray, this lexicographical monument may not have been even started,[7] let alone been accomplished. The dictionary was once justifiably called *Murray's Dictionary* and with good reason (e.g. Imazato and Tsuchiya 1984: 91–92).

3.2 Onions: the editor of the entry *surprise*

The following table shows who edited which sections and in what dates (The *OED*, Vol. I: xvii–xix). Actually, the *OED* was published in 124 installments, or fascicles, over a period of nearly 50 years. It was Onions who edited the entry *surprise* in compiling the fascicle 'Supple–Sweet' in 1918. (In the *Supplement* to the *OED* published in 1933, Craigie edited L–R and U–Z and Onions edited A–K, S and T.)

Table 1
Four editors and their compiled volumes and the dates

Murray	Bradley	Craigie	Onions
AB 1882–88			
C 1888–93	E 1888–93		
D 1893–97	F 1893–97		
H 1897–99	G 1897–1900		
IJK 1899–1901			

5) See the *OED* (Vol. I: xix). Let us also quote Elisabeth Murray, James Murray's granddaughter and the author of his biographical book *Caught in the Web of Words*. She writes, "It was very rarely that James' annual output was less than that of Bradley and Cragie, and in the end nearly half of the whole work (7,207 out of 15,487 pages) was produced by him" (1977: 284).

6) In the preface to *Caught in the Web of Words*, Burchfield describes Murray as "a lexicographer greater by far than Dr Johnson, though he lacks the lustre and legend associated with Johnson, and greater perhaps than any lexicographer of his own time or since in Britain, the United States, or Europe."

7) Landau (1989: 69), for instance, comments, "Far from being surprised at the time required to complete the project, we should be amazed that it was ever completed at all."

O 1902–04	L 1901–03	Q 1902	
P 1904–09	M 1904–08	R–Re 1903–05	
		N 1906–07	
T 1909–15	S–Sh 1908–14	Re–Ry 1907–10	
	St 1914–19	Si–Sq 1910–15	Su–Sz 1914–19
		V 1916–20	
	W–We 1920–23	U 1921–26	XYZ 1920–21
		Wo–Wy 1927	Wh–Wo 1922–27

IV. Onions' treatment of the 'passive of *surprise* + *by*' construction

4.1 Illustrative quotations with *surprised* + *by*

I have presented the fifteen quotations containing *surprised by* in §2.1. We will be able to determine who adopted which quotation. The result is the following list, in which the editors and the quotations represented by the date are shown:[8]

Murray: 1844, 1844, 1878
Bradley: 1786, 1794, 1816, 1823, 1830, 1838, 1845, 1865
Craigie: 1794, 1840, 1855, 1879, 1889
Onions: none

Eight out of the sixteen quotations are in Bradley's volumes, five quotations in Craigie's and three in Murray's. There is no quotation of *surprised by* in the volumes that Onions compiled (i.e. Su–Sz, X, Y, Z, Wh–Wo, and A–K, S and T of the *Supplement*).

It is not surprising if we consider the number of pages Onions edited (1,495 pages including 657 pages for the *Supplement*), which is substantially less than the numbers of pages edited by the three other editors (cf. Murray edited 7,207 pages, Bradley 4,590 pages and Cragie 3,062 pages including 210 pages for the *Supplement*). Nevertheless, it is still perplexing that no

---

[8] As the 1794 quotation was used by the two editors (i.e. Bradley and Craigie), it is counted as two occurrences.

illustrative quotations of *surprised by* are adopted in Onions' volumes. Did Onions fail to perceive the existence of the construction or did he lack the quotation slips with the construction in question in his editing room?

We must say that the answers are negative. First, as a number of popular and renowned writers of the Late ModE period had already used the construction. Onions himself may have read the works of these writers and realized its existence. It would be difficult to imagine that he had not read such writers as Johnson, Austen, Dickens, Trollope, Collins, Conrad, Hawthorne and so forth.

4.2 Quotations contributed by the volunteer readers

Secondly, the Bibliography of the *OED* shows that all the writers mentioned in §2.2, if not all of their works, were read by the voluntary readers for the dictionary,[9] who may have cited sentences containing *surprised by* used in their writings. This speculation may not be too far-fetched, considering one of the twelve directions given to readers as to how they should select words (*OED*, Vol. I: xv; E. Murray 1977: 347), which is as follows:

> make a quotation for every word that strikes you as rare, obsolete, old-fashioned, new, peculiar, or used in a peculiar way.

Readers who encountered the sentences with *surprised by* and found them 'peculiar' must have collected them as illustrative quotations. There may have been many of them as Morton (1994: 95), the author of *The Story of Webster's Third*, makes the following remark:

> Among Murray's chief problems with the volunteers was . . . readers collected too many citations of unusual words and too few of ordinary words.

In fact, a large number of quotations of these writers have found their

---

9) Hundreds of volunteer readers contributed to the compilation of the *OED* (e.g. Baugh, 1935: §234). The dictionary would not have been completed in the form as it is now, without their dedicated contribution. For instance, a reader by the name of Thomas Austin contributed as many as 165,000 citations and another reader named William Douglass (of London) made a contribution of 136,000 citations (*OED*, Vol. I: xxi).

way into the *OED* and we can find them by the hundreds or even thousands by the 'quotation search' of its CD-ROM. From Dickens, 8,536 quotations are retrieved, Johnson 5,751, Eliot 3,153, Hawthorne 1,651, Trollope 1,432, Jane Austen 1,072 and so forth. Considering this, chances are probably not remote that a number of sentences containing *surprised by* were found and contributed by the readers.

4.3 Rapport with senior editors

Onions had been an assistant editor to Murray and then to Bradley for twenty years before he became an independent editor (Baugh, 1935: 408; E. Murray, 1977: 287). While he was working under their supervision, especially when he was working under Bradley, Onions may have seen quotations containing *surprised by*, which Bradley utilized. Landau (1989: 69) explains how assistant editors collaborated with the editor.

> Each of the 5 million citations had to be painstakingly collected—a process conducted largely from 1858 to 1881—subsorted (i.e., alphabetized and divided in a preliminary way by sense); analyzed by assistant editors and defined, with representative citations chosen for inclusion; and checked and redefined by Murray or one of the other supervising editors.
>
> (Landau,1989: 69).

Onions, after becoming an independent editor, worked in the Old Ashmolen building with Bradley and Craigie, with only Murray working at the original location in Oxford. There seems to have been rapport between the editors in the Old Ashmolen, as is evidenced by Onions's statement (1917–20: 7) that "Professor Craigie was able to supply me with a quotation from an Italian novel of 1879 . . . " Onions may have been provided by Bradley with citations containing *surprised by*, or the existence of the construction may have been at least suggested to him. Onions may even have consulted the senior editors as to how the construction should be treated.

4.4 Onions' apparent disregard of *by*

It seems unlikely then that Onions failed to perceive the existence of the construction nor did he lack the quotations containing *surprised by* contributed by the readers in his editorial room. Why then did Onions not make any mention of it nor utilize the citations containing the construction for illustrative quotations? There may have been several reasons.

First, it may be that the quotation slips containing *surprised by* were simply not utilized even if they had been in the editorial room. This is because generally speaking, quotations which can be used for a dictionary may be a small portion of the whole body of quotations collected during the process of compiling the dictionary. According to Fisher (1997: 162), out of five million quotations contributed by the readers, 1,861,200 quotations were used in the first edition of the *OED* (also the Preface of the *OED*, Vol. I: v).

Secondly, Onions may have been influenced by the definitions made by senior editors of such typical psychological verbs as *annoy*, *delight*, *please* (edited by Murray) and *frighten* (by Bradley). Both Murray and Bradley made a reference to such prepositions as *at*, *with* or *of*, but not to *by* in the definitions.[10]

The verb *nettle* edited by Craigie is an exceptional case and it is given the following definition and description.

NETTLE v. 2b. In *pa. pple*. Irritated, vexed, provoked, annoyed. Const. *at*, *by*, *with*, etc.

It says that the verb in its past-participle form (i.e. the passive form) takes *by* as well as *at* or *with* as the agentive preposition.[11] Onions could have followed Craigie's suit and included *by* in the definition of *surprise* because the publication of the fascicle of '*N–Niche*', which includes *nettle*, was in 1906, more than ten years before the editing of the entry *surprise* began.

Thirdly, in terms of semantics, I argued that the 'passive of *surprise* + *by*'

---

10) However, examples of the passives of these verbs taking *by* were abundant in 19th century English. A text-search of *annoyed* (*delighted*, *pleased*, *frightened*) + *by* yields a number of quotations used for illustrating other entries. In fact, Bradley adopted the following quotation to illustrate the verb *frighten*, in which *by* is used: 1883 In fearing that England would go into schism the pope was frightened by a shadow.
 A search of the phrases in the COHA also produces many samples in which the agentive *by* is used with these verbs.
11) A search of the COHA yields 48 instances of *nettled* occurring with *at* and 30 instances with *by* during the period from 1810 to 1900.

construction seems to have been undergoing a semantic shift during the Late ModE period. This shift in meaning from physical to psychological was shown using a spectrum in Chapter 5. Sentences with quasi-psychological meanings, bordering on physical, physiological or psychological, may have caused the editor to hesitate to make any reference to *by* in defining the psychological use of the verb.

4.5 *Surprised by* as a non-standard usage

Last, but most importantly, Onions may have judged that the 'the passive of *surprise* + *by*' construction in a psychological sense had not established itself as a proper and legitimate usage. The agentive *by* was a comparative newcomer as an agentive preposition with the English passives, compared to other prepositions such as *from, of, through, with*, etc. (see §6 in Chapter 1). The quotations with *surprised by* are neither as numerous as, nor have appeared as early as, those of *surprised at*.

With these historical facts, Onions may have decided that the usage of the agentive *by* with *surprised* had not gained ground yet, just as some of the present-day dictionaries a few decades earlier still did not seem to consider it as accepted and established. Onions' decision may have been influenced by a number of great authors of the 19th century such as Lewis Carroll, Sir Arthur Conan Doyle, Mark Twain and Andrew Lang, who hardly used the agentive *by* with the passive of *surprise*.

V. Onions' prescriptivism

We will examine why Onions may have disregarded the agentive *by* with the passive of *surprise* in editing. Then I will argue that it may have to do with grammatical prescriptivism prevalent in his day and that Onions might have possessed it.

5.1 Onions' educational background

Onions was born in 1873. When he was growing up and acquiring the English of the late 19th century, the 'passive of *surprise* + *by*' construction in a psychological sense must have been taking root, as is demonstrated by a number of writers of the Late ModE period who used it. Unlike the *surprised at* construction which had been in use since the 17th century, the *surprised by* construction may not have been deemed to be established yet by the editor although it had become quite common more than half a century before Onions became an assistant editor in 1905.

It may be possible to speculate that Onions chose not to include any reference to *by* in the definition presumably because he was a prescriptivist, whether he was conscious of it or not, and the *by*-agent with *surprised* did not fit his prescriptive standards. Once he had written the definition, in which no reference to *by* was made, Onions may have felt inhibited thereafter from adopting the quotations containing *surprised by* for other entries in subsequent parts which he compiled.

This is also a speculation, but Onions' supposed prescriptivism may have to do with his educational and career backgrounds.[12] Onions had an education at a boarding school and at a secondary school in Birmingham, where he is said to have learnt the basics of grammar. After that he went on to Mason College (the present University of Birmingham) and later to the University of London. At Mason College, Onions was taught by Sonnenschine (1851–1929), a professor of classics and author of grammar books, two of which are *A New English Grammar* (1916) and *The Soul of Grammar* (1927). The former is a typical school grammar of English based on Latin grammar (Konishi and Deguchi 1967: 132). A sense of prescriptivism may have been nurtured and developed in Onions during his school and university days, especially when he was under the supervision of a professor who seems to have been strongly inclined toward prescriptivism.

After obtaining a B.A. from the University of London in 1892, Onions became a secondary schoolteacher. He was engaged in teaching until 1895, when he was invited to join the editorial staff of the *OED*. He may have taught, or may have had to teach, schoolchildren how to read and write by

---

12) For Onions' background, see Konishi and Deguchi (1967: 10–13), Matsunami et al. (1983: 1140–41) and Sasaki and Kihara (1995: 256–7). Also see the "Historical Introduction" of the *OED* (Vol. I: xviii).

referring to prescriptive grammar. Blake (1996: 287) says that "the private schools taught grammar from Lindley Murray's grammar,"[13] which was a typical prescriptive school grammar.

5.2 Onions and grammatical prescriptivism

Grammatical prescriptivism was prevalent in those days. Michael (1991: 12) says that a total of 856 grammar books were published in Britain by a conservative estimate during a period of 100 years from 1801 to 1900. This may have induced the prescriptivism to thrive in Britain in the 19th century. Matsunami *et al.* (1983: 436) confirm this, saying that after 1850 the British tradition of prescriptive grammar came to be in the spotlight again after having been eclipsed by American grammars during the first half of the 19th century. It is hardly surprising if Onions should have been influenced by the prescriptivism that was prevalent in society.

Onions himself wrote a grammar book titled *An Advanced English Syntax* in 1904 when he was thirty-one. Although the book is said to be a historical descriptive grammar (Konishi and Deguchi 1967: 23–25), it contains some prescriptive statements as 'Caution(s)', as in the following:

> Avoid the erroneous use of the Perfect Infinitive which is exemplified in such sentences as 'I should have liked *to have gone*', 'He had intended to have written'. We must say I should have liked *to go*', 'He had intended *to write*'. The 'pastness' belongs to the finite verb and not to the Infinitive. (p.130)
>
> The Participle must always have a proper 'subject of reference'. A sentence like the following is incorrect because the word to which the Participle refers grammatically is not that with which it is meant to be connected in sense: '*Born* in 1850, a part of his education was received at Eaton'. Correct thus: '*Born* in 1850, *he* received part of his education at Eaton'. (p.133)
>
> Avoid the Split Infinitive, in which an Adverb comes between the 'to' and the verb-noun. (p.152)

---

13) Lindley Murray was an American lawyer and businessman. He moved to Britain for health reasons and wrote a grammar book titled *English Grammar* for girls at a school he was religiously affiliated with. The book became so popular that it ran into many editions and it was translated into many other languages.

Onions apparently possessed characteristics of a prescriptivist and by writing a grammar book, he may have further developed a sense of prescriptivism.

I have argued that Onions' apparent disregard of *by* occurring with the passive of *surprise* may be ascribed to his prescriptivism and that it may have derived from his educational and career backgrounds. This is of course not meant to be a criticism of Onions. I have simply provided facts and figures about the historical usage of the 'passive of *surprise* + *by*' construction and presented my own views and speculations, based on the data obtained from computer corpora. In defense of Onions, I would say that the editor must have made the best possible decision that could have been made, making the most of what was available to him at the time of editing, approximately a century ago, when data-collection was not as convenient as it is now and grammatical prescriptivism must have been extremely dominant.

VI. Summary

The passive of *surprise* in a psychological sense is observed to have occurred chiefly with the agentive preposition *at* in Late Modern English but many examples are also found in which the agentive *by* is employed. Famous and popular writers such as Jane Austen, Charles Dickens, Wilkie Collins, Joseph Conrad and so forth utilized *by* with the predicate. Contrary to the conventional notion, the agentive *by* seems to have been used more often than our expectations.

How is this construction treated in the *OED*? The editor who compiled the entry *surprise* is Onions. Onions does not include any reference to *by* when it is used in the passive in the definition of the verb (i.e. *surprise* v. 5a). Nor is there any illustrative quotation with the construction under the entry. This treatment does not seem to reflect the real linguistic situations of the day. I have attempted to demonstrate that the editorial attitude of Onions may be responsible for this seemingly insufficient treatment of the construction.

A text-search of the *OED* retrieves fifteen quotations containing *surprised by* as an illustrative quotation for other entries. They are all adopted by the other editors and Onions did not adopt a single quotation in the volumes that he compiled.

Onions must have realized that the construction had existed and been used quite widely during the Late ModE period. He may have had the citation slips containing the construction contributed by the voluntary readers. Onions could have used them for illustrative quotations. Why did Onions apparently disregard the construction?

I argued that Onions may have judged the construction to be unestablished and that this decision of his may have had something to do with the grammatical prescriptivism thriving in Britain during the 19th century. The sense of prescriptivism, whether Onions was conscious of it or not, is assumed to have developed in him as he had been constantly exposed to it.

A large number of grammar books were written during the period and Onions was taught by a professor at college who wrote a prescriptive grammar. Onions became a schoolteacher and he must have taught his pupils with a grammar book. Onions wrote a grammar book himself and included a number of prescriptive comments as 'Cautions' in it.

These experiences may have imbued a sense of prescriptivism in him. When he was engaged in editing the *OED* as the fourth editor, his editorial attitude may have been influenced by his prescriptive inclination. It may have made him reluctant to accept non- or sub-standard usages like the passive of *surprise* with the agentive *by* and led to his disregard of it in the treatment of the verb *surprise* in the *OED*.

Chapter 9

How Bradley treated the 'psych-passive + *by*' construction in the *OED*

In Chaucer's *The Canterbury Tales*, the reeve tells a tale about a miller and there is a line, which goes: *A Sheffield thwitel baar he in his hose* ("He carried a Sheffield knife in his pouch", *The Reeve's Tale* 3933). Sheffield has been known as a town of cutlery since the middle ages and Henry Bradley worked in one of the cutlery firms in Sheffield. While working as a corresponding clerk to deal with foreign clients, he dedicated himself to studying languages and philology. Although he did not have much academic background and was a self-taught scholar, Bradley rose to the position of the *OED* editor.

I. Introduction

How Onions, the fourth editor of the *OED*, treated the 'passive of *surprise* + *by*' construction was the theme of the previous chapter. I argued that Onions was so imbued with a grammatical prescriptivism that he may have been hesitant to accept the *by*-agent as a legitimate usage. Consequently he may have avoided including the reference to it in the definitions in the *OED*.

We will probe how Bradley dealt with the 'psych-passive + *by*' construction in this chapter and show that he used it in defining entry words and adopted illustrative quotations containing it much more than the other editors. I will demonstrate that Bradley's editorial policy may have come from his educational and career backgrounds. I will then argue that an editor's personal background together with his personal disposition may affect the way he compiles a dictionary, by examining how Samuel Johnson edited his dictionary.

II. The treatment of the 'psych-passive + *by*' construction

2.1 Psych-passives and the agentive prepositions in the definitions

We will see how psych-verbs are treated in relation to the agentive prepositions in the *OED*. The verbs we will deal with are not only *surprise* and its synonymous verbs but also other psych-verbs.

The verb *please*, for instance, is provided with the following definition, usage description and illustrative quotations.

> Please 4.a. Passive. To be pleased: To be gratified, delighted, or agreeably satisfied. Const. *with*.
> 1535 Then shalt thou be pleased with the sacrifice of rightuousnesse.
> 1718 Every One is pleased with such an Occasion of shewing the Superiority of his Understanding.
> 1850 Nor can God be pleased with the perverted adoration.

The verb is shown to be used in the passive and to take *with* as an agentive preposition. This description is illustrated by the three quotations.[1]

We will treat the following verbs. They are typical psych-verbs commonly used in our daily conversation and writings.

> *alarm, amaze, amuse, annoy, astonish, bewilder, bother, chagrin, charm, confuse, deject, delight, depress, disappoint, disgust, dismay, displease, enchant, excite, fascinate, frighten, grieve, interest, offend, overwhelm, perplex, please, puzzle, rejoice, satisfy, scare, shock, startle, stun, surprise, terrify, vex, worry*[2]

The editors of the *OED* are James Murray, Henry Bradley, William Craigie and Charles Talbut Onions. Who edited which verb in the list above?

---

1) In the Third Edition (the *OED Online*), the following quotation containing the agentive *by* is added: 1845 C. Darwin Let. 25 Aug. in Corr. (1987) III. 242 I was much pleased by Lindley picking out my Extinction paragraphs & giving them uncurtailed.

2) Verbs like *appall, astound, concern, content* and *thrill* are excluded because there is not any reference to *by* in their definitions nor are the illustrative quotations with their passives occurring with *by* found under the entry and by the text-search. *Baffle* is also excluded because it almost always occurred with *by* in Late Modern English.

168

Chapter 9

The following list shows who edited which letter (*OED*, Vol. 1: xvii–xix).

Murray : AB, C, D, H, IJK, O, P, T
Bradley : E, F, G, L, M, S–Sh, St, W–We
Craigie : Q, N, R, Si-Sq, U, V, Wo–Wy, Supplement: L-R, U–Z
Onions : Su–Sz, Wh–Wo, XYZ, Supplement: A–K, S, T

From this information, we can determine who edited which verb, as shown below.

Murray: *alarm, amaze, amuse, annoy, astonish, bewilder, bother, chagrin, charm, confuse, deject, delight, depress, disappoint, disgust, dismay, displease, interest, offend, overwhelm, perplex, please, puzzle, terrify*
Bradley: *enchant, excite, fascinate, frighten, grieve, satisfy, scare, shock, startle, stun*
Craigie: *rejoice, vex, worry*
Onions: *surprise*

2.2 Agentive prepositions in the definitions and quotations

I have examined the definitions, usage descriptions and illustrative quotations of the verbs listed above. The examination reveals that the verbs, when they are used in the passive,[3] occur with such prepositions as illustrated below.

alarm	(*at, by, with*)
amaze	(*at, with*)
amuse	**with**, **by**, **at**
annoy	***after**, ***for**, ***of**, (*with*)
astonish	(*at, of, with*)
bewilder	———
bother	(*with*)
chagrin	(*at, by*)
charm	(*with*)

---

3) Some of the past-participle forms such as *amazed, frightened, pleased*, etc. are listed as a distinct headword in the dictionary. We will include them in our analysis.

169

confuse	——
deject	(*by*)
delight	**with, at,** *in
depress	(*by*)
disappoint	**in, with,** *of
disgust	**from, of, against,** (*at, with*)
dismay	——
displease	**with, at,** **of,* *against
enchant	(*at, with*)
excite	——
fascinate	(*by*)
frighten	**at, of, for,** (*by*)
grieve	**with,** (*at, by*)
interest	(*about, by, in*)
offend	**with, at**
overwhelm	(*with*)
perplex	(*with*)
please	**with**
puzzle	(*by*)
rejoice	**at,** **in,* *of
satisfy	**with, at, of,** **in,* (*by*)
scare	(*at, by*)
shock	**at,** (*by*)
startle	(*of, with*)
stun	(*by, with*)
surprise	**at,** *with
terrify	——
vex	**at, with**
worry	(*about, by, with*)

In the above table, prepositions in bold letters are the ones which are explicitly described in the definitions. The prepositions in the parentheses are the ones used in the illustrative quotations even if there is no explicit reference to them. —— shows that under the entry word, there is no description nor is there any illustrative quotation in which the preposition is used with its passive. An asterisk mark means that the preposition was obsolete.

Only *amuse* is provided with the explicit description of the agentive *by* occurring with its passive, which goes as follows:

> to be **amused** *with* a toy or whimsical person, *by* a story told me, *at* an incident, the self-complacency of another

It shows that the use of *by* is permissible with a particular type of object word, that is, "a story" in this case. No quotation is given, however, to illustrate this usage.

Judging from the fact that there is no description of the *by*-agent in the definitions except for the verb *amuse*, it may be said that the 'psych-passive + *by*' construction was not considered to be a standard or an acceptable usage yet at the time when the *OED* was being edited.

2.3 Illustrative quotations under the entry word

Even if there is no reference to the agentive *by* in the definitions, we find quotations under the entry word in which *by* is used with their passives. The following are such verbs and they are shown together with their quotations. The name of the editor who edited the verb is shown in the square brackets.

> *alarm* v.5 1653 The King was again Alarum'd by the Protestation. [Murray]
> *chagrin* v.2 1878 Surprised and chagrined by the coldness of her manner. [Murray]
> *deject* v.5 1625 The king was much dejected by a Lettre received from Denmark. [Murray]
> *depress* v.6 1806 We came . . . amidst rain and wind, and depressed by ill-forebodings. [Murray]
> *frighten* v. a 1883 In fearing that England would go into schism the pope was frightened by a shadow. [Bradley]
> *grieve* v.5 1841 He was grieved by the corrupt speech of his son. [Bradley]
> *interest* v.5 1791 She had been too much interested by the events of the moment. [Murray]
> *puzzle* v. 1870 Like a schoolmaster puzzled by hard sum. [Murray]
> *satisfy* v.7 1611 If any doubt hereof, he may be satisfied by examples enough. [Bradley]

scare v.1 1671 When they should find themselves more skarred than hurt by His Threats. [Bradley]
shock v.4 1849 Every moderate man was shocked by the insolence, cruelty, and perfidy with which the nonconformists were treated. [Bradley]
stun v.2 1802 Lady Catherine was stunned by this distinct refusal. [Bradley]
worry v.7 1867 Men when they are worried by fears . . . become suspicious. [Craigie]

Bradley provides six illustrative quotations. Murray six, Craigie one and Onions none. Bradley adopts more quotations than the other editors if we consider the number of pages compiled by each editor.[4]

2.4 Illustrative quotations containing the psych-passive + *by*

Through the text-search of the *OED* on CD-ROM, we will be able to find quotations containing the 'psych-passive + *by*' construction used for illustrating other entry words. For instance, we come across the following quotation, which illustrates the word *card*:

> 1876 **Astonished by** an invitation to dinner, which she declines, and then by cards for parties, which she refuses. (*card*, n.)

Many samples containing the construction are retrieved and appropriate examples are obtained after sieving inappropriate ones.[5] There are cases in which the same quotation is cited for the different entry words by two editors.[6] We count them as two examples. There is a quotation in which two psych-verbs are used side by side and this is also counted as two samples.[7]

---

4) The total pages edited by each editor are: Murray 7,207, Bradley 4,590, Craigie 3,242 and Onions 1,395.

5) Inappropriate examples include non-psychological uses (*A man is stunned by a blow with a stick on the head*), inadequate collocations (*Her Majesty hath been . . . pleased, by Writ, to Call [him] to the House of Lords*) or the occurrence of *by* in coordination with the passive of a non-psychological verb (*Small children are likely to be worried and drummed into apathy by dogmatic catechisms*).

6) The following sentence is quoted in two words, *bitter* a. & n. edited by Murray and *sweet* n. edited by Craigie: 1749 Fielding *Tom Jones* iii. vi. Surfeited with the sweets of marriage, or disgusted by its bitters.

The illustrative quotations that we have collected are those of the Late ModE period (1700–1900). This is the period when many prescriptive grammar books were written and a sense of prescriptivism began to emerge and spread throughout British society. It is my assumption that this prescriptivism, or a trait which makes an editor less permissive of non-standard or unacceptable usages, may have influenced the editor's attitude in compiling a dictionary.

The results of the investigation are shown in Appendix I and II. Appendix I is a table which shows the number of illustrative quotations used for each verb by each editor. Appendix II is a list of the illustrative quotations found by the text-search.

Appendix I shows that Murray provides 82 quotations, Bradley 77, Craigie 42 and Onions 16. As the total editing pages differ from editor to editor, the frequency per 1,000 pages for each editor are shown for the sake of fair and easy comparison. Bradley's figure of 77 quotations, or 16.8 quotations per 1,000 pages is by far the higher figure than the figures of the other editors (Murray 11.4, Craigie 13.0, Onions 11.5). It means that Bradley utilized far more illustrative quotations containing the construction than the other editors.

2.5 The psych-passive + *by* used in the definitions

Not only does Bradley adopt many illustrative quotations containing the construction, but he also uses it in defining a word or a phrase. The following are such words or phrases and the definitions written by Bradley.

> *excitement* 2c.: In recent use: The condition of being mentally excited, whether by pleasurable or painful emotion.
> *fear-struck*: struck with or overwhelmed by fear.
> *get over*: to cease to be troubled or surprised by.
> *glad of* (c): joyful account of, delighted or pleased by (an event, a state of things)
> *grimalkined* pa. pple.: (nonce-wd.). vexed by a 'grimalkin'.

---

7) 1859 Much excited and pleased by your accounts of your daughter's engagement. (*engagement* n.)

> *mind* v. 8a.: (Not) to object to, be troubled or annoyed by, dislike (something proposed, something offered to one, etc.)
> *scare* v.3: To take a scare (see scare n.2); to be alarmed by rumours or the like.
> *shade* n. 6c: Orig., in humourous invocation of the spirit of a deceased person, as likely to be horrified or amazed by some action or occurrence.
> *weak* a. & n.: Hence allusively in *weaker brethren* . . . who are in danger of being shocked by extreme statements of principle or policy.

Aside from Bradley's nine examples above, Murray has seven examples, Craigie three and Onions two. Bradley makes the most use of the construction in defining headwords.

What is remarkable is that Bradley seems to make a conscious distinction in the use of the agentive prepositions. Bradley used *with* or *by* in defining the phrase "glad of", depending on the prepositional complement. Let us compare the two definitions of the phrase.

> *glad of* (a): make happy or joyful, delighted or pleased with (an object possessed) (obs.)
> *glad of* (c): joyful account of, delighted or pleased by (an event, a state of things)

Evidently, Bradley thought that the agentive *by* with *delighted* or *pleased* was acceptable if the prepositional complement was "an event" or "a state of things".

From the observations made so far, we now realize that Bradley adopted the largest, if relatively, number of illustrative quotations containing the 'psych-passive + *by*' construction and made the most use of it in defining words. This suggests that Bradley may have been more lenient or permissive of the construction than the other editors.

How can we explain Bradley's lenient and permissive trait? I will propose a hypothesis that Bradley may have been free from the grammatical prescriptivism prevalent in his day and that his editorial attitude may have been influenced by his academic and occupational careers.

Chapter 9

III. Bradley's education and career

3.1 Bradley's education

I argued that Onions' prescriptivism may have come from his academic and career backgrounds. Onions went to university, where he must have studied prescriptive grammar. He worked as a schoolteacher, whose job it was to teach prescriptive grammar to his pupils. Later he wrote a grammar book with a number of prescriptive remarks in it. All these experiences may have ingrained the prescriptivism in Onions, whether he was conscious of it or not.

Bradley's career seems to make a stark contrast to that of Onions (Matsunami et al. 1995: 1101; Sasaki and Kihara, 1990: 32–33). Robert Bridges, a poet laureate and Bradley's friend, describes Bradley's life in his memoir dedicated to the posthumous collection of Bradley's papers (1928: 3–56). The following brief summary of Bradley's early and later life is based on Bridges' memoir.

Born in 1845 to the gentle and genial parents of John and Mary Bradley, Henry was a very precocious child and started going to Chesterfield Grammar School in Derbyshire in 1855. Thanks to "his superior mental gifts, his gentle manners, his patience, his modesty . . .", Bradley was well-liked and worshipped by boys. He obtained "the mass of his information" through "his inordinate love of reading" and was praised for "the excellence of his essays." His old notebooks show that "he was reading Homer, Virgil, Sallust, and the Hebrew Old Testament at the same time." Bradley left school because his master, the Reverend Frederick Calder "advised his leaving, since there was nothing more that he could learn in class." He spent the next couple of years as a tutor, teaching and living together with a physically delicate son of an affluent physician at a farm-house in the moors he had built for his son. After this tutoring post, Bradley got a similar tutorship position with another physician's son.

3.2 Bradley's learning while working as a corresponding clerk

Due to poor health, Bradley abandoned the hope of studying at university, and began to work as corresponding clerk to Messrs Taylor, an exporting cutlery firm in Sheffield at the age of eighteen. During his twenty years at this firm, he was engaged in the work of corresponding with foreign clients. For the sake of occupational need and for his own interest he learnt many languages and was versed in them: classical languages like Latin and Greek as well as modern languages like German, French, Spanish and even Hebrew. Henry Bradley was a self-taught scholar, just as James Murray was.[8]

Bradley preoccupied himself in academic and scholarly activities and contributed philological articles to the local *Sheffield Independent* newspaper[9] and he also read papers at the Philological Society.

3.3 Editor of the *OED*

In December of 1883, after he had been disengaged from the job at the cutlery firm,[10] Bradley went to London with his family to make a living and partly to improve his wife's health. Was it because Fortune smiled on him that the first fascicle (*A–Ant*) of the *OED* (then the *New English Dictionary*) was published in January of 1884? Bradley was asked to write a review of the fascicle by James S. Cotton, Editor of *The Academy*, a weekly literary journal. Elisabeth Murray, a granddaughter of James Murray and the author of Murray's biography (1977: 234), lauds Bradley as follows:

> In England, there were few scholars qualified to appreciate the work, but Henry Bradley, the future co-editor of the Dictionary . . .

E. Murray (1977: 234) introduces the Bradley's assessment of the fascicle as in the following:

> if the level of excellence reached in this opening part be sustained throughout, the completed work will be an achievement without parallel in the lexicography of any living language. (*The Academy*, 16 February, 1884)

---

8) Winchester says (2002: 149) that "Bradley's life and career . . . was in many respects rather like Murray's (except that Bradley had had far better than a Scottish village education)".
9) From *Hollamshire Worthies*. This is *Who's Who* in South Yorkshire.
10) "The business-house that he was serving gave him notice that their foreign trade could no longer support a special agent, and that they must therefore reluctantly dismiss him with the honorarium of six months' pay . . . " (Bridges, 1828: 12)

This review that Bradley wrote on an unopened moving package caught the eye of James Murray and he "got in touch with Bradley and began consulting on etymological problems"[11] (E. Murray, ibid.). Murray came to realize Bradley's gift and talent in languages and lexicography and invited him to join the editorial staff when Bradley "asked whether there might be work for him on the Dictionary staff" (E. Murray, ibid.).

After working for several years as an assistant editor to Murray, Bradley was "acknowledged as Joint Editor in 1888, responsible for his own sections" (Bridges, 1928: 15). Bradley became Chief Editor on the death of James Murray in 1915 and his editorship continued till his death in 1923. The total pages that Bradley edited amounted to 4,590 pages, next to Murray's 7,207 pages. Bradley had been eclipsed by James Murray but his dedication and achievement should have been given more credit and recognition. The compilation of the dictionary may have taken a different course if he had not written the review of the first fascicle and had not joined the editorial staff in 1885.

IV. Bradley's philosophy on language

4.1 Freedom from prescriptivism

As already noted, Bradley did not attend university and worked at a cutlery firm from his late teens. At such a young age, a person would be likely to be affected by the worldly circumstances surrounding him. Bradley must have been constantly exposed to Yorkshire dialect or non-standard English of the people working and associating with him. He may have developed a sense of leniency or permissiveness for non-standard or sub-standard English usages. When corresponding with foreign clients, Bradley may have encountered foreigners' unacceptable or ungrammatical English. These experiences in the real world, not a secluded academic society in which an ordinary scholar or lexicographer resides, may have accustomed him to the English usages considered to be non-standard or unacceptable.

---

11) Bradley had written articles on etymology, place names and personal names while he was in Sheffield (Bradley, 1928: 59–124).

Bradley was a self-taught scholar and may have been distant from the grammatical prescriptivism that had been dominant at that time. He did not have a formal higher education nor did he experience a career of a school-teacher, which may have made a prescriptive scholar out of Onions.

4.2 Bradley's view on language change

Bradley published a renowned book on the history of the English language, *The Making of English*, in 1904 when he was sixty. It was the same year when Onions published his book, *An Advanced English Syntax*. Unlike Onions' grammar book, which contains a number of prescriptive comments, Bradley considers language change as the shift from non-standard to standard usage. He seems to think of the decline of standard usages as something natural or inevitable in the history of a language.

The following descriptions in the book, for instance, illustrate how Bradley views the English language and language change.

> Except for a few irregular plurals, all modern English substantives are declined with the endings (written -'s and -es or -s) which descend from the Old English -es and -as. Now this is obviously an instance of the famous principle of 'survival of the fittest.' (pp. 35–36)
> A considerable amount of new grammatical material has been introduced, to serve the needs of expression in cases where the old machinery has become inefficient through phonetic change and other causes, or where it was from the beginning inadequate for its purpose. (p. 53)
> The analogous passive forms, as in 'the house is being built', 'he was being taught to ride', were hardly known till near the end of the eighteenth century, and long afterwards they were condemned by sticklers for grammatical correctness. Yet the innovation was clearly needed . . . the language has found means for representing shades of signification which had previously no accurate expression. (p.70)

The description about morphology on pp. 35–36 says that the principle of "survival of the fittest" applies to language change. It is intended to mean that non-standard expressions would survive to become a standard usage if they should fit the actual linguistic situation of a society in which the language is spoken. The description on p. 53 indicates that a new usage would be born to replace a certain standard usage if it should become inappropriate or outdated. The description about the passive progressive on p.70 seems to be intended to ridicule the grammarians who obstinately stick to the prescriptive rules. It seems that Bradley was not a type of scholar who possessed or adhered to grammatical prescriptivism. Rather, he may have developed an inclination or trait for descriptivism and try to describe linguistic phenomena as they are.

4.3 Slang as a legitimate usage

Bradley's tolerance or permissiveness for non- or sub-standard English seems to be illustrated by his interest in slangs, or non-standard words or phrases associated with a particular context or society. He contributed an article titled "Slang" to *Encyclopaedia Britanica* (1910, Vol. xxv: 207–10). Generally speaking, slangs are supposed to lie at the periphery of a language and they have been treated as if they were illegitimate and even disdained with contemptible eyes (Baugh, 1935: §225). Bradley, however, considers slangs as a legitimate element of a language and analyzes them as an appropriate object of language science in his 5,000-word article.

Although slangs are non-standard vocabulary or expressions, some of them are said to have entered standard vocabulary (Bradley 1904: 175; 1928: 154–5). Bradley treats slangs in the framework of language change from non-standard to standard. Judging from his attitude toward slangs, Bradley did not seem to harbor any prejudices against non-standard or unacceptable usages; rather he seems to have permissiveness and understanding toward it. Bradley's distance from grammatical prescriptivism or his trait of descriptivism to accept illegitimate or unacceptable usages may have had an influence on his editing of the *OED* in adopting illustrative quotations and defining words.

4.4 How prescriptive or descriptive are other editors?

It might be better to know whether other editors are prescriptive or descriptive. Murray (1837–1915) was another self-taught scholar and had a career as a schoolteacher for many years (Sasaki and Kihara, 1995; 247–48).

Having been a schoolteacher and a man of a generation earlier than the younger editors may lead to the low figure of 11.4 in the use of the construction.

Craigie (1867–1957) was a university-educated scholar but he had no experience as a schoolteacher. He was a scholar of the Scandinavian languages (Sasaki and Kihara, 1995; 60) and it may have made him less interested in prescriptivism. Whether this may be the reason or not, Craigie makes a reference to the *by*-agent in the definition of the verb *nettle*.[12] These factors may lead to his figure of 13.0, slightly higher than that of Murray or Onions.

Robert Burchfield (1923–2004) is the editor of *Supplement to the OED* (1972–86). Burchfield is not the object of our present analysis,[13] but he is said to exhibit less prescriptivism and more descriptivism in editing the third edition of *Fowler's Modern English Usage* (1996). This book has been reputed to be an authority of English usages for many years. Usage books like Fowler's provide prescriptive statements as to whether a certain word or a phrase is appropriate or not. When one is at a loss which to use, for instance, *will* or *shall*, *to not go* or *not to go*, and so on, one can resort to these books for guidance for a proper usage. Burchfield seems to be descriptive in editing this book at the expense of being prescriptive. He is criticized by the book's reviewers for his "permissive stance" or "passive acceptance of the misuses" (Horobin, 2016: 53). A lexicographer could be prescriptive or descriptive, depending on their backgrounds or personal characteristics.

V. Dr. Johnson's characteristic way of editing

Lexicographers must be attempting to achieve a scientific and objective way of editing a dictionary. However, it seems inevitable that their personal dispositions or characteristics may affect the way of editing and as a result, dictionary editing may become a subjective endeavor.

---

12) *nettle* v.2b. In *pa. pple.* Irritated, vexed, provoked, annoyed. Const. *at*, *by*, *with*, etc.
13) An analysis of his editing may not necessarily bring forth an appropriate comparison with other editors. This is because a large time lag exists and there has been a subsequent change in English, that is, the increase of the agentive *by* with psych-passives.

Chapter 9

Lexicographers have their own academic careers and scholarly experiences. Different careers and experiences may lead to their own views of what a language is and their own ideas of what a dictionary should be like. It may result in their distinctive and characteristic way of editing a dictionary.

Samuel Johnson (1709–1784), for instance, is well-known to be subjective or even eccentric in the way of defining words in his dictionary, *A Dictionary of the English Language* (1755).[14] First of all, there are words whose "definitions reflect Johnson's disposition" (Hayashi, 1968: 1). The definition of a "lexicographer" is shown in the introductory anecdote of the previous chapter. Another famous definition is "oats", which are defined as "a grain, which in England is generally given to horses, but in Scotland supports the people." It is said to show Johnson's dislike of Scotland.

As for illustrative quotations, Johnson, utilizing his proper judgments based on his own philosophy and learning, is said to have determined which quotation to adopt. Of course he adopts such quotations as would best and most properly illustrate the entry words, but Johnson supposedly made it a rule to collect and utilize such quotations as to be a model or an exemplar in various fields of learning and literature. Furthermore, according to Boswell, who wrote Johnson's biography as his dedicated admirer, Johnson did not adopt the sentences of the writers which may harm and endanger religious minds and morality (Imazato and Tsuchiya, 1985: 61). It is in the fourth edition (1773), the virtually revised edition, that this is typically represented.

In the fourth edition, the quotations of religious flavor are adopted in large numbers. The Bible is a source of many quotations throughout the first and second volumes of the fourth edition and so are the quotations from the seventeenth-century advocates of the Anglican Church or the Royalists who were opposed to the Puritans (Reddick, 1990:141–42). Let us show some quotations.

O Lord, make haste to *help* me. *Psalms* (HELP, v. a. "1. To assist; to support; to aid.")

---

14) This is said to be the best and most important dictionary before the publication of the *OED*. Dr. Johnson compiled the dictionary all by himself with an assistance of several sub-editors. It records 40,000 entry words and contains 110,000 illustrative quotations.

181

God *himself* is with us for our captain. *Chron.* (HIMSELF, pron. "2. It is added to a personal pronoun or noun, by way of emphatical discrimination.") (Reddick: 141)

To illustrate *help* or *himself*, these quotations do not seem to be linguistically optimal or the most appropriate quotations, nor do they seem to be essential to illustrate these words. It seems that they are adopted simply for the sake of "quoting from the Bible." Any quotations from the Bible might have served Johnson's purpose and intention.

I have argued that a lexicographer can be subjective or even idiosyncratic in the way of editing a dictionary and my argument may be substantiated by examining the way Dr. Johnson edited his dictionary.[15]

VI. Summary

This chapter attempts to clarify how Henry Bradley, the second editor of the *OED*, treated the 'psych-passive + *by*' construction in defining words and adopting illustrative quotations. Psych-passives are supposed to be occurring with prepositions other than *by*, but we have seen an increasing use of *by* in Present-day English. In the latter part of the Late ModE period, when the *OED* was being compiled, psych-passives with the agentive *by* were not necessarily recognized to be an acceptable and legitimate usage. In spite of that, we find them used in defining words and their illustrative quotations adopted by the *OED* editors.

Bradley is the editor who made the most of the construction of the four editors. Why is this? My assumption is that Bradley was free from grammatical prescriptivism, which was prevalent then and may have caused Onions to hesitate to accept with the agentive *by* with the passive of *surprise* as a legitimate usage. Bradley's freedom from it may have contributed to his rather ample employment of such unacceptable usage as the 'psych-passive

---

15) The subjective or idiosyncratic way of editing may be true of present-day dictionaries as Horobin (2016: 68) says, "*Urban Dictionary*'s contributions frequently reflect the subjective bias and personal prejudices of its users."

+ *by*' construction.

Bradley did not go to university and worked as a corresponding clerk at a cutlery firm in Sheffield from his late teens for twenty years. Bradley was a self-taught scholar; he taught himself languages and philology. Without university education nor a career as a schoolteacher, his exposure to the real world may have distanced himself from academic snobbishness and may have failed to imbue the prescriptivism in him. Instead, he may have developed a sense of descriptivism in treating various linguistic phenomena. His estrangement from prescriptivism and his familiarity with descriptivism may have been responsible for his leniency and permissiveness toward non-standard or unacceptable usages like the construction in question.

A lexicographer's editorial attitude can be affected by his personal dispositions as well as by his academic or career backgrounds. It can be seen in Samuel Johnson's editing his dictionary. Some of his definitions are famous for being subjective or even eccentric. The illustrative quotations are chosen from his own viewpoint of morality and his religious faith. The editor's scholarship and philosophy on language and lexicography, together with his personal disposition, may affect the way a dictionary is compiled. The same may have been true of the *OED* and its editors when they faced the treatment of the psych-passives and the agentive prepositions. It would be little wonder if Bradley had had a good mind to use the 'psych-passive + *by*' construction in defining entry words and adopting the quotations containing it.

Appendix I

Number of quotations with the psych-passive + *by* in the *OED*

	Murray	Bradley	Craigie	Onions
alarm	6	5	3	2
amaze	2	1	0	0
amuse	2	2	2	1
annoy	6	4	2	1
astonish	1	1	0	0
bewilder	3	2	1	1
bother	1	0	0	1
chagrin	1	0	0	1
charm	2	3	2	0
confuse	2	1	0	1
deject	2	1	0	0
delight	0	1	0	0
depress	1	0	1	0
disappoint	2	1	2	0
disgust	4	1	2	2
dismay	1	0	0	0
displease	1	0	0	0
enchant	1	1	0	0
excite	2	3	2	0
fascinate	1	1	0	0
frighten	5	10	2	0
grieve	4	3	0	0
interest	1	1	1	1
offend	3	1	0	0
overwhelm	0	2	0	0
perplex	2	0	2	1
please	0	3	0	1
puzzle	1	0	0	2
rejoice	1	0	0	0
satisfy	2	1	1	0
scare	4	4	2	1

shock	2	1	2	0
startle	6	8	4	0
stun	2	3	1	0
surprise	3	8	5	0
terrify	2	1	4	0
vex	3	1	0	0
worry	0	2	1	0
Total	82	77	42	16
per 1,000 pages	11.4	16.8	13.0	11.5
Total pages	7,207	4,590	3,242	1,396

Appendix II

Illustrative quotations with the 'psych-passive + *by*' construction in the *OED* (The number in parentheses is the frequency of occurrence of the construction. The word in parentheses is the headword and its part of speech)

alarm (16)

a1716 Alarmed by an experience of the baseness, and the exceptiousness of men. (*exceptious*, a.); 1791 They were alarmed ... by the tramping of horses near the abbey. (*tramp*, v.); 1800 The people of the vale had been a good deal alarmed by the appearance of that unaccountable being water-horse. (*water-horse*, n.); 1851 You will not be alarmed by my use of pruning-knife. (*prunig-knife*, n.); etc.

amaze (3)

1667 The tender tremulous Christian, 'tis easie to discern how much he must be distracted and amaz'd by them. (*tremulous*, a.); 1850 I started first, as some Arcadian, Amazed by goatly God in twilight grove. (*goatly*, a.); 1876 You are amazed by the profusion which is characteristic of Nature. (*profusion*, n.).

amuse (7)

1774 He then placed them in a cage at his chamber window, to be amused by their sportive flutterings. (*sportive*, a.); 1816 Had there been no pain to her friend... in the waverings of Harriet's mind, Emma would have been amused by its variations. (*wavering*, n.); 1858 Amused by a couple of rams butting at each other. (*butt*, v.); 1879 You would be screamingly amused by one. (*screaming*, a.); etc.

annoy (13)

1834 Sadly annoyed he is sometimes by her malapropisms. (*malapropism*, n); 1838 The men, though they affected to call me a poor little creature, squint-eyes, knock-knees, red-head, and so on, were evidently annoyed by my success. (*squint-eye*, n.); 1844 My reception has been so large, that I am not annoyed by receiving this or that superabundantly. (*superabundantly*, ad.); 1876 Washington was annoyed by shoals of selfish importuners. (*importuner*, n.); 1885 We have been greatly annoyed of late by a lot of tin horn gamblers and prostitutes. (*tinhorn*, a.& n.); etc.

astonish (2)

1876 Astonished by an invitation to dinner, which she declines, and then by cards for parties, which she refuses. (*card*, n.2); 1883 Never was more astonished than by Lady Arabella's gaucheness (*gaucheness*, n.).

bewilder (7)

1751 I was bewildered by an unseasonable interrogatory. (*interrogatory*, n.); 1837 Bewildered by long terror, perturbations and guillotinement. (*guillotine* v.); 1855 Bewildered by his own skillful word-juggling. (*word* n.); 1909 The chorus-singers seemed a little bewildered by his batonless movements. (*batonless*, a.); etc.

bother (2)

1846 I really am bothered by this confounded dramatization of the Christmas books. (*dramatization*, n.); 1923 If you are particularly bothered by the proximity of wires, it is worth while to try the effect of substituting a 'capacity earth' for the ordinary earth connection... (*capacity*, n.).

chagrin (2)

1878 Surprised and chagrined by the coldness of her manner. (*chagrin*, v); 1928 Mr. Churchill was deeply chagrined by being compelled to withdraw his proposed kerosene tax. (*kerosene*, n.)

charm (7)

1801 He was... strongly charmed by the sight of a watch-chain and seals.

(*strongly*, ad.); 1849 Men were in no humour to be charmed by the transparent style and melodious numbers of the apostate. (*number*, n.18); 1852 Miss Eva... appeared to be fascinated by her wild diablerie, as a dove is sometimes charmed by a glittering serpent. (*diablerie*, n.);

confuse (4)

1711 She was perfectly confused by meeting something so wistful in all she encountered. (*wistful*, a.); 1822 This man being confused by the pervicaciousness of all. (*pervicacious*, a.); 1857 We were soon confused by numerous logging-paths. (*logging*, n.); etc.

deject (3)

1638 Yet in the meridian of his hopes [he] is dejected by valiant Rustang. (*meridian*, n.); 1712 But how comes it to pass, that we should take delight in being terrified or dejected by a Description (*pass*, n.); etc.

delight (1)

1796 I am extremely delighted by the attentive perusal of musico-philosophical letters. (*musico-*, a.).

depress (2)

1804 We came... amidst rain and wind, and depressed by ill-forebodings. (*depress*, v); 1844 Had he allowed himself to be depressed by every unpleasantry. (*unpleasantry*, n.);

disappoint (5)

1648 [You] might have found yourself as sensibly disappointed by her Grant (*grant*, n); 1688 Greatly disappointed by this loss [of a horse] which was all the Teame he had. (*team*, n); 1880 They were wofully disappointed by the results of their intended sociability. (*sociability*, n.); etc.

disgust (9)

1794 Emily was disgusted by the subservient manners of many persons. (*subservient*, a.); 1840 Very much disgusted by Mr. Elton walking out in the last scene. (*walk*, v.); a1852 In popular governments, men must not... be disgusted by occasional exhibitions of political harlequinism. (*harlequinism*, n.); etc.

dismay (1)

1854 Somewhat dismayed by this specimen of barrack-life. (*barrack*, n.).

displease (1)

1822 I was so displeased by the jookeries of the bailie... (*jokery*, n.).

enchant (2)

1664 The more general Notion of Enchantment, Agrippa defines to be nothing but The conveiance of a certain mirificent power [L. *mirabilis virtus*] into the thing enchanted by virtue of the words and breath of the Enchanter. (†*mirificent*, a.); 1750 We are enchanted by a stupid Kennel of Stock-Jobbers. (*kennel*, n.)

excite (7)

1823 Excited, as he said, by the drollness of the scene. (*droll*, a.); 1858 Excited by... the waggery of his more intellectual neighbours. (*waggery*, n.); 1872 The Dutch were not excited by those visions of American gold and silver. (*vision*, n.); etc.

fascinate (2)

1773 Eyes fascinated by Mammon the god of this world. (*Mammon*, n.); 1852 Miss Eva... appeared to be fascinated by her wild diablerie, as a dove is sometimes charmed by a glittering serpent. (*diablerie*, n.)

frighten (17)

1794 If he supposes I am to be frightened by his pompous accusations, he has much mistaken his man. (*mistake*, v.); 1821 I am not to be frightened by fee, faw, fum. (*fee-faw-fum*, n.); 1856 But if he still delayed his marriage, it was probably... because he was frightened by her denunciations... (*denunciation*, n.); 1879 Let not women be frightened by the scaring name. (*scaring*, a.); 1884 I am not at all frightened by the word 'sectarian'. (*sectarian*, n.); etc.

grieve (7)

1775 By lack whereof, they have been oftentimes touched and grieved by subsidies given. (*lack* n.); 1802 I am more grieved than I can express by a cruel contretemps. (*contretemps*, n.); 1899 Lovers of old London have been grieved by the news that No. 47, Leicester-square... was to be made over to the house-knackers. (*knacker*, n.); etc.

interest (4)

1830 I have been gratified and interested by going over one of the largest manufactories of this place. (*go*, v.); 1861 Albinia had been strongly interested by the touching facts, so untouchingly narrated. (*untouchingly*, ad.); etc.

offend (4)

1829 He dared not contest obstinately against persons of quality, who would be offended by his discourse. (*contest* v.); 1830 I myself am offended by the obtrusion of the new lections into the text. (*lection*, n.); 1842 The Tartars call themselves Turks, and feel highly offended by being called Tartars. (*Tartar*, n.); etc.

overwhelm (2)

1849 Clarendon was overwhelmed by manifold vexations. (*manifold*, a.); 1866 Not only was I myself overwhelmed by these accounts of foreign travel when I was a We, but I noticed. (*we*, pro.).

perplex (5)

1770 Perplexed by sophistries, their honest eloquence rises into action. (*sophistry*, n.); 1869 Perplexed for a moment by the suddenness of the tidings. (*tiding*, n.); a1871 A young person is perplexed by the dissentient judgments. (*dissentient*, a.); etc.

please (4)

1855 His haughty spirit could not be pleased by the subordinate part. (*subordinate*, a.); 1859 Much excited and pleased by your accounts of your daughter's engagement. (*engagement*, n.); etc.

puzzle (3)

1858 Like a schoolmaster puzzle by a hard sum. (*puzzle*, v.); 1928 There is no anti-Britishism here, but I am puzzled by the objection to our being pro-American. (*anti-British*, a.); etc.

rejoice (1)

1858 I have just had cockles of my heart rejoiced by a letter from Lyell (*cockle* n.).

satisfy (4)

a1631 we are sufficiently cleared and satisfied by the Authority of the Holy Spirit of God. (*clear* v.); 1663 I was thereby much satisfied and confirmed by his uptaking of the nature and notion of faith. (*uptaking*, n.); 1701 When a lover becomes satisfied by small compliances without further pursuits. (*pursuit*, n.); etc.

scare (11)

1756 I will not... be scared out of my senses by improbabilities and maybe's. (*maybe*, n.); 1817 Scared by the faith they feigned each priestly slave Knelt for his mercy. (*priestly*, a.); 1845 We are not scared by all this towering indignance. (*indignance*, n.); 1855 It is difficult to believe that a Prince would have been scared by so silly a hoax. (*hoax*, n.); 1901 I was oppressed and scared by the far-reachingness. (*far-reaching*, a.); etc.

shock (5)

1851 Were Peter Damian still upon earth, To be shocked by such ungodly mirth. (*ungodly*, a.); 1871 The young ladies... were unanimously and consentaneously shocked by seeing him talk familiarly to a... governess. (*consentaneously*, ad.);

1881 It has never occurred to him that people would be shocked by seeing him 'tout' at Albany. (tout , v); etc.

startle (18)

1854 I was startled by the loud honking of a goose. (*honk*, v.); 1854 I was startled by something descending, with a great flop, on to my hat. (*flop*, n.); 1856 He was startled by the growing weakness of the ice. (*weakness*, n.); 1865 I have been startled by hearing it urged in sober earnest. (*sober*, a.); 1873 They were startled by an exclamation from Ingran. (*exclamation*, n.); etc.

stun (6)

1786 Stunned by their gibbering. (*gibbering*, n.); 1856 Perfectly be stunned by those insufferable cicale. (*cicala*, n.); 1865 He is only stunned by the unvanquishable difficulty of his existence. (*unvanquishable*, a.); etc.

surprise (16)

1786 At the desert I was very agreeably surprised by the entrance of Sir Richard Jebb, who stayed coffee. (*stay*, v.); 1838 Miss Merton was surprised by the beauty of the young fairy before her. (*fairy* n.); 1845 I was a good deal surprised by finding two species of coral, possessed the power of stinging. (*sting*, v.); etc.

terrify (7)

1658 When thy are most terrified and huspil'd by these Ghosts. (*huspil, -el*, v.); 1712 we should take delight in being terrified or dejected by a Description. (*pass*, n.); 1897 A person had been terrified by hearing the curtains of the bed rustle. (*rustle*, v); etc.

vex (4)

1748 We are to live on at this rate (are we?) vexed by you, and continually watchful about you. (*watchful*, a.); 1873 This young lady . . . was . . . vexed by the incomprehensible conduct of her reputed admirer. (*admirer*, n.); 1890 His order-loving soul was daily vexed by reason of the irregularities. (*order*, n.); etc.

worry (3)

1867 Men when they are worried by fears . . . become suspicious. (*worry*, v); 1869 Young Mr. Blucher was a good deal worried by the constantly changing 'ship time'. (*ship*, n.); 1881 Worried by a severe aunt and a grand-aired cousin. (*grand-aired*, a.)

Chapter 10

Psych-verbs in the past-participle form: Adjectives or passives?

The Strange Case of Dr. Jekyll and Mr. Hyde is an R. L. Stevenson's masterpiece published in 1886. In this novel, one person is represented in such two identities as Dr. Jekyll and Mr. Hyde. They are the same entity but they make a different appearance depending on the situation. This double character may be true of psych-passives we are dealing with: at one time they look like adjectives, and at another time they turn out to be passives. Which is the true self? We will look into this issue in this chapter.

I. Introduction

1.1 Adjectival use

The past-participle form of *surprise* can be considered to be adjectival if it has a static meaning and is followed by the agentive *at*, while it can be taken to be a passive when it is dynamic in meaning and occurs with *by*. It has been claimed by a school of linguists, however, that sentences with psych-verbs in the past-participle form are nothing but adjectives. Advocates of the adjectival theory claim that the following sentence, for instance, is an adjectival sentence, not a passive.

(1) I was astonished by his stupidity/John. (Yasui and Hasegawa, 2000: 9)

Their claim is true to some degree because there exist a number of sentences with adjectival characteristics, as in (2). The examples in (2a) are attributive uses modifying nouns and those in (2b) are used predicatively.

Chapter 10

(2) a. "No–never!" replied the **astonished** Mr. Pickwick. (Dickens, *Pickwick Papers*, 1837); The first **amazed** look that he cast on her, slowly darkened, (Collins, *Hide and Seek*, 1854); etc.
 b. At this discovery she became more **alarmed** than ever, (Dickens, *Barnaby Rudge*, 1841); Sylvia looked **perplexed** at these strange words, (Gaskell, *Sylvia's Lovers*, 1860); and she tried to treat it as a matter of course, but she was not the less **surprised**; (Trollope, *The Warden*, 1855); etc.

As Bailey (1996: 225–6) notes, "The drift of participles toward adjectives ... was well-established before the beginning of the century ... This process of participles becoming adjectives continued to accelerate during the nineteenth century." There is no denying that past-participle forms of psych-verbs may have been functioning as adjectives in increasing numbers but it cannot mean that all the past participles of psych-verbs have become adjectives.

1.2 The definitions in the *OED*

While some psych-passives show adjectival features, there are psych-passives which are to be judged as passives. This observation may be confirmed by the definitions of such typical psych-verbs as *delight, please, shock* and *surprise* in the *OED*.

delight 1. Frequently in *pass*. (const. with *at*, †*in*, or with infin.)
please 4.a. Passive. *To be pleased*. Const. *with*.
shock 4. Often in *passive*.
surprise 5. Often *pass*., const. *at* (†*with*) or inf.

In the definitions, the verbs are shown to be used in the passive. It follows that the *OED* editors decided that these verbs in the past-participle form function as the passives.

I will present evidence in the next section that psych-verbs in the past-participle form are not always adjectives but can be passives.

II. The evidence for the passive

2.1 Active- and passive-voice correspondence

When a psych-verb appears in the active voice and the same verb is used in the past-participle form in the same context, these two sentences are considered to be active and passive pairs. Let us examine the following sentences from Late Modern English.

(3) a. I sat counting the time . . . and waiting to be **startled by** the sight of the gloomy face, whose non-arrival **startled** me every minute. (Dickens, *David Copperfield*, 1850)
b. Its failure never **surprised** me; but I have been **surprised by** the success of Doctor Thorne. (Trollope, *Autobiography*, 1883)

The past-participle forms of *startle* and *surprise* occurring with the agentive *by* ought to be taken to be passive predicates as there are corresponding active sentences within the same context. Active-passive correspondence intended by the authors seems to be obvious. There may have been a consciousness in the minds of the authors that where there was an active sentence with a psych-verb, the sentence with the same psych-verb in the past-participle form was a passive sentence corresponding to the active counterpart.

The sentences in (4) are examples from Present-day English.

(4) a. You know, I'd like to say I was **shocked by** it, but nothing that Miss Ruiz does now **shocks** me. (COCA, Spoken, 2002)
b. "You delved into his personal archives. What **surprised** you the most?" "I was **surprised by** how the — the personal stories translated to what people read in the magazine." (COCA, Spoken, 2017)

In (4a), the verb *shock* is used in the active and passive voice in the same sentence, so the active-passive correspondence is evident. In (4b), the verb *surprise* is used in the active and passive voice in the question-answer sequence, so the correspondence is much more obvious.

Chapter 10

Considering the examples presented above, the sentences with psych-verbs in the past-participle form should be interpreted to be passives when they correspond to the active counterparts lying nearby. There seems to be no way of interpreting them to be adjectives.

2.2 Co-occurrence with a real passive predicate
There are sentences in which the past-participle form of a psych-verb is used in coordination with the passive of other regular verbs. Let us show the sentences taken from the writers of Late Modern English.

(5) They leaped upon their horses and departed, leaving the whole party of Christian spectators **amazed** and **rebuked by** this lesson . . . (Irving, *Captain Bonneville*, 1837); Ralph Nickleby and Gride, **stunned** and **paralyzed by** the awful event which had so suddenly overthrown their schemes . . . (Dickens, *Nicholas Nickleby*, 1838–39); Why should she be **shocked** or **warned by** this reiteration? (Dickens, *Hard Times*, 1854)

In (5), the past-participle forms of *amaze*, *stun* and *shock* are used in coordination with the past participle forms of such verbs as *rebuke*, *paralyze* and *warn*, respectively. *Rebuke*, *paralyze* and *warn* are all non-psychological verbs and therefore their past-participle forms are nothing but passives. Since the past participles of *amaze*, *stun* and *shock* are coordinated with these passives, the psychological predicates must be judged to be passives as well.

The same holds true of the sentences from Present-day English in (6).

(6) But on the other hand, we were **inspired** and **amazed by** what happened afterward. (COCA, Magazine, 2017); The Iowa farm boy had been **shucked** and **shocked by** Sunset. (COCA, Spoken, 2012)

Inspired and *shucked* are the passive predicates of non-psychological verbs. The past participles of *amaze* and *shock* are used in coordination with the passives of these verbs, the psych-verbs are to be judged as passives as well. This offers further evidence that the past-participle forms of psych-verbs are not always adjectives, but they can also be passives.

2.3 The occurrence with *that*-clauses and *to*-infinitives

To identify the characteristics of psych-passives whether they act more like adjectives or passives, let us examine how they occur with *that*-clauses or *to*-infinitives. The occurrence with these clauses suggests that the predicates are behaving as adjectives as some grammarians (Quirk et al.,1985: 1227–28; Biber et al. 1999: 618,718) describe them as "participial adjectives".

The examples of psych-passives taking these clauses are collected from the BNC and the COHA (1970–2010). Let us show some examples.

(7) Greene is **amazed that** people still think of California as an endless job market. (BNC, Magazine, 1973); I'm **astonished that** she consented to marry an American. (COHA, Fiction, 2005); He was too **shocked to** give any account of what had happened. (BNC, News, 1985); Valerian is too **stunned to** speak. (COHA, Movie Script, 1981); etc.

Figure 1 below shows the frequency of occurrence of psych-passives occurring with the clauses except for *surprise*.[1]

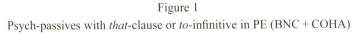

Figure 1
Psych-passives with *that*-clause or *to*-infinitive in PE (BNC + COHA)

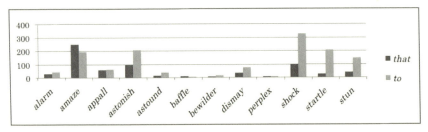

Some verbs in their past participles have a strong tendency to occur with *that*-clauses or *to*-infinitives. To occur with these clauses is sure to be a sign

---

1) *Surprise* shows such an unproportionally large number of occurrences: 895 times with *that*-clauses and 1,840 times with *to*-infinitives. It is nearly seven times larger than the second and third largest *amaze* or *shock* and may dwarf the graphs, so it is excluded from this chart. Without a doubt, however, *surprise* has the stronger adjectival characteristics than other psych-verbs.

of adjectival characteristics as mentioned above. Biber et al. (1999: 530, 672, 718) list *alarmed, amazed, astonished, shocked* and *surprised* as the examples of adjectival predicates.

Verbs like *baffle, bewilder* and *perplex*, on the other hand, occur with these clauses very rarely or hardly at all. It shows that their past participles are not likely to behave as adjectives. Not occurring with *that*-clauses or *to*-infinitives may be synchronizing with their tendency not to occur with the agentive *at*, but to occur chiefly with *by*, an indication that the psych-passives are acting as passives. Biber et al. (1999) do not include their past participles as adjectival predicates.

We may be able to conclude that some psych-passives, which rarely or hardly occur with *that*-clauses or *to*-infinitives, are not adjectival, but they are more likely to be acting as passives.

III. Passives as well as adjectives

From the observations and the arguments we have made so far, a conclusion may be drawn that sentences with psych-verbs in the past-participle form are not always adjectival sentences, but they can be passives, especially when they are accompanied by the agentive *by* and when the prepositional complement is dynamic in meaning.

Epitomizing the adjectival theory, Yasui and Hasegawa (2000: 8–11, 66) enumerate adjectival features of the construction and present their arguments to substantiate their theory. They seem to overlook the fact, however, that there are cases where psych-verbs in the past-participle form have the obvious features of the passive, as we have seen in the previous section.

They also seem to be oblivious to the real linguistic situation. They say that the frequency of occurrence of the 'psych-passives + *by*' construction is not very high (ibid., 10). Their claim, however, may be called in to question as we have shown an abundance of examples, where the agentive *by* has been used with psych-passives in increasing numbers.

Psych-verbs are not the monolithic group of verbs. The adjectival advocates seem to take into consideration only the verbs which show the adjectival characteristics (e.g. *amaze, astonish, surprise*) and overlook the behaviors of the verbs which act like passives by mainly taking the *by*-agent and hardly occurring with *that*-clauses or *to*-infinitives (e.g. *baffle, bewilder, perplex*).

My view that psych-passives are not always adjectival may be supported by Fukumura's (1965, 1998²: 179) following remarks:

> Psychological verbs containing unpleasant feelings may involve passivity. It cannot be said that psychological verbs in the form of passive do not subsume passivity at all.

Nevertheless, psych-passives and adjectival constructions are sometimes difficult to distinguish as we discussed in Chapter 2. We cited Denison (1998: 229) and Huddleston and Pullum (2002: 1436), who use the terminology "adjectival passives" (vs. "verbal passives") to refer to the psych-passives with adjectival features and this may be an appropriate concession.

IV. Summary

Psych-verbs in the past-participle form, or psych-passives, take the structure of the passive but they may function as adjectives as well as passives, depending on the connotation involved and the agentive preposition they occur with. As mentioned previously, however, there is a school of linguists who claim that psych-verbs in the past-participle form are nothing but adjectives. Of course, there are many cases where the sentences of this construction behave as adjectives but there also are plenty of instances which act as passives.

I have presented evidence which may serve as counter-arguments to that claim. First, there are examples in which a sentence with a psych-verb in the active and the corresponding passive sentence exist side by side in the same context. When there is the obvious active and passive correspondence, the psych-passive predicate must be judged to be a passive, not as an adjective.

Secondly, there are examples where the past-participle forms of a psych-verb and a regular verb are used in coordination. Since the past-participle form of the regular verb is a true passive, the psych-verb counterpart must be taken to be a passive as well.

Thirdly, the past-participle forms of such verbs as *amaze, astonish, shock* and *surprise* have a strong tendency to occur with *that*-clauses and *to*-infinitives, a sign that they are functioning as adjectival predicates. On the other hand, verbs like *baffle, bewilder* and *perplex* very rarely or hardly occur with these clauses. Not occurring with them would mean that they do not function as adjectival predicates. Their occurring almost exclusively with the *by*-agent is conversely a sign that they are behaving as passives. Psych-verbs of the *surprise* group are not monolithic and some of them have a strong ten-dency to act as passives, hardly showing any characteristics of adjectives.

I have shown a number of examples which would constitute counter-arguments to the adjectival theory. In the final analysis, the past participles of psych-verbs can be passives as well as adjectives, just like many scholars have claimed in their grammar and usage books.

Chapter 11

Concluding remarks

In concluding this book, allow me to introduce the title of another Shakespearean play, *All's Well That Ends Well*. Actually, this is not the phrase coined by Shakespeare himself, but it seems to have existed as a proverb since the Middle Ages. Shakespeare may have borrowed it from a book of proverbs published in the 16th century. Whatever the origin, this seems to be an eternal axiom and I hope I shall be able to end this last chapter like the title of this play.

It seems generally acknowledged that a scholar's mission is in pursuit of academic truths and if the scholar is a philologist or a linguist, he is expected to discover new facts about a language and if possible, he should be able to uncover some linguistic principles or rules hidden in linguistic phenomena. I am pleased to say that some achievements have been made in that a number of new facts have been discovered and presented in the previous chapters. Hopefully, some principles of language have also been uncovered and visibly presented to the readers.

We have seen various aspects of psych-verbs in the passive form and the agentive prepositions they have occurred with from a historical perspective. Let us summarize some interesting and even amazing facts we have found out. The following are the conclusive comments that can be made about what we have explored.

Chapter 1 clarified the frequency of occurrence of the agentive prepositions *at* and *by* with the passive of *surprise*. The occurrence rate of *by*, being roughly one-fourth of that of *at* in Late ModE, has surpassed considerably that of *at* in PE; in fact *by* may be occurring nearly twice as frequently as *at* in the most recent decade.

Chapter 2 examined the determining factors for the choice of *at* or *by* with the passive of *surprise* in PE. There seems to be a certain tendency in the choice and some of the characteristics are: *at* occurs with *how*-clauses, in a near-idiomatic expression as *I'm surprised at you!* and with reflexive pronouns, while *by* tends to be used with such complements as abstract nouns, pronouns like *that, this* or *any* in spoken English and in journalism and legal English.

Chapter 3 revealed how the passives of psych-verbs synonymous to *surprise* behave with agentive prepositions from Early ModE to PE. The psych-verbs after being examined turn out not to be monolithic in their behavior: some verbs tend to occur with *at*, some are likely to occur with *by* and others occur with *at* and *by* more or less equally. In PE, *by* occurs nearly twice as frequently as *at* despite the occurrence rate of them being almost equal in Late ModE. The increasing use of the *by*-agent possibly acts as a presage that the dominance of *by* may be taking place with the psych-passives just as the agentive *by* had become the chief agentive preposition with the English passives in general several centuries earlier.

Chapter 4 dealt with the English of Charles Dickens, who preferred to use *by* with the psych-passives. The novelist used *at* and *by* with the passive of *surprise* in almost equal numbers in his major novels and this is an unusual rate compared to his contemporary writers. Moreover, Dickens apparently replaced *at* with *by* in his later novels. The choice of *at* or *by* seems to depend partly on style, *at* in speech and *by* in narrative. Dickens preferred to use *by* with other psych-passives as well. His unusual preference for *by* may be attributed to his innovative writing style. A great writer like Dickens may help a new usage to be accepted and established in society.

Chapter 5 was an attempt to clarify the semantic shift of the 'psych-passive + *by*' construction from physical to psychological. At the 'intermediate' stage, psych-verbs carried physical or physiological meanings as well as psychological and they occurred with the *by*-agent, so the construction should be taken to be the passive. The occurrence of *by* at this stage may have induced it to occur with the psychological use as well.

Chapters 6 and 7 examined how and why the decrease of gerunds and the increase of *how*-clauses with psych-passives have been taking place. Gerunds are observed to have been declining considerably from Late ModE to PE, contrary to the general idea that they are gaining ground in some environments. Their decline may be explained by the replacement of them with *to*-infinitives, or *that*- or *how*-clauses partly to eradicate ambiguity inherent in gerunds.

A rapid increase of *how*-clauses with psych-passives with or without a preposition has been seen in PE, especially in the recent few decades. There may be stylistic reasons involved in the choice of the *how*-clause or the *by* + *how*-clause. The increase of *how*-clauses with a preposition may have occurred by analogy with *what*-clauses already existent in the earlier period. It may also have occurred through the replacement of *the way*-clauses or *the N with which*-clauses with *how*-clauses to achieve more lucid and plain style plus an exclamatory effect.

Chapters 8 and 9 attempted to explore how the *OED* editors treated agentive prepositions occurring with the passives of *surprise* and other psych-verbs. Onions may have been prescriptive, while Bradley seems to have been more descriptive than prescriptive. This editorial difference may have led to Onions' apparent disregard of *by* in the definition of *surprise* and Bradley's employment of the 'psych-passive + *by*' construction in defining some entry words. It may also explain Bradley's adoption of illustrative quotations containing the construction for other entries more than the other editors. The difference in their editorial attitudes may come from the difference of their academic and career backgrounds, as well as their personal dispositions. This may be confirmed by the examination of the way that Dr. Johnson edited his well-known dictionary.

Chapter 10 dealt with the issue whether the past-participle forms of psych-verbs are adjectives or passives. Although there has been the claim by one school of linguists that they are nothing but adjectives, I presented evidence to refute their claim. First, there are abundant examples of an obvious active-passive correspondence. Secondly, the coordination of the past participle forms of a psych-verb and a regular verb is an obvious indication that the psych-verb is used as a passive. Thirdly, the past participles of *baffle*, *bewilder* or *perplex*, which rarely occur with *that*-clauses or *to*-infinitives, do not seem to function as adjectival predicates.

Chapter 11

The theme I have treated in this book is language change. A language changes with time. No language can escape from the force of change. Natural or innate changes may take place when children invent a new way of saying things. Chaucer makes a child utter the following sentence with a *do*-periphrasis, a novel usage in his day: *Fader, why do ye wepe?* (*Monk's Tale*: 2334).

Drastic changes that could alter the face of a language can also happen. They are often triggered by the big change of the society or the transformation of its culture. It will be evident if we consider what happened in the English language after the Danish Invasions or the Norman Conquest, the Renaissance or the Reformation.

Another kind of language change may be conceivable. It is something that can be instigated by an individual person. Let us imagine a situation in which a language change may be caused through the influence of a great individual in a society. A novelist's idiosyncratic usage or style, for instance, may become an established one through the imitation of it by ordinary people. When it has been adopted by the whole society, it will eventually become a part of the language. Milroy's following statement (1992: 221) shows how an innovative expression will become an established usage:

> an innovation in a speaker's output is not a linguistic change until it has been agreed on and adopted by some community of speakers.

This is not a change that only happens in English but it may be seen in other languages. Soseki Natsume (1867–1916), a novelist during the Meiji Era of Japan, is credited with transforming the Japanese language from the old, feudalistic tongue to the modern language through his innovative writing style in his novels.

Grammarians or lexicographers may have their share of contributing to the development of a language. They may be an instigator of language change or a conservative keeper of its stability. Some scholars describe the changing usages and by doing so, make them acceptable and legitimate. Others could fix a language by writing a prescription of what should be appropriate usages. Language is not an autonomous entity but it is something that would develop through the interaction of the people in the society where they live. When we deal with a language or language change, would it not be necessary to consider the people who use it or the society in which they live?

This research started out of sheer curiosity to find out how the agentive *by* has been occurring with the passive of *surprise* in Present-day English. That was nearly twenty years ago. With some intermission periods, I kept conducting research and writing articles without any intention of making the results into the form of a book. I am pleased with and humbly proud of having made the outcome of the two decades into something whole and complete.

I am now convinced that a trivial interest or curiosity could turn itself into a decent academic subject, to be explored as seriously and earnestly as any important academic themes. Many of the Japanese Nobel laureates invariably seem to say that their curiosity or inquisitiveness eventually led to the award of the prize after many years of strenuous research. A simple and even naïve curiosity could yield an achievement like this book, a humble and modest one as it may be. Hopefully, this book born out of a mere curiosity will be useful and beneficial to those who have a keen interest in the structure and function of English and its historical development.

Bibliography

Aijmer, Karin and Bengt Altenberg ed. 1991. *English Corpus Linguistics*. Harlow: Longman.
Aston, Guy and Lou Burnard. 1998. *The BNC Handbook: Exploring the British National Corpus with Sara*. Edinburgh: Edinburgh University Press.
Bailey, Richard W. 1996. *Nineteenth-Century English*. Ann Arbor: The University of Michigan Press.
Barber, Charles. 1993. *The English Language: A Historical Introduction*. Cambridge: Cambridge University Press.
Baugh, Albert C. 1935. *A History of the English Language*. London and New York: D. Appleton-Century.
Benson, Larry D. ed. 1987. *The Riverside Chaucer*. 3rd. Boston: Houghton Mifflin.
Biber, Douglas, Susan Conrad and Randi Reppen. 1998. *Corpus Linguistics*. Cambridge: Cambridge University Press.
Biber, Douglas, Johansson Stig, Geoffrey Leech, Susan Conrad and Edward Finegan. 1999. *Longman Grammar of Spoken and Written English*. Harlow: Longman.
Blake, N. F. 1981. *Non-standard Language in English Literature*. London: André Deutsch.
Blake, N. F. 1996. *A History of the English Language*. London: Macmillan.
Boswell, James. 1791. *The Life of Samuel Johnson, LL.D*. London: Henry Baldwin. Knopf [Everyman], New York, 1992.
Bradley, Henry. 1904. *The Making of English*. London: Macmillan.
Bradley, Henry. 1928. *The Collected Papers of Henry Bradley*. Oxford: Clarendon Press.
Bridges, Robert. 1928. "A Memoir of Henry Bradley", in Henry Bradley. 1928.
Brook, G. L. 1970. *The Language of Dickens*. London: André Deutsch.
Burchfield, Robert ed. 1972–86. *Supplement to the Oxford English Dictionary*, 4 vols. Oxford: Clarendon Press.
Burchfield, Robert ed. 1996. *The New Fowler's Modern English Usage*. Oxford: Oxford University Press.
Cawley, A. C. ed. 1958. *The Canterbury Tales*. London: Dent. [Everyman] Reprint, 1992.
Chapman, R. W. ed., 1964. *Jane Austen's Letters: to Her Sister Casandra and Others*. Oxford: Oxford University Press.

Close, R. A. 1975. *A Reference Grammar for Students of English*. Harlow: Longman.
Coghill, Nevill. tr. 1951. *Geoffrey Chaucer: The Canterbury Tales*. London: Penguin Books. Reprint with revisions, 2003.
Crystal, David and Derek Davy. 1969. *Investigating English Style*. London: Longman.
Crystal, David. 1995. *The Cambridge Encyclopedia of the English Language*. Cambridge: Cambridge University Press.
Curme, George O. 1931. *A Grammar of the English Language*. Vol. II: *Syntax*. Boston: D. C. Heath. Reprinted by Verbatim, Essex, Connecticut, 1977.
Davies, Mark. 2012. "Expanding horizons in historical linguistics with the 400-million word Corpus of Historical American English". *Corpora*, Vol. 7 (2). Edinburgh: Edinburgh University Press. 121–157.
Declerk, R. 1991. *A Comprehensive Descriptive Grammar*. Tokyo: Kaitakusha.
Denison, David. 1998. "Syntax", in *The Cambridge History of the English Language*, Vol. 4. ed. by Suzanne Romaine. Cambridge: Cambridge University Press.
Evans, G. Blakemore. ed. 1974. *The Riverside Shakespeare*. Boston: Houghton Mifflin.
Fergusson, Rosalind. ed. 1992. *The Penguin Dictionary of English Synonyms and Antonyms*. Revised. London: Penguin Books.
Fischer, Andreas. 1997. "The *Oxford English Dictionary* on CD-ROM as a historical corpus: *To wed* and *to marry* revisited", in *From Ælfric to the New York Times: Studies in English Corpus Linguistics* ed. by Udo Fries, Viviane Müller and Peter Schneider. Amsterdam: Rodopi. 161–172.
Foster, Brian. 1968. *The Changing English Language*. London: Macmillan.
Golding, Robert. 1985. *Idiolects in Dickens*. London: Macmillan.
Gordon, Ian A. 1966. *The Movement of English Prose*. Harlow: Longman.
Gowers, Sir Ernest. 1973. *The Complete Plain Words*. Revised by Bruce D. Fraser. London: Penguin Books.
Hitchings, Henry. 2005. *Dr. Johnson's Dictionary: The Book that Defined the World*. London: John Murray.
Hori, Masahiro. 2004. *Investigating Dickens' Style: A Collocational Analysis*. London: Palgrave and Macmillan.
Hornby, A. S. 2005[7]. *Oxford Advanced Learner's Dictionary of Current English*. 7th edition. Oxford: Oxford University Press.
Horobin, Simon. 2016. *How English Became English: A Short History of a Global Language*. Oxford: Oxford University Press.
Huddleston, Rodney and Geoffrey K. Pullum. 2002. *The Cambridge Grammar*

of the English Language. Cambridge: Cambridge University Press.
Hughes, Geoffrey. 1988. *Words in Time: A Social History of English Vocabulary*. Oxford: Blackwell.
Hughes, Geoffrey. 2000. *A History of English Words*. Oxford: Blackwell.
Jespersen, Otto. 1909–49. *A Modern English Grammar on Historical Principles*. 7 vols. Reprinted. London: George Allen and Unwin.
Jespersen, Otto. 1922. *Language: Its Nature, Development and Origin*. New York: Henry Holt.
Jespersen, Otto. 1938. *Growth and Structure of the English Language*, 9th ed. Oxford: Blackwell.
Johnson, Samuel. 1755, 1773[4]. *A Dictionary of the English Language*, 2 vols. Reprinted by Forgotten Books, London. 2015.
Kruisinga, E. 1931. *A Handbook of Present-day English*. Part II: *English Accidence and Syntax*, 5th ed. Groningen: Noordhoff. Reprinted by Hon-No-Tomo-sha, Tokyo. 1995
Landau, Sidney I. 1989. *Dictionaries: The Art and Craft of Lexicography*. Cambridge: Cambridge University Press.
Leech, Geoffrey. 1989. *An A–Z of English Grammar and Usage*. London: Edward Arnold.
Leech, Geoffrey and Jan Svartvik. 1975. 2003[3]. *A Communicative Grammar of English*, 3rd ed. Harlow: Longman.
Marckwardt, Albert H. 1958. *American English*. New York: Oxford University Press.
McDermott, Anne ed. 1996. *Samuel Johnson: A Dictionary of the English Language on CD-ROM*. Cambridge: Cambridge University Press.
Michael, Ian. 1991. "More Than Enough English Grammars", in *English Traditional Grammars: An International Perspective* ed. by Gerhard Leitner. Amsterdam/Philadelphia: John Benjamins. 11–26.
Milroy, James. 1992. *Linguistic Variation and Change: On the Historical Sociolinguistics of English*. Oxford: Blackwell.
Morton, Herbert C. 1994. *The Story of Webster's Third: Philip Gove's Controversial Dictionary and Its Critics*. Cambridge: Cambridge University Press.
Murray, J. A. H., H. Bradley, W. A. Craigie and C. T. Onions. 1933. *The Oxford English Dictionary*, 12 vols. and Supplement. Oxford: Clarendon Press.
Murray, K. M. Elisabeth. 1977. *Caught in the Web of Words: James A. H. Murray and the Oxford English Dictionary*. New Haven and London: Yale University Press.
Mustanoja, Tauno F. 1960. *A Middle English Syntax*. Part I: *Parts of Speech*. Helsinki: Société Néophilologique.

Nevalinen, Terttu. 2006. *An Introduction to Early Modern English*. Edinburgh: Edinburgh University Press.

Odom, W., the Rev. 1926. *Hallamshire Worthies: Characteristics and Work of Notable Sheffield Men and Women*. Sheffield: J. W. Northend Ltd.

Onions, C. T. 1904. *An Advanced English Syntax*. London: Routledge and Kegan Paul.

Onions, C. T. 1911. *A Shakespeare Glossary*. Oxford: Clarendon Press. Enlarged and Revised by Robert D. Eagleson. 1986.

Onions, C. T. 1917–20. "SU words in the N.E.D." in *Transactions of Philological Society*. 7–11.

Osgood, Charles Grosvenor. 1963. *A Concordance to the Poems of Edmund Spenser*. Gloucester, Mass: Peter Smith.

Page, Norman. 1972. *The Language of Jane Austen*. Oxford: Blackwell.

Palmer, F. R. 1975, 1988[2]. *The English Verb*, 2nd ed. Harlow: Longman.

Peters, Pam. 1995. *The Cambridge Australian English Style Guide*. Cambridge: Cambridge University Press.

Quirk, R., S. Greenbaum, G. Leech and J. Svartvik. 1985. *A Comprehensive Grammar of the English Language*. Harlow: Longman.

Reddick, Allen. 1990, 1996[2]. *The Making of Johnson's Dictionary 1746–1773*. Revised ed. Cambridge: Cambridge University Press.

Simpson, J. A. and E. S. C. Weiner. 1992. *The Oxford English Dictionary on CD-ROM*. Oxford: Oxford University Press.

Soanes, Catherine and Angus Stevenson. 2003. *Oxford Dictionary of English*, 2nd. Oxford: Oxford University Press.

Sonnenscheine, E. A. 1916. *A New English Grammar*. Oxford: The Clarendon Press.

Sonnenscheine, E. A. 1927. *The Soul of Grammar*. Cambridge: Cambridge University Press.

Sørensen, Knud. 1985. *Charles Dickens: Linguistic Innovator*. Aarhus: Aarhus University Press.

Stone, Harry. 1959. "Dickens and Interior Monologue." *PQ*. 38. 52–65.

Summers, Della et al. ed. 1993. *Longman Language Activator*. London: Longman.

Strang, Barbara M. H. 1970. *A History of English*. London and New York: Methuen.

Svartvik, Jan. 1966. *On Voice in the English Verb*. The Hague and Paris: Mouton & Co.

Swan, Michael. 1980, 1995[2]. *Practical English Usage*, 2nd ed. Oxford: Oxford University Press.

Taketazu, S. 1989. "A Historical Study of Psychological Verbs from Middle

English to Early Modern English". *Okinawa International University Journal*. Vol.16. 29–60.
Taketazu, S. 1994. "*It*-construction with Psychological Verbs from ME onwards". *Nagasaki Prefectural University Journal*. Vol. 27, No. 4. 105–162.
Taketazu, S. 1999(a). "*Be surprised at* or *by*?: The choice of preposition in Present-day English". *Nagasaki Prefectural University Journal*. Vol.33, No. 1. 1–18.
Taketazu, S. 1999(b). "*Be surprised by* in the Corpus and the *OED*". *Nagasaki Prefectural University Journal*. Vol. 33, No. 2. 191–213.
Taketazu, S. 1999(c). "Onions and his treatment of *be surprised by* in the *OED*". *Nagasaki Prefectural University Journal*. Vol. 33, No. 3. 9–28.
Taketazu, S. 2001. "The decline of *be surprised at/by* + gerund". *Nagasaki Prefectural University Journal*. Vol. 35, No. 4. 75–88.
Taketazu, S. 2002. "Dickens's use of (*be*) *surprised by* construction". *Nagasaki Prefectural University Journal*. Vol. 36, No. 2. 1–17.
Taketazu, S. 2015(a). "'Psych-passives + *at* or *by*' in Dickens' English: in the case of psych-verbs synonymous to *surprise*". *The Faculty of Economics Journal, The University of Nagasaki*. Vol. 48, No. 4. 53–84.
Taketazu, S. 2015(b). "'Psych-passive + *by*' Constructions in the *OED* and Henry Bradley's Lexicographical Philosophy". *The Faculty of Economics Journal, The University of Nagasaki*. Vol. 49, No. 1. 1–31.
Taketazu, S. 2015(c). "'Psych-passives with *at* or *by*' in Late Modern English and its historical shift from Early Modern to Present-day English". *The Faculty of Economics Journal, The University of Nagasaki*. Vol. 49, No. 2. 1–39.
Taketazu, S. 2016. "The semantic shift of the "psych-passive + *by*' constructions: in the case of *surprise* and its synonymous verbs". *The Faculty of Economics Journal, The University of Nagasaki*. Vol. 50, No. 2. 1–25.
Tieken-Boon van Ostade, Ingrid. 2009. *An Introduction to Late Modern English*. Edinburgh: Edinburgh University Press.
Ule, Louis. 1979. *A Concordance to the Works of Christopher Marlowe*. Hildesheim and New York: Georg Olms Verlag.
Visser, F. Th. 1963–1973. *An Historical Syntax of the English Language*. 3 parts in 4 vols. Leiden: E. J. Brill.
Waley, Arthur. 1960. *The Tale of Genji*. New York: Modern Library.
Winchester, Simon. 2003. *The Meaning of Everything: The Story of the Oxford English Dictionary*. Oxford: Oxford University Press.
Yamamoto, Tadao. 1950, 2003[3]. *The Growth and System of the Language of Dickens*. Osaka: Kansai University Press. (3rd ed., Hiroshima: Keisuisha)

荒木一雄・宇賀治正朋. 1984.『英語史ⅢA』(英語学大系10) 東京：大修館書店. (Araki, Kazuo and Masatomo Ukaji. 1984. *The History of English* ⅢA. Tokyo: Taishukan-shoten.)

池上嘉彦. 1975.『意味論』東京：大修館書店. (Ikegami, Yoshihiko. 1975. *Semantics*. Tokyo: Taishukan-shoten.)

池上嘉彦. 1978.『意味の世界』東京：日本放送出版協会. (Ikegami, Yoshihiko. 1978. *The World of Meanings*. Tokyo: NHK Publishing Co.)

今里智晃・土屋典生. 1984.『英語の辞書と語源』東京：大修館書店. (Imazato, Tomoaki and Tsuchiya Norio.1984. *English Dictionaries and Etymology*. Tokyo: Taishukan-shoten.)

宇賀治正朋. 1981.「シェイクスピアの受動文における動作主名詞句を導く前置詞」『現代の英語学』東京：開拓社. 389–403. (Ukaji, Masatomo. 1981. "Prepositions introducing Agentive Noun Phrases in Shakespeare's Passive Sentences", in *Current English Linguistics*. Tokyo: Kaitakusha. 389–403.)

江藤秀一・芝垣茂・諏訪部仁. 2002.『英国文化の巨人 サミュエル・ジョンソン』東京：港の人. (Etoh, Hidekazu et al. 2002. *A Giant in British Culture: Samuel Johnson*. Tokyo: Minato-no-hito.)

大塚高信・中島文雄監修. 1982.『新英語学辞典』東京：研究社. (Otsuka, Takanobu and Fumio Nakajima ed. 1982. *The Kenkyusha Dictionary of English Linguistics and Philology*. Tokyo: Kenkyusha.)

小西友七編. 1980.『英語基本動詞辞典』東京：研究社. (Konishi, Tomoshichi. ed. 1980. *A Dictionary of Word Grammar on Verbs*. Tokyo: Kenkyusha.)

小西友七・出口義勇. 1967.『C. T. アニアンズ／E. A. ソネンシャイン』(不死鳥英文法ライブラリ2) 東京：南雲堂. (Konishi, Tomoshichi and Yoshio Deguchi. 1967. *C. T. Onions / E. A. Sonnenshine*. Tokyo: Nan'un-do)

斎藤俊雄・中村純作・赤野一郎編. 1998.『英語コーパス言語学』東京：研究社. (Saito et al. ed. 1998. *English Corpus Linguistics*. Tokyo: Kenkyusha.)

佐々木達・木原研三編. 1995.『英語学人名辞典』東京：研究社. (Sasaki, Tatsu and Kenzo Kihara ed. 1995. *The Kenkyusha Biographical Dictionary of English linguistics and Philology*. 1995. Tokyo: Kenkyusha)

竹田津進. 2002.「*OED*における「心理受動文 + *by*」構文と Henry Bradley」長崎県立大学論集第35巻第4号. 343–64. (Taketazu, S. 2002. "'Psych-passive + *by*' constructions in the *OED* and Henry Bradley". *Nagasaki Prefectural University Journal*. Vol. 35, No. 4.)

竹田津進. 2005.「Dickens は *be surprised at/by* 構文をどう使い分けたか？」田島・末松編『英語史研究ノート』東京：開文社. 266–70. (Taketazu, S. 2005. "How Dickens differentiated *be surprised at /by* construction?", in *Notes on The History of the English Language*. ed. by Tajima・Suematsu. Tokyo: Kaibunsha.)

竹田津進. 2008.「シェフィールド時代の Henry Bradley」田島・末松編『英語史研究ノート』東京：開文社. 339–43. (Taketazu, S. 2008. "Henry Bradley in Sheffield days", in *Notes on the History of the English Language*. Tokyo: Kaibunsha. 339–43.)

竹田津進. 2008.「*OED* の見出し語 'slang' と Henry Bradley」田島・末松編『英語史研究ノート』開文社. 294–99. (Taketazu, S. 2008. "Headword 'slang' in the *OED* and Henry Bradely", in *Notes on the History of the English Language*. Tokyo: Kaibunsha. 294–99.)

竹田津進. 2013.「心理述語 (*be*) surprised + *by* 構文の意味変化」*The Kyushu Review*. *The Kyushu Review* の会. 27–49. (Taketazu, S. 2013. "The Semantic Shift of (*be*) surprised + *by* Construction" *The Kyushu Review*. Fukuoka: The Society of *the Kyushu Review*. 27–49.)

田島松二編著. 1995.『コンピューター・コーパス利用による現代英米語法研究』東京：開文社. (Tajima, Matsuji et al. ed. 1995. *Computer Corpus-based Studies on Current British and American Usages*. Tokyo: Kaibunsha.)

寺澤芳雄・川崎潔. 1993.『英語史総合年表』東京：研究社. (Terasawa, Yoshio and Kiyoshi Kawasaki. 1993. *A Comprehensive Chronology for the Study of the English Language*. Tokyo: Kenkyusha)

中原章雄. 1999.『「辞書のジョンソン」の成立―ボズウェル日記から伝記へ―』東京：英宝社. (Nakahara, Akio. 1999. *Johnson, the Lexicographer: From Boswell's Diary to Biography*. Tokyo: Eihosha.)

永嶋大典. 1983.『ジョンソンの『英語辞典』：その歴史的意義』東京：大修館書店. (Nagashima, Daisuke. 1983. *Johnson's Dictionary of the English Language: Its Historical Significance*. Tokyo: Taishukan-shoten.)

林哲郎. 1968.『英語辞書発達史』東京：開文社. (Hayashi, Tetsuro. 1968. *The Developmental History of English Dictionaries*. Tokyo: Kaibunsha.)

福地肇. 1995.『英語らしい表現と英文法』東京：研究社. (Fukuchi, Hajime. 1995. *Typical English Expressions and English Grammar*. Tokyo: Kenkyu-sha.)

福村虎次郎. 1965, 1998^2.『英語の態：Voice』東京：北星堂書店. (Fukumura, Torajirou. 1965, 1998^2. *Voice in English*. Tokyo: Hokuseido-shoten.)

松浪有・池上嘉彦・今井邦彦編. 1983.『大修館英語学辞典』東京：大修館書店. (Matsunami, Tamotsu, Yoshihiko Ikegami and Kunihiko Imai ed. 1983. *Taishukan Dictionary of English Linguistics*. Tokyo: Taishukan-shoten.)

安井稔・長谷川ミサ子. 2000.「心理動詞の -ed 形について」『英語青年』東京：研究社. 8–11, 66. (Yasui, Minoru and Misako Hasegawa. 2000. "On the *-ed* form of Psychological Verbs". *Rising Generation* (*Eigo-Seinen*), Tokyo: Kenkyu-sha. 8–11, 66.)

Dictionaries

井上永幸・赤野一郎編. 2013.『ウィズダム英和辞典 第3版』東京：三省堂. (Inoue・Akano ed. 2013. *The Wisdom English-Japanese Dictionary*. 3rd ed. Tokyo: Sanseido.)
河村重治郎編. 1995.『新クラウン英和辞典 第5版』東京：三省堂. (Kawamura ed. 1995. *The New Crown English-Japanese Dictionary*. 5th ed. Tokyo: Sanseido.)
木原研三編. 2001.『新グローバル英和辞典 第2版』東京：三省堂. (Kihara ed. 2001. *The New Global English-Japanese Dictionary*. 2nd ed. Tokyo: Sanseido.)
小西友七他編. 2012.『プログレッシブ英和中辞典 第5版』東京：小学館. (Konishi et al. ed. 2012. *Shogakukan Progressive English-Japanese Dictionary*. 5th ed. Tokyo: Shogakukan.)
高橋作太郎編. 2012.『リーダーズ英和辞典 第3版』東京：研究社. (Takahashi ed. 2012. *Kenkyusha's English-Japanese Dictionary for the General Reader*. 3rd ed. Tokyo: Kenkyusha.)
竹林滋他編. 2005.『ルミナス英和辞典 第2版』東京：研究社. (Takebayashi et al. ed. 2005. *Luminous English-Japanese Dictionary*. 2nd ed. Tokyo: Kenkyusha.)
竹林滋他編. 2010.『新英和中辞典 第7版』東京：研究社. (Takebayashi et al. ed. 2010. *Kenkyusha's New College English-Japanese Dictionary*. 7th ed. Tokyo: Kenkyusha.)
野村恵造他編. 2013.『オーレックス英和辞典 第2版』東京：旺文社. (Nomura et al. ed. 2013. *O-Lex English-Japanese Dictionary*. 2nd ed. Tokyo: Obunsha.)
南出康世編. 2015.『ジーニアス英和辞典 第5版』東京：大修館書店. (Minamide ed. 2015. *Genius English-Japanese Dictionary*. 5th ed. Tokyo: Taishukan-shoten.)
宮部菊雄・杉山忠一編. 1990.『ロイヤル英和辞典』東京：旺文社. (Miyabe・Sugiyama ed. 1990. *Royal English-Japanese Dictionary*. Tokyo: Obunsha.)

Computer Corpora

BNC = British National Corpus (Shogakukan version, Brigham Young University = BYU)
CASO = Corpus of American Soap Opera (BYU)
CLIC Dickens (University of Birmingham)
COBUILD = Cobuild Direct Corpus (Collins)
COCA = Corpus of Contemporary American English (BYU)

COHA = Corpus of Historical American English (BYU)
Corpus of US Supreme Court Opinions (BYU)
Dickens concordance (http://www.concordance.com/dickens.htm., now unavailable)
EEBO = Early English Books Online (BYU)
MEC = Modern English Collection (University of Virginia, now unavailable)
TIME = *Time* Magazine Corpus (BYU)
VLSA = Victorian Literary Studies Archives (Nagoya University)
Wordbanks = Collins WordBank (Shogakukan version)

Index (Names)

A

Academy, The (journal) 176
Advanced English Syntax, An 164, 178
Ainsworth, W. H. 61, 76
America, -n 9, 11–13, 16, 21, 35, 41, 49–51, 57–62, 64–5, 119, 124, 141, 164
Anglican Church 181
Astoria (Irving) 107–8
Austen, Jane 2, 10, 38, 76, 88–9, 105, 116, 122, 153, 159, 160
~ *'s Letters* 89, 89f
Australian English Style Guide 133

B

Bailey, Richard 86f, 193
Baugh, Albert C. 48, 156f, 159f, 160, 179
BBC 12f, 33
Biber, Douglas et al. 196–7
Bible, the 44, 47, 181–2
Blake, Norman 86, 115, 125, 125f, 164
BNC (corpus) 3, 11, 11f, 12, 15, 26, 29–32, 41, 64–7, 100, 103, 111, 117–8, 120–1, 124, 124f, 138–9, 142–5, 196
Bolinger, D and R. Ilson 21, 24, 28, 76
Boswell, James 87f, 181
Bradley, Henry (*OED* editor) 111, 148, 151–2, 156–8, 160–1, 167–91
Bridges, Robert 175, 176f, 177
Brigham Young University 11f, 13, 16, 34f
Britain, -tish 9, 11, 12, 35, 41, 48–51, 56, 58–66, 87, 119, 124, 132, 141, 144, 164, 173
Brook, G. L. 71, 86
Bunyan, John 46–7
Burchfield, Robert 153, 155, 157f, 180

C

Canterbury Tales, The 17–18, 167, 203
Carroll, Lewis 10f, 162
CASO (corpus) 4, 13–5, 26, 28–32, 142, 144
Caught in the Web of Words (Elizabeth Murray) 157f, 176
Chapman, R. W. 89f
Chaucer, Geoffrey 17–18, 167, 203
CLiC Dickens (corpus) 71
Close, R. A. 21
COBUILD (corpus) 3, 11–2, 15, 32–3, 75
COCA (corpus) 3, 13–5, 26, 29–32, 41, 64–7, 117–8, 120–1, 138–9, 143–5
COHA (corpus) 3, 16–7, 26–32, 41, 63–7, 100, 103, 107, 119, 121, 129, 137–43, 144f, 145–6, 148, 161f, 196
Coleridge, Herbert 156f
Collins, Wilkie 38, 49f, 61, 76, 116, 159
Conrad, Joseph 2, 10, 61, 76, 159
Cotton, James S. (*Academy* editor) 176
Craigie, William (*OED* editor) 152, 157–8, 158f, 160–1, 168–9, 172–4, 180
Crystal, David 34, 86, 127f, 148
Crystal, D and D. Davy 34
Cummins, Maria S. 61
Curme, George O. 123f, 125, 127

D

Darwin, Charles 10f, 155
David Copperfield (Dickens) 70, 74
Davies, Mark (BYU) iv, 138
Declerk, R. 22–3, 25
Defoe, Daniel 44–45, 47
Denison, David 23, 198
Dickens, Charles iii, 2, 10, 38, 49f, 70–96, 102, 122, 153, 159, 160
Dictionary of the English Language, A (Dr. Johnson) 88, 103, 180–2
Doyle, Arthur Conan 10f, 162
Dreiser, Theodore 61

E

Early Modern English (EModE) 3, 8f, 9,

215

37, 39, 41–8, 67–8, 134–6
EEBO (corpus) 3, 8, 135–6
Eliot, George 116, 160
Emerson, R. W. 156
Encyclopaedia Britannica 179
English Grammar (Lindley Murray) 164
Etoh, H. et al. 87f

F
Faerie Queene, The (Spenser) 42–3, 68, 134
Fielding, Henry 61, 102, 105
Fisher, Andreas 5, 5f, 161
Follet, Ken 2, 74f
Foster, Brian 34
Fowler's Modern English Usage 180
Fukuchi, Hajime 126f, 147
Fukumura, Torajirou 198
Furnival, F. J. 156f.

G
Gaskell, Elizabeth 49f, 61
Genius (dictionary) 115f, 123, 132, 152
Genji (*The Tale of* ~) 97
Gissing, George 38, 61, 76, 109
Goldsmith, Oliver 61
Gordon, Ian A. 88
Gowers, Sir Ernest 148, 148f
Gulliver's Travels (Swift) 45

H
Hallamshire Worthies 176f
Hard Times (Dickens) 76
Hardy, Thomas 76
Hawthorne, Nathaniel 10, 61, 105, 156, 159, 160
Hayashi, Tetsuro 181
Heike (*The Tale of* ~) 114, 130
Hitchings, Henry 88
Horatio, Alger 61
Horobin, Simon 180, 182
Huddleston, R and G. Pullum 23, 198
Hughes, Geoffrey 34

I
Ikegami, Yoshihiko 100, 111–2
Imazato, T and N. Tsuchiya 157, 181
Irving, Washington 61, 107–8, 156
Ishiguro, Kazuo 2, 74, 130

J
James, Henry 116
Jekyll and Mr. Hyde, Dr. 192
Jespersen, Otto 17, 48, 126–7
Johnson, Samuel 10, 61, 76, 87–8, 103, 105, 151, 157f, 159, 160, 180–2

K
King James Bible, The 44, 47
Kipling, Rudyad 61
Knight's Tale, The (Chaucer) 17–8
Konishi, Tomoshichi 21, 24f, 133–4
Konishi, T and Y. Deguchi 163, 163f, 164
Kruisinga, E. 123

L
Landau, Sidney I. 153f, 156f, 157f, 160
Lang, Andrew 10f, 61, 162
Late Modern English (LModE) 2, 9–10, 14–7, 22, 25, 35, 39, 49–64, 67–8, 73, 85–6, 103, 105, 109, 116–7, 119–21, 122, 124–5, 131, 136–7, 140, 155–6, 173, 194–5
Leech, Geoffrey 27f
Leech, G and J. Svartvik 21, 48, 147
Lewis, C. S. iii, 4
Linguistic Innovator (*Charles Dickens:* ~) 86
Little Dorrit (Dickens) 75
London, Jack 61–2
Longman Language Activator 132
Luminous (dictionary) 21, 76f, 151

M
Making of English, The (Bradley) 111, 178–9
Markwardt, Albert H. 50

Index

Marlowe, Christopher 42, 46–7
Mason College (U. of Birmingham) 163
Matsunami, Tamotsu et al. 163f, 164, 175
Matsuoka, Mitsuharu (Nagoya U.) v, 9
MEC (corpus) 3, 9–10, 41, 87f, 100, 103, 116–7, 116f, 124, 136–7
MEG (Jespersen) 17, 126
Melville, Herman 61
Michael, Ian 164
Middle English (ME) 17–8, 67
Milroy, James 203
Milton, John 46
Modern English (ModE) 3, 10
Monk's Tale (Chaucer) 203
Morton, Herbert C. 159
Murray, Elisabeth 157f, 159, 160, 176–7
Murray, James (*OED* Chief Editor) 151–2, 156–61, 167–7, 172–4, 176–7, 179
Murray, Lindley 164, 164f
Murray's Dictionary (= *OED*) 157
Mustanoja, Tauno 17, 48

N

Natsume, Soseki 203
Nevalainen, Terttu 50
New College (dictionary) 115, 124, 132
New Crown (dictionary) 132
New English Dictionary (= *OED*) 176
New English Grammar, A 163
Nicholas Nickleby (Dickens) 70
Norman Conquest 203
NPR (radio broadcast) 12f, 33

O

OED (on CD-ROM) iii, 1, 3, 5–8, 10, 38, 76, 99–100, 104–5, 134–5, 151–166, 167–91, 193
OED Online (Third Edition) 153f, 168f
Old Ashmolen 160
Old English (OE) 48f, 67, 111, 178
Old French 111
O-Lex (dictionary) 115f
Oliver Twist (Dickens) 70

Onions, Charles Talbut (*OED* editor) 43, 104, 151–66, 167–9, 172f, 172–5, 178, 180
Otsuka, T and F. Nakajima 27f
Oxford Dictionary of English 39
OZ news (Australian news) 12f, 32–3

P

Page, Norman 89
Palmer, F. R. 22
Paradise Lost (Milton) 46
Penguin Dictionary of English Synonyms and Antonyms, The 40
Peters, Pam 133
Philological Society 156f, 176
Pilgrim's Progress (Bunyan) 46
Plain English Campaign 148
Poe, Edgar Allan 61
Present-day English (PE) 2, 11–7, 20–2, 25, 39, 48, 64–7, 72–4, 103, 109, 117–22, 124, 132, 138–9, 140, 148, 194–5
Progressive (dictionary) 115

Q

Quirk, R. et al. 22, 25f, 30, 125, 125f, 146, 147f, 196

R

Rambler, The (Johnson) 76, 87–8
Readers (dictionary) 115f
Reddick, Allen 181–2
Reeve's Tale, The (Chaucer) 167
Renaissance 203
Riverside Shakespeare, The 104
Robinson Crusoe (Defoe) 44
Royal (dictionary) 115, 132

S

Sasaki, T and K. Kihara 163f, 175, 179–80
Scott, Walter 61
Sedgwick, Catharine 41f, 61
Shakespeare, William 17–8, 41, 43, 47, 104–5

217

Shakespeare Glossary, A (Onions) 43, 104
Sheffield 167, 175–6, 177f
~ *Independent* (newspaper) 176
Simms, William 61
Sørensen, Knud 72, 72f, 86, 86f
Sonnenschine, E. A. 163
Soul of Grammar, The 163
Spenser, Edmund 41, 42–3, 47–8, 134
Stevenson, R. L. 61, 192
Stone, Harry 72
Story of Webster's Third, The 159
Stowe, Harriet Beecher 61
Strang, Barbara 115
Supplement to the OED 153, 157–8, 180
Surprised by Joy (C. S. Lewis) iii, 4
Swan, Michael 21, 24f, 25, 101
Swift, Jonathan 45–7

T

Tajima, Matsuji et al. 124
Thackeray, W. M. 61
Tieken-Boon van Osted, Ingrid 86
Time Magazine (corpus) 33–4
Times, The (newspaper) 12f, 33
Timon of Athens (Shakespeare) 104
Titus Andronicus (Shakespeare)104
Today (newspaper) 12f, 33
Trollope, Anthony 2, 10, 61, 76, 153, 159, 160

Twain, Mark 61

U

UK 12f, 32–3, 75
US 12f, 32–3, 35
US Supreme Court Opinions (corpus) 35–6

V

Victorian 9
Visser, F. Th. 17
VLSA 3, 9–10, 41, 49–57, 59, 63–4, 79, 116–7, 119–20, 130, 136–7

W

Waley, Arthur 97–8
Washington, George 61
Wharton, Edith 156
Winchester, Simon 176f
Winter's Tale (Shakespeare) 104
Wisdom (dictionary) 115f, 133
Wordbanks (corpus) 11–2, 15, 26, 29–32, 64–7, 138–9, 142–3

Y

Yasui, M and M. Hasegawa 192, 197
Yonge, C. M. 61

[f = footnote]

Index (Subjects and Words)

A

abstract (noun) 22f, 25–8, 73, 74f, 88, 110, 148
academic (text) 11, 13
accusative (case) 122, 125, 125f
active (voice) 17, 22, 43, 78, 152, 194–5
adjectival 21–5, 98, 192–3, 196–8
　~ passive 23
　~ predicate 196
adjective iii, 17, 21–5, 43, 111, 192–8
　participial ~ 22, 194
adverb (-ly ~) 147
afraid (~ *of*) 17, 17f
agency 17, 43
agent iii, 25–6, 29–30 (semi-), 31
agentive
　~ noun 25f, 43, 88, 102–3, 108, 110
　~ preposition 1, 3, 6–9, 17–8, 22, 25, 25f, 30–2, 37–9, 42–8, 60, 66, 70, 99, 110, 151, 168
agentivity 25–6
aim (to do, at ~ing) 124
alarm 39, 42. 44–5, 47, 51, 56–7, 60–1, 79, 83–5
amaze 39, 42–8, 51–2, 56–7, 60–1, 65–6, 80, 83–5, 135, 137, 139, 141–2, 195–6, 198
ambiguity 126–7
amuse (*amused with* or *by*) 171
analogy 103, 110, 146
annoy 161
appall 39, 48, 52, 56–7, 60–2, 80, 83, 85
appearance (agentive noun) 102–3, 109
　nouns of ~/*entrance* 102, 109
　surprised by ~ 102–3
aspect (perfect ~) 122, 144–5
astonish 39, 42–8, 52, 56–7, 60–1, 80, 83–5, 97–8, 135, 137, 139, 172, 192, 198
astound 39, 48, 53, 56–7, 60, 81, 83
authority 89, 103, 180

B

baffle 39, 48, 53, 56–7, 60, 81, 83, 85, 197
bewilder 39, 48, 53, 56–7, 60, 81, 83–5, 197

C

case (accusative, genitive) 122, 125, 125f
clause 127, 133
　how- ~ 2, 23f, 27–8, 73–4, 114, 126–7, 130–50
　N with which- ~, *the* 146–9
　non-finite ~, the 4
　that- ~ 124–7, 196–7, 198
　way- ~, *the* 27f, 147
　what- ~ 27, 144f, 146, 147
cognate 148
collocation 4, 103
colloquial 13, 127, 142, 148
colonial lag 50
competition, -tive 111, 123–4, 127
complement (prepositional ~) 2, 22f, 23f, 26–8, 31–3, 72–4, 97–8, 114, 116, 118, 174, 197
complementary distribution 145
computer corpus (corpora) iv, 3–5, 9, 11, 23, 41, 71, 134, 165
concealed exclamation 126, 147
concordance (Shakes., Spenser, etc.) 41
concrete a. 27f, 112
coordinated 30, 40, 78
coordination (*in* ~ *with*) 24, 30, 77, 195
cutlery (firm) 167, 175–6

D

deep (vs. *profound*) 111
definition 5–6, 38–40, 88, 98, 104, 153, 156, 161, 167–74, 180–1, 193
delight v. 161, 161f, 193
descriptive, -vism 164, 179–80
dialect, -al 124, 177 (Yorkshire ~)

219

dialogue 28
dictionary 21, 115, 132, 151–2, 156, 161
dismay 39, 42–8, 54, 56–7, 60, 81, 83, 85
dynamic (meaning) 21, 26, 27f, 101, 197

E
editor 151–2, 156, 160, 168, 173, 176
   assistant ~ 160, 163, 177
emotion, ~nal iii, 2, 21, 24f, 28, 37, 76, 142
English
   American ~ 9, 16, 64, 124, 142
   British ~ 9, 11, 64, 124
   colloquial ~ 142
   journalism ~ 32–4
   legal ~ 34–5
   19th-century ~ 50, 74
   plain ~ 127, 148, 148f
   spoken ~ 14, 28–32, 75, 142, 144
   written ~ 75
entrance (agentive noun) 102–3, 109
entry (~ word) 155–6, 161, 167, 171–2, 181, 181f
etymology, -gical 98, 177
exclamation 147–8
   concealed ~ 126f, 147
exclamatory 28, 126, 147–8
existential *there* 122

F
fascicle 156–7, 161, 176–7
fiction (text) 11, 13, 64, 136f
frequency 48, 48f
frighten 37, 161, 161f, 169f
from (agentive) 17, 39, 67, 162

G
genitive 122, 125–6
genre (of texts) 11–12, 32–3, 64, 136–7
gerund iii, 22f, 23f, 27, 73, 114–29
glad of 174
grammar 2, 20, 22, 60, 86, 89, 124, 130, 163–5, 173, 175
grammarian 21–3, 132, 179, 203

grammatical 2, 25f, 34, 37, 38, 86, 130, 162, 165, 167

H
historical, -ly iii, 2–3, 5, 16, 17, 37, 143, 162, 164–5, 200, 202, 204
how-clause 2, 23f, 27–8, 73–4, 114, 126–7, 130–50

I
I am surprised at you(!) 14, 28–9, 30 (~ *by you*), 73, 75
idiomatic 28, 44, 73, 144, 201
infinitive 123–4, 127, 135, 164, 196–8
innovation, -tive 77, 86–7, 178, 203
innovator (linguistic ~) 86, 87f, 89
instrument (semantic role) 48
intermediate (~ stage) 22f, 99–103, 104, 106–10
intransitive verb iii, 37

J
journalism English 32–4

L
language change iv, 111, 123, 178–9, 180, 202–3
legal English 34–5
lexical 72f, 103
lexicographer 21, 132, 153, 157, 177, 180–2
linguistic, -ally iv, 2, 6, 20, 34, 37, 50, 58, 77, 84, 115, 118, 131, 149, 152, 155, 179, 182
linking verb (seem, look, etc.) 1f, 4, 25
logarithmic scale 117–8, 120–21

M
magazine (text) 2, 11, 13, 33–4, 64, 136f
meaning 25, 28, 31, 40, 79, 97–113, 123–4, 162
modifier 31–2
morpheme (one-word ~) 148

Index

morphology 178

N

N with which-clause, *the* 147–8
narrative (style) 75, 90
negative 122
nettle 161, 180
newspaper (text) 2, 11, 13, 33–4, 64, 136f
non-fiction (text) 64, 136f
non-finite clause 4
non-standard 77, 86, 153, 177–9

O

oats 88f, 181
of (agentive) 6, 17–8, 39, 67, 161–2

P

participial 4, 22, 194
~ adjective 23, 196–7
passive (voice) iii, 1–3, 6, 8, 17, 20–6, 30, 37, 42–6, 60, 62, 67, 72, 77–8, 87, 109–11, 114, 122, 132, 143, 151, 162, 168–74, 192–8
adjectival ~ 23, 198
progressive ~ 178–9
pseudo- ~ 22
semi- ~ 22
true ~ 22
verbal ~ 23
~ voice 194–5
past participle 1, 17, 21, 25, 77–8, 161–2, 169f, 192–7
permissive, -ness 173–4, 179, 180
perplex 42–7, 54, 56–7, 60, 63–6, 81, 85, 135, 137, 197–8
phrase (noun ~, nominal ~) iii, 2, 25–6
physical (meaning) 4, 22, 25, 31, 43f, 98–102, 106–8, 110–2, 133, 162
physiological (meaning) 100–1, 106, 108–10, 162
please 37–8, 152, 161, 168, 193
prescriptive (grammar) 163–4, 178–80
prescriptivism (grammatical ~) 162–5, 167, 174, 178–80
profound (vs. *deep*) 111
pronoun 27, 73
demonstrative ~ 32
indefinite ~ 32
interrogative ~ 146
reflexive ~ 29–30
psychological (meaning), -ly iii, 2–5, 8, 31, 43f, 45, 55f, 87, 98–112, 133, 153, 162
psych-passive iii, 23, 30, 37–9, 47–8, 51, 58, 62, 67–8, 78, 85, 119, 131, 137, 146, 151–2, 167–8, 172–4, 193
psych-verb iii, 18, 30, 37–46, 51–5, 60–2, 78–82, 100, 111, 151–2, 161, 168, 193–7

Q

quotation (illustrative ~) 5f, 6, 76, 103–5, 115, 131f, 132–3, 153–6, 158–60, 167–74, 179, 181
quotation-search 160

R

ratio (of *at* and *by*) 8–10, 11–16, 26, 31, 41, 48, 50, 55f, 58, 63–4, 67, 72, 74, 78, 84–5, 97f, 109, 124
readers (voluntary ~ of *OED*) 156, 159f, 159–61
replace, -ment 3, 39, 75, 100, 123–7, 146–8, 179
reporter (newspaper ~) 34–5, 86

S

scare 152
school grammar 2, 163
schoolteacher 163, 175, 179–80
semantic, ~s 25f, 48, 97–113, 162
shock 39, 48, 54–7, 60–2, 66, 82–5, 139, 142, 193–7
slang 179
soap opera (CASO) 13
speech 13, 75, 86, 148

221

spoken 11, 13–4, 28–9, 32–3, 58, 75, 142, 144, 149
standard (non- ~, sub- ~) 10, 38, 86, 89, 97, 115, 124, 132, 152, 171, 177–9
startle 39, 48, 55–7, 59, 60–1, 66, 82–5, 108–9, 141, 194
static (meaning) 21, 26, 27f, 110
statistics iii, 27f, 58, 82–4, 115, 117–21, 135, 137, 148
stimulus (semantic role) 30, 48, 98
stun 39, 45, 48, 55–7, 60, 82–5, 110–1, 142
style 32, 75, 88, 127
   colloquial ~ 127
   plain ~ 127
stylistic, -cally 76, 130, 141, 143–6
subject (grammatical) 98, 122, 124–5
sub-standard (grammar) 77, 86, 153, 177
surprise iii, 1–10, 20–35, 37–9, 42f, 45, 70–8, 87–96, 97–107, 114–9, 122–7, 130–48, 151–63, 165, 167–70, 192–4, 196–8
synonymous (verbs to *surprise*) 39–41, 67, 78–9, 131, 146f, 168
syntactic, -ally iii, 4, 20, 77, 87f, 146–7
syntax 89, 164

T

tense 126–7, 141
text 4, 9, 11–4, 16, 64, 64f, 136–7, 142
text-search 6, 105, 134, 153, 155, 161f, 172
that-clause 124–7, 196–7, 198

through (agentive) 17, 39, 67, 162
to-infinitive 123–4, 135, 196–7, 198
traditional grammar 2, 86–7
TV/radio news 2, 33–4

U

unconventional (language) 86–9
usage 10, 20, 22–4, 34, 38, 43, 60–1, 89, 124, 132–3, 148, 153, 162, 173, 179–80

V

variant form 4, 6, 153
variation (stylistic ~) 14, 28, 75–6, 141, 143
very 24, 24f
voice
   active ~ 99, 194
   passive ~ 194

W

way-clause, *the* 27f, 146–7
what-clause 27, 144f, 146, 147
with (agentive) 6–8, 17–8, 38, 42–8, 153, 161–2
worry 23, 152
written 11, 58, 75

Y

you'd (you'll) be surprised 133, 143–4

[Agentive prepositions *at* and *by* are omitted due to their very frequent appearance]

[About the author]

Susumu Taketazu was born in Oita prefecture. He went to Osaka University of Foreign Studies and earned a BA in English. He then went on to obtain an MA in Linguistics from San Jose State University in Califorinia. After teaching at Kitakyushu College of Technology and Okinawa International University, he has been teaching at a public university in Sasebo, Nagasaki Kenritsu Daigaku.

His main interest lies in the historical change of syntax and vocabulary from the Middle English period. His academic articles include "*It*-construction with Psychological Verbs from ME onwards", "The Prefix *a-* + Psychological Verbs and their Passives in Middle English", "*Do you have ~ ?* 構文の初出年代をめぐって", "『欽定訳聖書』に使われた *wroth* と *angry*".

The publication of this book was aided by a grant from the Academic Association of the university (Sasebo Campus).

Psychological Passives and the Agentive
Prepositions in English: A Historical Study　［検印廃止］

2019 年 3 月 15 日　初版発行

著　者	竹 田 津　進
発 行 者	安 居 洋 一
印刷・製本	モ リ モ ト 印 刷

〒162-0065　東京都新宿区住吉町 8-9
発行所　**開文社出版株式会社**
TEL 03-3358-6288　FAX 03-3358-6287
http://www.kaibunsha.co.jp

ISBN978-4-87571-588-2 C3082
©2019 Susumu TAKETAZU